Daniel S. Gregory

**Christ's Trumpet-Call to the Ministry**

The preacher and the preaching for the present crisis

Daniel S. Gregory

**Christ's Trumpet-Call to the Ministry**
*The preacher and the preaching for the present crisis*

ISBN/EAN: 9783337313982

Printed in Europe, USA, Canada, Australia, Japan

Cover: Foto ©Lupo / pixelio.de

More available books at **www.hansebooks.com**

# CHRIST'S TRUMPET-CALL TO THE MINISTRY.

# CHRIST'S TRUMPET-CALL TO THE MINISTRY

OR

The Preacher and the Preaching for the
Present Crisis

BY

DANIEL S. GREGORY, D. D., LL. D.

*Author of "Christian Ethics," "Why Four Gospels?" Editor of
the "Homiletic Review," Late Managing Editor
of "The Standard Dictionary," etc.*

———

NEW YORK
FUNK & WAGNALLS COMPANY
LONDON AND TORONTO
1896

Copyright, 1896,
BY
FUNK & WAGNALLS COMPANY

[PRINTED IN THE UNITED STATES]

# PREFACE.

The following pages embody the thoughts and reasoned convictions of the writer on a subject that has been prominently before his mind during much of the last thirty years of a somewhat active life. They lie along the line of a belief which he shares in common with many other Christians, that the Church of Christ has come to the great crisis in her history and work—a crisis big either with unspeakable disaster and misery for all the future, or with decisive victory and the conquest of the world for Christ. They are presented with the profound—almost overwhelming—conviction that the questions discussed are, for the ministry and the Church, life-and-death questions that every preacher of the Gospel should, for the glory of the Master and for the sake of a lost world, take up, consider carefully, and settle in the light of the Word of God, without an hour's delay. They have been expressed in the popular and practical form that permits the repetition and even reiteration of important facts and principles that require emphasis by presentation in various aspects and relations. They are addressed especially to preachers of the Gospel, for the reason that upon the preacher as leader in the work of the Church, more than upon all else, will depend the final result.

New York City, April, 1896.

# CONTENTS.

| CHAPTER | | PAGE |
|---|---|---|
| I. | The Preacher's Present Commission, | 1 |
| II. | The Preacher's Message, | 53 |
| III. | The Preacher and His Furnishing, | 130 |
| IV. | The Preaching for these Times, | 205 |
| V. | The Preacher as a Pastor in these Times, | 304 |

# CHRIST'S TRUMPET-CALL TO THE MINISTRY.

## CHAPTER I.

### THE PREACHER'S PRESENT COMMISSION.

The Apostle Paul wrote to the Christians at Corinth:

" For after that, in the wisdom of God, the world by wisdom knew not God ; it pleased God by the foolishness of *preaching* to save them that believe."

" Preaching" is, therefore, the one supreme requirement of this lost world; and the "preacher" is thus lifted to the supreme place of initiative, leadership, dignity, and responsibility in the work of Christ for the lost world. The preacher's position and work, always peculiarly important, have assumed vastly more of importance in the present crisis of the enterprise of the Church in carrying out the Great Commission. The preacher who at all takes in the situation can hardly help asking, in view of this crisis, such questions as the following :

What is the present immediate requirement that the Great Commission makes of me as a preacher?

What is the message that must constitute the

burden of my preaching in order to meet that requirement?

What is the special furnishing that will best fit me for the effective delivery of that message?

What must be the aim, and what the characteristics, of the preaching that will meet the demands of the times and the crisis in saving men and the world?

What must be my character as pastor, and what the character of my work of pastoral oversight and direction, in order that I may do what needs to be done for those saved through preaching?

There is obviously nothing new in the form of the preacher's commission. Its language is the same to-day as in the Apostolic age. It is familiarly known as "The Great Commission." It came originally from the Head of the Church, the Lord Jesus Christ himself. As recorded by the Evangelist Matthew, it reads:

*The Great Commission.*

"All power is given unto me in heaven and in earth. Go ye therefore and teach all nations, baptizing them in the name of the Father, and of the Son, and of the Holy Ghost: teaching them to observe all things whatsoever I have commanded you. And, lo, I am with you alway, even unto the end of the world. Amen."

As recorded by the Evangelist Mark, it reads:

"Go ye into all the world, and preach the gospel to every creature. He that believeth and is baptized shall be saved; but he that believeth not shall be damned."

These are certainly among the most solemn words ever addressed to a company of mortals. They take hold on life and death; they involve the issues of the judgment and of eternity. The mission to which they give expression is the most important ever entrusted to men. It is the evangelizing of the whole race of lost men, the making over of the world in righteousness.

That mission was doubtless intended, in a very real and pregnant sense, not for the Apostles only, but for all the disciples and followers of Jesus there present when they were uttered, and for all the Church of the ages as represented by them. But, with as great certainty, in the highest and most pregnant sense, they were intended especially for those who were to be officially the Apostles, or "Missionaries," of our Lord to the world, and for all those in the ages since who have officially represented, or who now officially represent, the Master in the great work of the Church for the salvation of mankind. To these has been entrusted the special task of directing, leading, inspiring, and impelling the Church in its great work.

It is not necessary to enter into the general exposition of the language of this commission, nor to show the application of the whole to the Church at large in its entire membership. Preachers are familiar with these things; besides, it would be quite aside from the present purpose. That purpose requires, as preliminary to its statement, two points of special significance and application. These preliminary points are involved or expressed in two words of the preacher's commission: "Go ye." *Two Special Points.*

The verb "Go" is in the imperative mode. The words are words not simply of permission nor of entreaty, but of *command.* As Christ utters them to the Church and to the ministry, he implies that he has a claim upon those whom he addresses, for the employment of themselves, and for the use of all their powers and possessions, in the great work of evangelizing the world. He bases his claim upon the absolute authority given him for the conquest of the world in redemption. This claim of Christ assuredly rests upon the highest conceivable grounds, whether scripturally or rationally considered. The Church and the ministry are Christ's by right of production in creation, by virtue of his essential Deity; by right of purchase in redemption, by virtue of his vicarious and sacrificial death; and by right of gift, by virtue of the sinner's voluntary consecration at his conversion. They can only get away from the duty by repudiating Christ's right to them as Creator, by denying his claim as Redeemer, and by casting off their vows of fealty to Christ as Lord in the Kingdom of God, and casting away with these their hope of salvation.

The command is issued to them to carry out the Great Commission. As addressed to *the Church*, that includes and is summed up in the requirement *to furnish the messengers of salvation to carry the Gospel into all the world, and to supply the pecuniary means and the moral and spiritual support needed to sustain them in the completion of the world-wide task assigned by the command.* As addressed to *the ministry*, it includes the requirement that, as the messengers and mouthpieces of Christ and the official leaders and guides of the Church, they shall *take up the great task and push it to its completion*, keeping the commission always before the Church, and instructing, guiding, leading, inspiring, and impelling her to the accomplishment of her divinely assigned task. And so upon the preacher rests the supreme responsibility in the work of the Gospel, the duty of making the Kingdom of Christ coextensive with the world of mankind.

The command, "Go ye," is in the *present tense*, not in the future. That means, "Do it *now*." It means, "Do it, *ye* to whom the words are addressed." It has been taken up by the Church and the ministry through the ages, as presently and directly applicable to them. That command, with the obligation it carries for the salvation of the lost world, has rested upon every generation of the Christian membership and the Christian ministry, from the beginning until to-day; and Christ has held every generation responsible from the beginning until now—unless it could give the best of reasons for not fulfilling the requirements of the Great Commission. If, in any particular age or generation, the Church and her messengers have been able to give a valid reason for failure to accomplish the appointed task well, either from lack of men or lack of means or lack of opportunity, the reason has been so far accepted and approved. The means of the Church may have been limited; the world of heathendom may have been inaccessible to Christendom; the nations may have been closed to the Gospel—these and other excuses have been reasonably urged in extenuation of past failures. The past has been able to give at least a partial reason for lack of complete success in this so great enterprise; and beyond that, and so far as its reasons have not been adequate, it has suffered even to judgment for those failures.

Does Christ demand of the Church *that she shall give the Gospel to all the world now*, in this present generation to which we belong, which we constitute, and whose responsibilities are ours?

Does Christ require of the preacher *that he shall be a leader of the Church in immediately evangelizing the world?*

These are the first questions that the preacher of the present day should ask himself in connection with his commission from Christ.

**The Test Questions.**

In the past history of the Church, two, and only two, reasons have been given—when the Great Commission has been urged as a present duty—for a negative answer to these two questions:

First.—The world is inaccessible to the messengers of the Gospel.

Second.—The Christian Church can not furnish the pecuniary means necessary to send these messengers immediately into all the world.

Do these hold as valid reasons still; or have they come to be mere pretexts to cover up the unwillingness of the Church to obey the command of her Lord?

Now we think it clear that, altho the form of the preacher's commission is the same to-day as always, there has been an absolute change in its present and immediate requirements and responsibilities. The world has changed front. Christendom has come to the fore. The learning and wealth and power of the world are in its hands. God calls upon the Church and the ministry to complete the conquest of the world for Christ—not one, five, ten, twenty generations hence, but *absolutely now, in this present generation.* The first task of the preacher of the Gospel in this age, as the bearer of the Great Commission, is, therefore and necessarily, to understand that commission in its present pressing demands, that he may understand his own mission and responsibility so as to enter intelligently, energetically, and enthusiastically upon his task of leadership, inspiration, and impulse, in the

Church, in the accomplishment of the work of evangelizing the world. If he misunderstands the situation or fails to take it in, he will be found wanting in his place of leadership and direction; the Church will be hindered or fail in her work; and the world will remain still unevangelized and the travail of the Redeemer's soul still unsatisfied.

In answering the critical questions just propounded, and in meeting the first of the objections so often urged, he will need to study diligently the teaching of the Word of God and to read with broad sweep of vision the signs of the times. He will find by such study and reading, if we mistake not, that, as surely as all Scripture and all providences pointed to the time when the light of the first morning sun shone upon that cradle in Bethlehem as "the fulness of times" for the Incarnation, so now the light of every morning sun, as it glances along the mountain-peaks from east to west around the globe, points to "the fulness of times" for the world's completed redemption.

In meeting the second objection, he will need to study earnestly the teachings of the Word of God concerning the principles of beneficence, and to try the conduct of the Church in the matter of giving for the cause of Christ, in the light of the scriptural principles of Christian giving and of the marvelous wealth that the present age has poured into her coffers.

And when he has learned the true answers to the questions and the present worthlessness of the old objections, the preacher's commission requires that he should see to it that the whole truth in the matter should be made known to the Church, and that the Church be roused, as with trumpet-call from God, to consider and take up the mighty and glorious task and complete it. That is the part of his commission that is *new* and for the living present. For that, in this materialistic and sordid age, he will need the baptism of the Holy Ghost and the "tongues of fire."

We propose to take up and consider somewhat in detail the two standing objections, already adverted to, **The Standing Objections.** in order to show their futility, and at the same time to make clear precisely what, in the light of the divine word and providence, the preacher's commission requires him to proclaim to the Church, in the present crisis, regarding these so vital matters.

## SECTION FIRST.

### The Whole World is Now Accessible to the Church.

We suggest some special points, in order to help clear the field of vision, and make manifest the breadth and scope of present Christian and ministerial duty.

I. THE WORLD NOW PHYSICALLY ACCESSIBLE TO THE CHURCH.

The preacher's commission authorizes and requires him, in the light of God's providences, to proclaim to the delaying Church that the excuse that the world is physically inaccessible to the messengers of the Gospel can no longer be honestly pleaded for her delay in the work of evangelizing the world.

This excuse may once have been valid; the obstacles in the way may once have been actually insuperable. When the Apostles, the first Missionaries, went out into the Roman Empire with their message fresh from the lips of the Master, they found that the Roman had cast up highways for them across the Empire and that his law was omnipotent within the limits of his sway. But through the vast reaches of the heathen world beyond, there were no highways and no all-reaching and powerful law. Later, when the empire crumbled, paganism came in like a flood and seemed to sweep away much of what was best, in destroying the much that was evil—leaving centuries of chaos and darkness to settle down upon what had been the civilized world. The great world was then physically inaccessible.

But a most remarkable series of providences, reaching over the Christian ages, has made all the world physically accessible to Protestant Christendom of to-day. In Psalm cxi. we read that God "Hath showed his people the power of his works, that he might give them the heritage of the heathen." That word has been fulfilled, not only in God's providential dealings with Israel of old and with his Church in modern times, but also in another and remarkable sense, in which the "power of God's works" may be understood to mean the "forces of nature." Along with the Christian movement of the ages and the other providential movements, God has been revealing to the nations, especially to the Christian nations, and in a peculiar sense to the Protestant Christian nations, three great forces of nature, by which everything has been transformed and civilization made another thing from what it was in the distant past. Those three great forces are magnetism, steam, and electricity. Each of these has had its mission in the great plan of God, in making the world physically accessible to the Gospel message. *The Nature Providences.*

It may properly be admitted that, to begin with, in

the early centuries, the world, especially beyond the Roman Empire, was unknown and inaccessible. God revealed to man—no one knows how or when or where—the application of magnetism in the mariner's compass, and, with that as his guide, man went out over the earth in his work of discovery, and in process of time it became a known world. At the opening of the thirteenth century, A. D., about all the known world was a little strip of land around the Mediterranean Sea. But magnetism, in the mariner's compass, in the next three centuries practically opened the whole world to the knowledge of the civilized nations.

In due time, after the Reformation, with the awakened and earnest life of the Christian Church, there came the need for enlarged facilities for commerce and more rapid intercommunication among the nations. It was then, when the missionary idea began to take possession of men's hearts, that God gave to man the knowledge of the application of steam, in the steam-engine, to prepare the way for such increased intercourse. The bearing of this providential gift upon the problems of modern evangelization may readily be seen. It is to be observed that the knowledge of this power of steam was not given to the heathen nations, nor to the Mohammedan nations. It was not given first to the Roman Catholic nations; and it has not been largely applied by them. They are not to-day employing one-fourth as much steam-power as is employed by the Protestant nations. The gift was reserved until the Greater Spain, the Greater Portugal, and the Greater France were passing away, and the Greater Britain, representing Protestant Christendom, had come to the front. And all this wonderful power of steam is to-day mainly in the hands of the Protestant nations. Steam began the work of bringing the world closer together and making it easily accessible—the world that was before inaccessible, even after it had been made known through the mariner's compass. This was a marvelous step forward in the work of preparing for the evangelization of the world.

Following the revelation of magnetism and steam there has come, in this age, that of a new force—electricity, to be employed as an agency in bringing the nations of the earth together into practical unity. This new force of nature promises to be the great motor of the world for the coming generation, to cheapen transportation and intercourse, and to help in annihilating the vast interspaces that have hitherto kept the nations apart. It promises to make—is already making—revolutions in comparison with which what has been accomplished by magnetism and steam can not but appear insignificant. We have already seen the telegraph and the telephone advance in their reach, from the "short-distance" to the "long-distance"; until men can literally speak their messages across a continent or under a sea, in their own distinct and clear tones.

God in his providence has been making this threefold revelation of his power to his people, that he might give them the "heritage of the heathen." Christ has, so to speak, been gathering all the world into one mighty audience-chamber, to the remotest aisles of which every word for Christ may reach; and he is now waiting for the Church to look this condition of things in the face, and to acknowledge that, however it may have been in the past ages or generations, the excuse that the world is an inaccessible world can now no longer be honestly pleaded at the bar of God, and that it can not be regarded as worthy of serious consideration even by intelligent men.

## II. The World Governmentally Open to the Church.

The preacher's commission authorizes him, in the light of God's providences, to proclaim to the dilatory Church that the old excuse, that heathenism is governmentally closed to missionary effort, no longer holds at the bar of reason.

When, about fifty years ago, Dr. John Harris wrote the prize essay entitled, "The Great Commission,"—the most eloquent and stirring appeal that has been made to the modern Church in behalf of missions,—he proclaimed with almost prophetic foresight the dawning of a new era, and summoned with almost Apostolic fervor Christ's followers to the rescue of the world from sin and Satan. At that time the more earnest Christians were gathering, from month to month, to pray in concert for the breaking down of the barriers imposed by the governments of the nations, Roman Catholic and Pagan, to the spread of the true Gospel. These nations were then everywhere substantially closed against evangelical Christianity—the whole force of the governments being arrayed against it and on the side of error. Many are now living who can recollect when the "Monthly Concert of Prayer for Missions" was introduced into the churches. The Christian Church prayed unitedly for the opening of the world to Christianity.

In answer to this prayer God's providence has been moving in a most wonderful way in breaking down the barriers. The governmental obstacles interposed by the heathen nations have successively been removed —partly through internal revolution and partly through external pressure; partly by advances of commerce and the quickening of thought, and partly by mighty throes that have shaken the world—until the masses of Asia and of Africa and of the Islands of the Sea are almost as open to the Christian missionary as are the non-church-going multitudes in so-called Christian lands. At this very date we seem to be witnessing the completion of this work in the far East, in the great conflict between Japan and China, that is already throwing wide open the gates of the Hermit Nation, and that promises to shatter the walls that have hitherto barred the way of Christian civilization to most of the four hundred million inhabitants of the Flowery Kingdom. In the Papal world, on the Western Continent, from Mexico to Patagonia, and on the Eastern Continent, in Italy, Spain, Austria, and the other leading Roman Catholic nations, the religious changes that have taken place in the same period have opened vast and inviting mission fields to Protestant Christianity. Men of this generation have seen the lines of traffic and intercourse, with power of magnetism, steam, and electricity, reach out over the earth, until the network of inter-communication has become well-nigh complete. The Suez Canal and the transcontinental and international railway and steamship lines have brought Christianity right to the open doors of all the world. The lines of travel that, under control of the Protestant nations, pass through the straits of Gibraltar and the Suez Canal to the Great East, and those that are to be found in connection with the steamers

*Hostile Barriers Removed.*

on the great rivers, together with the great Indian and other railways, carry those who take them right to the doors of nine hundred millions of the human race who need the greater light that shines out from the open Bible—to the doors of all the great representative Papal nations, Portugal, Spain, France, Italy, Austria; of all the representative Mohammedan nations, the Barbary States, the two Turkeys, Egypt, Nubia, the Sudan and Eastern Africa, Arabia, Persia; and of all the representative Pagan nations, Afghanistan, Baluchistan, Hindustan, India, Farther China, Japan, Korea, and the inhabitants of the almost innumerable islands of the Pacific Ocean.

Every one will be ready to admit that this new route has vast significance for the commerce of the future, but the Christian can not help seeing that it will not have less for the Church in its work; for the very steamships that bear the traffic of the world along the Mediterranean, up the Nile, the Euphrates, the Indus, the Ganges, the Brahmaputra, the Irrawaddy, the Cambodia, the Yang-tse-Kiang, and the Hoang-Ho, into the very heart, nay, to the remotest bounds, of all these great nations, are ready to bear the missionaries of the Church to the same regions. The man of most exalted imagination can have but an inadequate view of the vast import, to the cause of Christ, of this new step in the onward movement of Providence.

*The Route of the World's Commerce.*

Viewed in its relation to the population of the globe, its bearings appear no less striking and important than when viewed in its relations to the nationalities. Estimating the total population of the globe in round numbers at fifteen hundred millions, more than nine hundred millions are found along this great thoroughfare! Of the remaining millions, the one half, along Northern Europe and Asia, are under the control of the Protestant and Greek Churches. The remaining millions inhabit the portions of America and Africa peculiarly under the moral influence of the United States and Great Britain.

Let the fact be emphasized, then, that the Protestant Churches, with all their new facilities for giving the world the Gospel, *now for the first time in history*, stand foremost at every one of the open doors of the world. A single month will soon suffice to place a band of missionaries far within the bounds of the most remote of these nations. The inquiry forces itself upon every one who gives this subject a moment's thought: What does it all mean? This almost incomprehensible increase in the facilities for propagating the Gospel among the unevangelized races, and the giving of them all into the hands of the leading Protestant states—do not these providences point Protestant Christians to a special duty? The creation of these facilities within the memory of men still living—does it not point to *present duty?*

*Protestantism at the Open Doors.*

Before the imperious demands of commerce the reluctant monarchs of the earth have withdrawn the barriers of government, and thrown open the portals of their nations to the trade of Christendom, and the missionary of the Church has to-day *practically free access with the Gospel to all the nations of the earth.* The commission of the preacher requires him, therefore, to announce and to demonstrate to the slow-going Church that she is henceforth barred from pleading, as an excuse for her delay in evangelizing the world, that impassable governmental barriers block the way of her messengers. That excuse has been shown to be no longer valid at the bar of reason, and it must be worse than vain at the bar of God.

### III. Roman Catholicism no Longer Dominates the World.

The preacher's commission warrants him, in the light of God's providence, in proclaiming to the hesitating Church of Christ that the excuse that Roman Catholicism dominates the world, however true it may have been in the past, is no longer valid and can no longer be urged.

A series of remarkable providences in modern times has brought Protestant Christendom practically into commercial, political, moral, and religious control of the world. These past four hundred years and more, since Columbus found the way to the New World, have been marvelous years. It is well to stop and think what has taken place in them. In recent years Columbus has been the one great figure brought into prominence, in connection with this Continent, by the Columbian Exposition. In the centuries since the discovery of America, the entire face of the Christian world has been changed.

*The Columbian Providences.*

Four hundred and fifty years ago, there was the Roman Catholic Church covering Europe—that was practically the extent of Christendom; and there was the Mohammedan world surrounding it on the south and east; while the two, in military array, were face to face at Constantinople and Grenada. It was a question whether Roman and Greek Christendom would conquer the Mohammedan world, or the Mohammedan world would conquer Roman and Greek Christendom, the Christendom of that day. When the Turk took Constantinople, in 1453, men thought that the world had almost come to an end. It seemed the great disaster of all time. The Turk, in getting possession of Constantinople, sat down across the gateway to India, whence riches came; and the lines of commerce were in his control and the riches of the world at his feet. Europe was shut out, and Christendom shut out, from that source of wealth. But the fall of the Eastern Empire spurred the Roman Christendom in the West to new and redoubled effort, and Spain, under Ferdinand and Isabella, aided by the military genius of Gonçalo de Córdova, conquered Grenada and expelled the Moor from Western Europe, only forty years after the fall of Constantinople, and so became the foremost power in Europe. A great nation, trained and disciplined into strength and enterprise and chivalrous spirit by seven hundred years of warfare with the Moors, was thus compelled to seek new channels of adventure and a broader field of action. It was these two great events, the one in the Orient and the other in the Occident, that changed the destiny of the modern world.

As one result of them, we have the reaching out over the world, until then unknown, by the great voyagers of the next seventy years after the fall of Constantinople, and thirty years after the conquest of Grenada. These events indirectly gave the inspiration, the impulse. They rendered it necessary that those three great voyages of all time should be made. In 1492 Columbus, seeking India by a new way, found this New World, a New India. In 1497 Vasco da Gama, again seeking India, found the way around the must, humanly speaking, be accomplished. Protestantism is practically supreme. The preacher must utter no uncertain sound on this subject, but must leave the Church stripped of its old excuse, for God himself has made it utterly baseless and worthless.

### IV. The Means Necessary for the Work in the Hands of the Church.

The preacher's commission requires him, in the light of God's providence and of his Word, to proclaim to a covetous Church that her old excuse, that her poverty stands in the way of her fulfilment of her mission, and that the Lord's money-tithes are inadequate to the work, has come to be an insult to God, to cover up a positive and long continued failure to meet this plain requirement.

Christians have in the past pleaded their poverty as a reason for not literally obeying Christ's last command. They have often claimed that proper provision for the present necessities of life, and the need of "laying by something against a rainy day," have exhausted their means and left nothing—at best a mere pittance—to give to the work of missions at home and abroad, for the saving of mankind. That this has usually been little more than a mere hypocritical pretext, the past experience of such bodies of Christians as the Moravians clearly shows. The time has now fully come when the preacher needs to show the Christian Church, beyond possibility of gainsaying, that the state of things on which she based her old excuse has passed away, and that the theory of Christian giving by which she has directed her conduct has no foundation in the Word of God.

Let it be emphasized that it is not the *poor Church* of the past, but the *marvelously rich Church* of to-day, that calls for consideration, and that must set the law and pace for Christian duty in the matter of giving and in the work of the Gospel.

A silent revolution,—a revolution almost inconceivable as we look back upon it,—that has been going on through the century, has resulted in throwing vast wealth into the hands of Christendom, and especially into the hands of Protestant Christendom.  1. A Revolution and its Causes. The remarkable revolutions of the past fifty years have been so numerous, and so silent, that even the best ecclesiastical statisticians and financiers scarcely understood the full meaning of that *rich Church* and its vast income, which so often enter into their calculations.

De Quincey, in some curious investigations, in his *Biographical Essays*, has shown that the dowry that Mary Arden, the mother of Shakespeare, brought to his father, John Shakespeare—the estate amounting at the lowest calculation to £100 and at the highest to £224, and the rent amounting at the lowest to £8 and at the highest to £14—was really a very respectable fortune. In these days, and that even after taking into account the difference in values, so greatly in favor of three centuries ago, such an income would be considered but a beggarly one for the most unskilful boot-black. Only seventy-five years ago, when Coleridge refused a half-share in *The Morning Post and Courier*, with the emphatic declaration that he would not give up his country life with the lazy reading of old folios, for two thousand times the income it offered; he added: "In short, beyond £350 a year I regard money as a real evil." Yet this would barely meet the wants of a first-class mechanic of the present day.

Manifold causes have wrought in producing an almost fabulous increase in the wealth of the Protestant nations, during the present century. One of these is found in the fact that steam furnishes the nervous power and steel the muscle of modern material civilization. The industrial arts have thus been revolutionized. The able-bodied working population of the globe is about 200,000,000; that is, the globe can furnish, in the form of productive man-power, about that number of days' work in a single day. A century ago, that constituted the major part of the work that could be done by mankind in a day. At the present time Great Britain alone, by machine-power with steam and electricity, is able to do from five to ten times that amount of work; while the United States can probably do even more, and Germany is making rapid advance in the same direction. This development of productive power has been the source of an immense increase of wealth.

Another cause may be found in the commerce, that has grown so immensely in consequence of this enlarged productive power, and that has made the world chiefly tributary to the leading Protestant nationalities.

A third cause is to be noted in those striking providences that seem to indicate the purpose of God to give the world to Protestant Christendom, among which may be enumerated those that in a century have increased the subjects of the British Empire from 13,000,000 to almost 400,000,000; those that have raised Prussia from the position of an insignificant state to a first place on the map of Europe, at the head of the German Empire with its 50,000,000 of people ; and those that have established on these western shores our great Republic with its almost 70,000,000 of free people, mostly Christian and Protestant.

Most marked perhaps of all has been the gift of the great gold and silver fields—Australia, California, South Africa, and the Ural region— to the Protestant or anti-papal nations. If these deposits of the precious metals had been discovered a little earlier, they would have gone into the hands of people holding other religions, and would have been used—as the wealth that Spain wrested from Mexico and Peru was used to spread Roman Catholicism—for the dissemination of those other religions. But they were reserved until Protestant Christendom was at the front and had substantial control, and they were then providentially given into the hands of the foremost Protestant Christian nations. *The Treasure-Fields of the World.*

There have been some strange things in connection with the opening up of these vast stores of riches. Dr. Stone gave the writer, several years ago, a little incident learned in connection with the Historical Society in San Francisco, that will show how wonderful these providences have sometimes been. Before we had taken California from Mexico, or about that time, the Jesuit Fathers became aware, through the Indians, of the fact of the existence of gold-mines in that region. They surveyed the mines, prepared their maps, and took ship for Spain just before California came into our hands, to inform the Spanish government and the authorities abroad of their wonderful discovery. But those charts and those Fathers were never heard of again! Had they reached the other side, Spain would doubtless have grasped California with a firm grip, or would have aided Mexico to hold fast to it, to prevent it from coming into the hands of the United States.

The increase of wealth resulting from these and other causes has almost outrun accurate statistics, and even imagination. So far as we have been able to ascertain by somewhat careful inquiry, an annual income of a million dollars is more common on this side of the ocean now than was an income of fifty thousand half a century ago. Three centuries ago, the ransom of the Inca Atahualpa, paid to that Spanish robber and butcher Pizarro, turned the brain of all Europe by its magnitude; yet it was less than the annual income of many of our merchant princes as the reward of legitimate business, and hardly a tithe of what many of our speculators manage to get hold of by illegitimate business.

The increase of national wealth in the aggregate has kept pace with that of individual wealth. The material progress of the nation, for the two decades from 1850 to 1870, will illustrate the earlier stages of the change. The total wealth of the nation in 1850 was $7,000,000,000; in 1860, $16,000,000,000; in 1870, according to the estimate of Special Commissioner Wells, $23,000,000,000, and, according to that of Judge Kelly, member of Congress from Pennsylvania, $43,000,000,000. The increase in twenty years, during five of which there was expended or wasted in civil war at least $10,000,000,000, was therefore somewhere from three to six fold. The gross product of the industry of the country about 1870, which may represent its gross annual income,

*2. Results of the Revolution.*

apart from the annual increase of aggregate values just referred to, Mr. Wells estimated at $6,825,000,-000. He proceeds, however, at once to show that this "is an under rather than an over estimate"; and in doing this gives data drawn from the wages of the lowest of the working classes, that indicate that $8,-000,000,000 would be a very moderate estimate. These statistics show that the product of the industry of the nation in 1870 equaled or surpassed the entire value of all its property twenty years before. A like marvelous increase took place in the wealth of Great Britain and an almost equal increase in the case of some other nations. The last twenty-five years has witnessed the continuance of this astonishing pace of material prosperity, as might readily be shown by statistics.

In view of these extraordinary facts, the question comes home with overwhelming force, Why has God so flooded the Protestant nations with wealth, and done it in these same years in which the way has been opened for the Gospel into all nations, and Protestant Christendom brought to stand foremost at all these openings? **3. Consequent Christian Duty.**

It cannot be claimed with a shadow of justice, or even a show of plausibility, that this vastly enlarged wealth is required for increased expenses of living. Nor can it be claimed, with any greater show of justice, that either the Scriptures or human experience warrants the hoarding up of these vast sums in private coffers. Mr. Lewis Tappan, well known once as a Christian merchant, and later as secretary of one of the benevolent societies of the country, in his little tract, "Is it Right to be Rich?" gives a forcible exhibition of the teachings of the Scriptures on this subject, in connection with many striking corroborative facts drawn from his extended observation and experience—an exhibition, the acquaintance with which can not but be helpful, even if one is not prepared to indorse all its presentations. How dangerous this unscriptural hoarding of millions is, to the possessors of great wealth and to their families, any one may learn by observation.

In short, nothing can be clearer than that the Head of the Church has not placed this vast wealth, just at this juncture, in the hands of his stewards, the members of the Christian Church, for the purpose of allowing them to indulge in enervating luxuries without stint, or to pamper their families, or for the purpose of giving them opportunity to store up millions of rusting treasure for their children to use and abuse. If there is any meaning in this wondrous chain of providences, taken together and in connection with the truths of God's absolute ownership of everything and the Christian's stewardship, that meaning must be this: that Christ does not purpose that the thousands of millions of the race for whom his blood was shed shall perish without the Gospel; and that, moreover, he has rolled upon the Church of this very time the responsibility of furnishing the entire pecuniary means requisite for the work in its completeness, at home and abroad, the world over. He who has the authority, given him by the Father, to call for the gold *at any time*, calls *now*. Can the Church, and especially its opulent members, give a valid reason for not furnishing the Lord's treasury with all that is needed *now?*

## V. THE NEEDED MESSENGERS AND MACHINERY READY.

The preacher's commission, in the light of the Divine Word and providence, and of existing industrial and financial conditions, demands that he should warn a worldly Church that the old excuse, that the messengers and the organizing and administrative power for such speedy completion of the work of the Gospel, are lacking, has lost all force and validity.

It may be true that, but a short time ago, the Church was unable to spare the messengers needed for the immediate accomplishment of such a work. It may be true that, one hundred years ago, there was need of well-nigh all the work of all the able-bodied men in the world, to take care of the world and meet the pressing necessities of mankind. One hundred years ago there were two hundred millions of able-bodied men, or rather, there were enough in the world to do the work of two hundred millions of able-bodied men. That was the working power of the world then. To-day, by the aid of steam and electricity, as has been seen, the able-bodied men represented in the working power of this country and Great Britain alone, are reaching up into the billions. Through these wonderful developments in the providence of God, we, in this country, can easily do the work of more than a billion men instead of the work of a few millions, say ten millions, that we could formerly do; and we are able at will to increase that ability indefinitely. And it is so, to a great extent, with the other nations, especially the Protestant nations. Vast multitudes have thus been set free, or may at pleasure be set free, from the necessity of manual labor in the old style—unless reenslaved by wrong economic principles and conditions.

That is one reason why we have so many idlers. God, in furnishing steam as the muscles and electricity as the nerve-power of this age, has freed from pressing necessity to labor a great multitude of the young and of the old. He has set them free for a purpose; they have not found out that purpose; and therefore are idling away or playing away life. The preacher has not given them the needed light upon the subject. Necessity is upon the Church, for her self-preservation, that they be used in God's way. God, by his providences and his Word, clearly demands that all this work be devoted, not to the increase of wealth, of the grandeur and the growth of our material civilization, which would bring luxury and vice and death; but for his glorious purpose in the Gospel, as expressed in the Great Commission.

It may have been true, fifty years ago, that, of the vast multitude of the laity in the Church, but few had any consciousness of a call from Christ to cooperate actively in giving the Gospel to all men, and that but few had any experience or even interest in such cooperation; but that is no longer true. The great awakening of 1858 was, as is shown more fully elsewhere, specifically an awakening of the laity, and having every appearance of being providentially intended to bring a chief and essential factor in the Church—theretofore only in small degree available—into proper prominence and rightful place in the Christian work of these times.

The period that has since elapsed has been especially a period for organizing, and getting into working order, the immense lay forces in Christendom. That awakening has inspired the world-wide movement of the Young Men's Christian Association, of the Young People's Society of Christian Endeavor, of the Epworth League, and manifold kindred organizations. It has compelled the hearty recognition of the layman, even in episcopally organized Churches. It has entered as a powerful factor, and a principal impelling and shaping force, into the more recent evangelistic work of Mr. Moody and other Gospel workers of kindred spirit all over the world, great numbers of whom have been simple laymen. It is an essential feature in the present vast and rapidly increasing work of the Salvation Army, in rousing the lapsed and submerged classes throughout the bounds of Christendom. It has given a new impulse to missions at home and abroad, and has already led thousands to consecrate themselves to mission work. There is only needed, in order to complete the preparation for the final triumphant movement against the forces of sin and Satan, that all the older and wiser heads in the Church should be roused and incited—as many already have been—to add the experience and wisdom of age to the energy and enthusiasm of youth; and that the preacher should come to an understanding of the situation, and a readiness to take his place of leadership, in the great final campaign; in short, there is only needed a new baptism of the Holy Spirit, to marshal all the forces of Christendom for the immediate conquest of the world for Christ.

It may likewise have been true, a century ago, that the Church was not possessed of the organization or the administrative power needed for the speedy completion of so vast a work; but it is not true to-day. As a natural and necessary

*Administrative Power Ready.*

result of the immense increase of wealth, and the vast extension of industry, trade, and commerce, this is the age of organization and of business enterprise on the scale of the world. While, therefore, it may still remain a fact that the preachers of the Gospel have no very large organizing or business ability, it is nevertheless a fact, more pertinent as well as more important, that the Church has among her members and office-bearers great numbers of men who have that capacity in a very unusual degree, tested by long and wide experience, and waiting to be used in this greatest enterprise of the ages, for the energetic and immediate urging forward of the work to which Christ calls now, in the present tense of that command, "Go ye!"

Many of these men of exceptional abilities, having tested their capabilities and accumulated fortunes, and having become dissatisfied with the sordid work and selfish scramble of money-getting, have retired from business, while yet in the full vigor and maturity of their powers, and are ignominiously rusting out, or sinking into the comparative imbecility that always results from strong powers unused, no less than from the selfish indulgence that so often attends upon such disuse of powers once developed. There are the best reasons for believing that many such men would be only too glad of the opportunity to take up and plan some task of a nobler order for the Master, if it were pointed out to them—some task that would prevent them from becoming nonentities in this world, and at the same time help them to retain and increase the strength that would fit them for the larger and better tasks of the other world. We know, too, that others are consciously and intelligently casting about for such tasks for themselves.

The late Colonel Elliot F. Shepard was a conspicuous illustration of this. When about to enter upon the career of a journalist, he divulged his plans to a distinguished citizen of New York. Immense wealth, and the power of rapidly increasing it, did not satisfy him as a Christian man. He said: "A man can accomplish very little that is worth his while with money." Distinguished position in the law and in society did not satisfy him. He rated fame as of little value in itself, and as conferring little added power upon a Christian man for doing good. He had determined to use his wealth in establishing a great secular journal that should advocate the application of Christian principles along all the lines of social, municipal, and national reform, and to devote his time and influence to giving it success. In this way he began, and for years carried on, the struggle for municipal reform in New York that culminated in the recent great political revolution in that city. At the same time, as a stanch advocate of the Christian observance of the Sabbath, he made his influence powerfully felt over the nation. And all the success that crowned his efforts in these directions did not turn him away from his churchly Christian duties, nor from a practical and princely interest in the work of missions, either at home—as is witnessed by church mortages paid off and churches endowed—or abroad—as is witnessed by the Christian school founded and endowed by him for the children of Paul's native city of Tarsus.

The story of such lives—this is but one of many—narrated by preacher or press, would doubtless furnish inspiration for others, and direct them to nobler purpose and better accomplishment in Christ's service, until, in God's own time and way, all the needed administrative and organizing ability should be subsidized in the interests of the Church, in carrying out her commission for a lost world.

The messengers can assuredly be had, as appears from the immense volunteer force—in connection with the Young People's Society of Christian Endeavor and other organizations, and in the Volunteer Missionary movement—waiting everywhere to be sent. The organizations necessary are all ready and prepared to handle the means, the men, and the work; as may be seen by inquiring into the character and scope of the great missionary societies of the nation and of the world. The business and administrative ability requisite for so great a work is all to be had for the asking—as may be seen by the increasing number of those who have been leaders in the world's business, who are now ready to devote something of their time and ability to this greater task; or who have already given up their worldly business and are ready to devote all their time and powers for their remaining days to the Lord's work, for the taking up of which their worldly successes have admirably prepared them.

The preacher who fails to understand all this, and to bring home the truth to the Church, in such a way as to inspire her with that truth, and who fails to lead his people to take up the work and carry it forward, will so far fail in fulfilling his commission. That commission most assuredly requires him to let it be known with all clearness that such an excuse as lack of messengers and organizations and administrative ability for the work, can no longer be rationally entertained or pleaded at the bar of human reason or of conscience,

*The Preacher's Duty.*

or innocently presented and urged at the bar of God, in extenuation of the sin of neglecting the command of Christ.

Let the preacher understand, then, and give himself to making all Christendom understand, that God has providentially taken away all the obstacles and excuses that have in the past delayed the work of evangelizing the world; that the Church stands to-day in the presence of him who gave her the commission, without shadow of excuse or pretext for further delay, and that, if the work is not done at once, the Church will be responsible for not doing it.

In doing this he will need to make clear as sunlight the providential drift of recent years and the resulting situation and duty. The Church needs, first of all, to have light on these subjects. She must be made to see that God has set the task of the world's evangelization right before her, and be forced to feel that her obligation is immediate and imperative.

The preacher must make it clear that God has removed the old natural and governmental barriers that stood in the way of missions, and opened all the world to them; that he has brought Protestant Christendom to the front and made it the dominant power in the world; that he has revealed to the Protestant nations the swift and subtile forces of nature wherewith to multiply inconceivably its working-power by machine production, and to emancipate vast multitudes to be his messengers to the world, and that he has given to these nations all the great treasure-fields and most of the commerce of the globe. He must bring the Church to realize the meaning of the immense wealth that the second half of the nineteenth century has poured into her coffers, and that will bring wreck and perdition if used for selfish ends and enjoyments instead of for the glory of God. He must press upon her attention, with urgent zeal, the significance of the Christian unity that has come to pervade her spirit and her hosts; of the universal rousing of the laity to a sense of the fact that they are coworkers with Christ in saving the world; of the world-wide organizations for effective service for Christ; and of the attitude of vast numbers, especially of the young men and the young women, in waiting to be sent to aid in establishing the Kingdom of God.

All this, in connection with the dreadful condition of the lost world, and the life and death urgency of the work, must be enforced and emphasized by the preacher until all Christians shall come to understand the situation, and be constrained to stop and consider, and to inquire what is their present duty in relation to the world's evangelization.

## SECTION SECOND.

### The Scriptural Law of Giving Provides the Needed Means for the Work.

But may not all this be true, and yet the Church be under no obligation to furnish, at the present time, all the pecuniary means needed to send the Gospel at once into all the world? So the Church—judging from her acts—seems to think.

A greater or more deadly error is hardly conceivable. There is not even the shadow of a foundation for it in the Word of God.

The supreme need of the hour, next to the outpouring of the Holy Spirit, is that *the Church should be set right in her theory of Christian giving.* She has been, and is still, directing her conduct in this matter in accordance with a false and unscriptural theory, that would prove fatal to her success even if her wealth were again multiplied a hundredfold, as it has already been multiplied a thousandfold—a theory that must always prove fatal *because* false and unscriptural. It therefore becomes a main part of the duty of the ministry, as the leaders in the Church, to set her right in this regard, that the world may be saved without delay. So general and so fundamental is the error on this point, and so inevitably fatal, that we are constrained to ask special and prayerful attention to its consideration, and to the teaching of the Word of God regarding it. If such error exists, the subject manifestly calls for such attention and consideration, and no leader in Zion can innocently avoid or evade the duty of making a complete investigation for himself.

<small>False Theories.</small>

Perhaps it is almost too much to speak of such a thing as *the Church's theory of Christian giving.* A vast number of professing Christians do not consciously hold any theory on that subject. Their practical theory, as formulated from their conduct, seems to be that, after they have ministered to their own necessities and enjoyments to the full and laid up a generous sum "against a rainy day," if there be anything left from their income, such driblets of this surplusage as the minister may extort from them by pathetic appeals, or the parish draw from them by oyster suppers and other pious entertainments, should go reluctantly to help carry out Christ's commission. The brother who thanked the Lord for a "free religion," and declared that tho he had been "a member of the Church for twenty-five years it had only cost him twenty-five cents," may be regarded as the typical Christian of this class. There is still another and large class who treat their giving very much as a matter of impulse, and so give without system. At a far remove from these is a small class of conscientious Christians who advocate systematic giving, according to the Jewish law of tithes, which, it is claimed, requires of every one a tenth of his income, either in the net or in the gross. The great fact remains, as will be seen, that the Church is giving *next to nothing of what she should give* for the carrying out of her commission from the Master.

And unless the preachers wake up and tell the Church the whole truth of God in this matter, there is no good reason to expect the world's conversion for a thousand years to come. The Church's theories are all wrong,—as demonstrated by the outcome,—and the preacher must make that plain beyond misunderstanding, doubt, or peradventure. If he is to do that, his watchword must be, "To the law and to the testimony." It is high time for him to go back to the Word of God to learn what is the law of Christian giving, in order to enforce it upon the rich Church of to-day.

### The Law of Christian Giving.

The law of Christian giving is the basal thing for the Church of the present time. If there are any principles involved in the matter, or if there are any rules that govern or should govern it, it is most assuredly of vital importance that the preacher should find out what they are, and that he should let the Church know just what they are and precisely what the Master requires of her.

It may be that we ought not to say "Christian *giving*," for the time is fast coming, if, indeed, it has not already come—when that expression must be abandoned. We cannot *give* to any one what already belongs to him. The Christian can not, strictly speaking, *give* to Christ what is already *his own by every possible title.* We should speak rather of "the Christian's use of wealth as the steward of Christ in the Kingdom of God."

The starting-point is with the requirements made through Moses, the Hebrew lawgiver. The old dispensation laid the foundation for the new. *According to the Mosaic code, what portion was the Jew required to devote to the cause of religion?*

**Old Testament Rule.**

The general notion is that he gave *one tenth.* That is clearly a mistaken notion, as any one will see by an examination of the Scriptures; and the theory founded upon it is utterly baseless.

The law, in its first enactment, required the Jew to give *one tenth* to the Levite. If he paid it in kind, well; if not, one fifth of one tenth was added. The Levite gave a tenth of his tenth to the Lord for the support of the high priest (see Levit. xxvii. 30–33; Num. xviii.). This first tenth was for the support of the priesthood. But the law required that the Jew should devote a *second tenth* to the yearly religious festivals. He was to take this tenth to the place appointed by the Lord for his worship (see Deut. xiv. 22–27). Then, every third year, he was to bring a *third tenth* of all his produce and share it with the Levite and the poor and the stranger, in festival rejoicing with them. This was enacted in Deut. xiv. 28, 29, and renewed in Deut. xxvi.

If its provisions have been read correctly, the Mosaic law demanded of the Jew *two tenths* every year, and every third year *three tenths*, or an average of two and one-third tenths yearly.

But may not the record have been read incorrectly? Certainly no argument against the result arrived at, based upon the greatness of the requirement, can for a moment stand, for, by accurate calculation, almost one half the time of the Jew was required in God's service. It was evidently the divine purpose to require great things of the chosen people. Indeed, it is necessary to go further and to take into account the fact that these tithes were *only a part* of the gifts of the Jew—the ordered and measured part—before we can appreciate the full extent of the means which he devoted to God's service. The other part consisted of *free-will offerings*, the largeness and frequency of which were left to the promptings of the individual heart, but which might, in some instances, even exceed the tithes. Moreover, in the case of the Jew, it was the *gross income* or product of his industry that was tithed, before anything had been used for his own purposes.

But we are rescued from all need of dependence on probabilities by finding just at hand reliable witnesses to the correctness of the above reading of the Mosaic law. Josephus, who lived at the time of the destruction of Jerusalem, says distinctly that one tenth was to be given yearly to the Levites; one tenth was to be applied to the festivals at Jerusalem; and one tenth was to be given every third year to the poor. Tobit, who probably wrote about 400 B. C., and Jerome, who wrote about 400 A. D., tell us the same thing. Now, these are all credible and competent witnesses to the Jewish understanding of the law, in their various days, and they all confirm our reading of the rule which was to govern the benevolence of the Jews.

But the pertinent question arises: Does this enactment of the Jewish lawgiver belong to that part of his code that, as is the case with the Decalogue, is of *perpetual obligation*, and, therefore, necessarily binding upon the Christian Church? Or, if not, what is the present rule that is to govern the Church in its Christian giving? *(New Testament Rule.)*

This involves the inquiry: *How did Christ and his Apostles treat the tithes system?* What rule did they acknowledge or lay down?

How did Christ, himself the greater lawgiver than Moses, treat the tithe system? It is learned from the Gospels that he ratified it, at least for the Jew. He did this when he reproved *(Christ's View.)* the Pharisees for their neglect of the weightier matters of the law: "Wo unto you, scribes and Pharisees, hypocrites; for ye pay tithes of mint, and anise, and cumin, and have omitted the weightier matters of the law, judgment, mercy, and faith; *these ought ye to have done*, and not to leave the other undone." This ratification is recorded in Matt. xxiii. 23, and in Luke xi. 42.

But was this ratification for any one besides the Jew? The considerations in favor of a negative answer appear to be conclusive—for the Jew clearly, since the Jew was still under the law of Moses, and this was but an affirmation of that fact; for none besides the Jew, since Jesus was himself "a minister of the circumcision," or of the old dispensation (see Rom. xv. 8), and, as such, enforcing the law of Moses. The new dispensation could not have its full beginning until its foundation had been laid in Christ's death. Taking into account the teachings of the Apostles, along with those of our Lord himself, there is nowhere any clear and sufficient evidence that he made the old Jewish law of tithes the law of that dispensation. There is nowhere even the shadow of evidence that he did.

If he did reaffirm the law, then the requirement would be that the Church should yearly devote at least *seven thirtieths* of its income to the objects of Christian benevolence: and this, too, in addition to all the free-will offerings for which the special favors of God give ten thousand occasions. If he did not reaffirm it, then more, rather than less, in some form, must be required of Christians as a body. If a reason be asked, it may be answered that, since the times of the Mosaic law, the grand truth of God's ownership of all things has given place to that of Christ's ownership of all things; that the motive has risen all the way up from law to love; and that the mission of the people in covenant with God has enlarged from the reception and conservation of the divine revelation in the little Jewish state to the propagation of the Gospel throughout the whole world. To the Christian, the Head of the Church can say: "Give as bought by my blood; as recreated by my Spirit; as you love me; as a perishing world needs."

But assuming that Christ did not make the Mosaic system binding under the new dispensation, did the Apostles, on whom devolved the work of organizing the primitive Church, do any such thing?

**The Apostles' View.**

We think the answer must be an emphatic negative.

The substantive expression for "tithe," and the twofold verbal expression for "giving tithes" and "receiving tithes," occur in the Apostolic writings, from the Acts to the Revelation, only seven times—never out of the Epistle to the Hebrews, and always in such connection as to preclude the basing upon them of any valid argument for the reenactment of the Jewish tithe law for the New Testament Church. It is hard to see how any one who does clear thinking can avoid coming to the same conclusion, with regard to the whole tithing system, that Blackstone reached with regard to the clergy of the Church of England, and that in spite of his notorious and almost slavish adherence to past usages, and which he expressed when he wrote in his *Commentaries*, "I will not put the title of the clergy to tithes upon any divine right, though such a right certainly commenced, and I believe as certainly ceased, with the Jewish theocracy." See Blackstone, *Commentaries*, bk. ii. ch. 8.

*What, then, is the Scriptural and Apostolic rule laid down to govern the Church in Christian giving?* We can barely call attention to the rule, as comprehensively stated by Paul for the Christians in Corinth, in 1 Cor. xvii. 2: "Upon the first day of the week let every one of you lay by him in store as God has prospered him." The Apostolic rule evidently knows no measure short of the steward's utmost ability, when wholly under control of love to Christ and a lost world. The single illustration from Christian conduct, to which we may refer, is that furnished by the mother Church of all, at Jerusalem, and recorded in the second chapter of the Acts of the Apostles. Living in that first great crisis in the spread of the Gospel, than which no greater has been

*The Apostolic Rule.*

known till that of the present day, those early Christians read with all clearness the demand of their ascended Lord, in his words and in the signs of the times, and, catching the spirit of their mission, devoted themselves and all their possessions to his cause.

If the views that have been presented are in accordance with the Word of God, there is no reasonable escape from the conclusion that *the Church is at present conducting her work for the world on a false and unscriptural theory.* Even the so-called "systematic giving," on the basis of the Jewish tithing system, is utterly untenable; while the other working-theories are absolutely indefensible as being both Christless and unchristian. While the latter are eminently fitted to furnish a cloak for all the meanness and covetousness possible to unregenerate human nature, and at the same time to dry up the springs of all true benevolence in regenerate human nature; the former can not fail to mechanize and minimize the whole matter of Christian giving and develop a spirit of self-righteousness, self-satisfaction, and self-gratulation. The tithing principle inevitably tends to make the tenth the maximum of gift, to which only one in perhaps tens of thousands will work up, and far below which the majority will contentedly fall; while it is apt to fix the attention of the giver upon the remaining nine tenths, rather than upon the supreme demands of the cause of Christ. It is pretty sure to start with the *net income*, rather than the *gross income* with which the Jew started. Leaving out the time that the Jew devoted to his religion, and the free-will offerings, it halves, or rather thirds, the amount that the Jew gave in tithes. Worst of all, it takes away Christian freedom, remands the man to rule and

*The Church's Unscriptural Theory.*

law, and in the end results in the obscuring of the interests of Christ's Kingdom by mechanism and legalism. These theories are therefore not only baseless, but also demoralizing and dechristianizing in the extreme. Until they have been displaced by the true and Scriptural theory, there can be no hope of any great progress in the work of the Church for a lost world.

Providence and the Scriptures, therefore, unite in sweeping away that old and sinful excuse of a covetous Church—that the Lord's money tithes are inadequate to the work clearly required of her—by bringing out clearly and emphasizing the *present tense* of the command, "Go ye!" In the more than calcium light which they cast upon her present rates of giving for Gospel work, her gifts—however great as compared with those of a generation or two ago—are *beggarly in the extreme!* The preacher's vocation demands that he shall turn on the light, and turn it on, and on again, until the Church is roused to a proper consideration, and apprehension, and comprehension of the existing condition of enormous wealth, and of Christ's requirements respecting the use of it. He is under obligation to press the facts and the divine law upon men, until they are constrained to bring their logic from the schools and the forum, and their arithmetic from the counting-room, the stock-exchange, and the marts of trade, and to make practical application of them to the questions of their own present duty, in view of Christ's pressing demand for the immediate carrying out of the Great Commission.

*Ample Provision Made.*

To apply arithmetic: the gross outcome of American productive industry for the year 1890 was, let us say, $10,000,000,000—figures far below the actual. By a low estimate, one half that sum, or $5,000,000,000, came into the control of those connected directly or indirectly with the Protestant Christian Church and acknowledging more or less fully Christian obligations. One tenth of that—a tithe—would be $500,000,000; two tenths, twice that, or $1,000,000,000; two and a third tenths—or what the old Jew gave—$1,166,000,-000! Is the rich Church able to give what is needed to save a lost world through the preaching of the Gospel? Let every adherent of Protestant Christianity apply his Christian arithmetic to that question and answer it for himself, as he expects to give account to God!

Or look at the possibilities of the problem from another point of view. There are in these United States fourteen million members of evangelical Protestant Churches. Leaving out of consideration the vast number of Church adherents who are not Church members, these millions of professing Christians control approximately one fifth of the wealth of the nation, and one fifth of the annual outcome of production. That would give them a gross income of $2,000,000,-000. One tenth of that is $200,000,000; two tenths, $400,000,000; two and a third tenths, $466,000,000. That would be what God would require of them yearly *if they were Jews,* under the old Jewish law of tithes; that, besides the free-will offerings in recognition of God's special mercies—for their Christian work for the world!

But this statement pertains to the Protestant Christian Church of this country only, leaving out all the rest of the Protestant nations. This emphasizes the question: *Is the Church able to furnish the means to send the Gospel into all this perishing world now?* Is she not herself perishing in wealth and luxury and corruption because she is not doing it? Let every Christian apply his arithmetic to this life-and-death problem and find its true solution, and measure his duty by the Gospel standard, by Christ's own standard.

Who can contemplate, without shuddering, the consequences that must follow from using this vast God-given wealth—given by God and, as shown by his providences, for this one great end of saving a lost world—for other purposes than that for which he has given it? And yet it is undoubtedly being so used ; and all the material show and grandeur gathered at the Columbian Exposition demonstrated that misuse. It is rapidly becoming manifest that the greatest danger to-day to society, to the Church, to this nation, and to the world, is the danger from misused wealth ; for the misuse of such wealth brings to the individual and to the nation luxury; it brings idleness ; it brings vice ; it must bring wreck. That is the natural penalty. That was the course run in the nations of antiquity; and in our case there will follow the same results, if we gather and hoard, or scatter and abuse, this vast wealth, and do nothing more or higher than that. *(Dangers from Hoarded Wealth.)*

Already thoughtful men are coming to recognize the fact that the most dangerous classes in society are not, after all, the men and women down in the slums ; but the rich people who have millions and nothing to do, except to try to get more, or to find something to kill time and out of which to get a passing enjoyment. These are the dangerous classes, because their position and wealth and show give them marvelous influence over all the *(Dangerous Classes.)*

middle classes, and thereby enable them to gloss over irreligion, immorality, and vice; to pervert the moral sentiment of the country and of the world; and to debase and debauch with equal ease the home-life, politics, and religion.

Now God's providences, in all past history, have shown that it was not his purpose that we should gather up all this wealth for ourselves, and keep it for ourselves—or, at least, that we can not do it without ruin. We ought to have learned this lesson in connection with the late Civil War. We kept the slave to make money by; but we learned that "God will have his own." He struck off the chains. He took ten thousand million dollars, in various ways; and that was probably as much as we had made by our oppression—or more. God will have his own! Men ought to learn it by the panics that come periodically, in consequence of their pushing on in their greed for wealth and thinking of nothing else. Every great panic has that lesson of God in it; and the financial crisis and stress through which the nation is passing at the present time has a lesson along the same line. Just so long as men use the gold and silver and steam and the electricity and all these forces of nature and humanity, that God has given them, for selfish ends, for the amassing of wealth, for pleasure and luxury and show—just so long they will find panics recurring, they will find stoppages of activity, they will find ruin overwhelming them from time to time. These providences are always coming and will keep coming; they are God's voice warning of error and danger and destruction, and calling to imperative duty and glorious privilege in Christian work.

*Perils from Misused Wealth.*

The exact situation, then, as it appears from providence and Scriptures, seems to be this: The rich Church, with her great possessions, is to-day confronting a lost world. Christ is holding up before her the ideal Christian, the man of service and of self-sacrifice, and is bidding her to go forward illustrating the ideal Christian character. It can readily be seen that, on the principles of the Old Dispensation, we would have enough in five years to send the Gospel into all the world. We could furnish enough at once, if we were disposed to do it. There is no reason why it should not be done. Every one would be better—and in the end richer too—for doing it. The Church can only refuse it at her peril. Will she consecrate her sons and daughters, and send them to this work? Or will she keep them at home, and pamper them with her wealth and destroy them? Will her wealth become a consuming canker? Or will it be wrought into a crown of glory? Christ calls her; he pleads his dying love and her solemn vows! She can not falter and fail without repudiating her Master, breaking her vows and her covenant, and giving up her hope of salvation. *The Present Problem.*

The preacher must bring home her responsiblity in this matter to the Church of Christ, until the truth has been burned into the very souls of all her members and they come to realize, as in the presence of the judgment, the exact situation!

In this critical condition of affairs, it was eminently appropriate that all the great American Missionary Societies should send, in the year of grace, 1894, "An Epistle to the Church concerning the World's Evangelization," and that they should call upon the Churches with which they are con- *The Missionary Call.*

nected to make "The Final Rally of the Century." We quote the opening of that call, as in essential harmony with the considerations that we have been urging:

> "For nearly nineteen centuries the vast majority of the populations of the globe have waited in vain for the Gospel of redemption that was committed to the Christian Church. It was said most truthfully, by the late Earl of Shaftesbury, that 'the Gospel might have been proclaimed to all nations a dozen times over if the Christian Church had been faithful to her trust.' It is appalling to think that sixty generations of the unevangelized heathen world have perished in darkness since our Lord established and commissioned his Church as a living and aggressive force in the world. And of all the generations ours is the most guilty in proportion to its greater opportunities. In some mission-fields it is already demonstrated that by the Spirit of God thousands may be gathered where there have only been hundreds or scores. 'Let us expect great things from God and attempt great things for God.'"

The call is for universal cooperation—to instructors in colleges and theological seminaries, to pastors and associate officers of churches, to superintendents and teachers of Sabbath-schools, to the women of the Church, to Young Men's Christian Associations, and Young Women's Christian Associations, to Societies of Christian Endeavor, to the Epworth League, to the St. Andrew Brotherhood, to all gilds and societies of the young in any branch of the Church, to join in one common effort for the salvation of the world, and to unite, with new meaning and emphasis, in the divinely prescribed petition, "Thy kingdom come, thy will be done on earth as it is in Heaven."

If any one thing is manifest to any one who stops for serious thought, it is that the Church can be *The Only Help.* emancipated from this worldly thraldom, and this greatest of obstacles can be removed, by the renovating power of the Holy Ghost, and by that alone. The baptism of the Holy Ghost is therefore the supreme need of the hour. In the interview of Jesus with his disciples, when he met them, on the evening following the first day of the week, after the crucifixion, with Thomas absent, he gave them a *promise* and a *command:*

"And behold I send the promise of my Father upon you. But tarry ye in the city of Jerusalem, until ye be endued with power from on high."

In the Acts of the Apostles, Luke states more fully the promise of baptism with the Holy Ghost :

"But ye shall receive power, after that the Holy Ghost is come upon you ; and ye shall be witnesses unto me both in Jerusalem and in all Judea and in Samaria, and unto the uttermost parts of the earth."

In the second chapter of the Acts of the Apostles Luke records the fulfilment:

"And when the day of Pentecost was fully come they were all with one accord in one place. And suddenly there came a sound from heaven as of a rushing mighty wind, and it filled all the house where they were sitting. And there appeared unto them cloven tongues like as of fire, and it sat upon each of them. And they were all filled with the Holy Ghost, and began to speak with other tongues, as the Spirit gave them utterance."

The immediate result on that day was the adding of three thousand souls to the number of the disciples. That pentacostal season has been regarded as typical of all great religious awakenings and conquests in the ages since ; and the "tongues of fire" have been the symbol of that baptism, or that pouring out, of the Holy Spirit which has been the only thing that has ever endued the Church with power in its work of saving the world.

Such baptism of the Holy Ghost is what the Church supremely needs to-day. The tongue of fire is what the preacher needs, if he is to be, in his official position, the agent in preparing the Church for such a baptism, and in saving lost sinners from the power of sin and death. That need is emphasized and made so imperative, by the great fact that, while, in this age as in every other age, he is to carry on the general work of his commission, the preacher has, at the present day, the added work and responsibility of bringing all Christians to a deeper sense of their deficiencies and of their responsibilities, and of leading them to seek, with an urgency that can not be denied, for the immediate and universal outpouring of God's Spirit, that the world may be saved *now*.

*The Preacher's Present Duty.*

Meanwhile, it is high time that the preacher should everywhere lead on the Church in the final rally of the century. The supreme demand upon him in this connection is that he should absolutely overwhelm his people with the momentous facts of providence, of history, and of the Word of God on this subject, until by the breath of the Spirit they shall be brought to feel, in every fiber of their being, that "covetousness is idolatry," that God hates it in them just as fiercely as —yea, much more fiercely than—he hated it in Achan of old, and in Ananias and Sapphira, when he crushed them with his thunderbolts, and that there is no escape from the bottomless pit for those who are under its dominion.

## Summary and Conclusion.

The considerations that have been urged make it clear that the Church is to-day passing through a great crisis. It is not simply a crisis in foreign missions, but a crisis in the entire work of evangelizing the race at home and abroad. The whole world is open to the Gospel, waiting for it, perishing for the lack of it. The Church has every means and facility for giving it that Gospel. The great Church and missionary agencies are already pushing on to take possession of the highways and byways of this nation and of all the nations. The command "Go ye" has at this hour a pregnant and momentous meaning that it never had before. The preacher's commission, as the official leader, director, inspirer, of the great forward movement, takes on a solemnity that it has never had before. Upon the preacher, under God, the great burden of responsibility supremely rests. The answer to the question, "What shall be done?" depends largely upon him. If he fails to grasp the situation himself, he cannot instruct the Church in her present duty.

It has been said that Christ has providentially taken away *every obstacle* to the spread of the Gospel, and that he has made worthless every one of the *old excuses* for delaying the work. **The One Only Obstacle.** That statement needs to be corrected: *He has taken away all obstacles except those in the hearts of professing Christians themselves.* It can not be reasonably denied that there is still deep spiritual lethargy resting upon the Church; deep insensibility to the needs of a perishing world; a wide-spread indifference to her obligation to the Master. We had better face the facts. There is nothing to be gained—rather everything to be lost—by blinking them. Hardness of heart is upon us to-day, as upon Israel of old. Worldliness wraps us about and lulls us into unconsciousness to-day, as it did priest and people and king of old. Gold dazzles us with its glitter, as it dazzled in the olden times, shutting out with its glare the glory of our mission and the glory of God. Money-getting is practically and the world over, in the view of the multitude, the chief end of man. The same sins—idolatry and the self-righteous formality of outward works—against which the later prophets strove, in seeking to bring the Chosen People to a sense of their mission, stand in the way of the progress of the Kingdom of God to-day. The influence of all this is powerfully operative with preacher and people alike; and in consequence of it the world is left to perish in its sin, while we keep up our self-deception by officially enacting our "Play of Missions"! Dr. Arthur T. Pierson has graphically summed up the present condition of affairs and the failure of the Christian centuries to push the Gospel, except so far as God has carried his own work majestically on, by his providence :

"Meanwhile, what are we doing ? Trifling with the whole matter of a world's evangelization ; trifling on a magnificent scale ! Since our Lord on Calvary breathed his dying prayer, fifty successive generations of human beings have passed away. In this awful aggregate twenty-five times the present population of the globe have perished without the Gospel ; and as yet the entire Christian Church sends less than 6000 laborers into the foreign field and spends less than $12,000,000 a year on the world-wide work !"

# CHAPTER II.

## THE PREACHER'S MESSAGE.

WHAT, in view of the present pressing requirement of his commission, is to be the preacher's message? What must it be in view of the great crisis of the hour? We answer:

*Bible Christianity as a Saving Power for the Sinner and for the World.*

The preacher's one essential message, under his commission, is the message of salvation: "Preach the Gospel to every creature." Christianity is essentially distinguished from all other religions, by being the religion of *salvation*. **Salvation the Key-Note.** It has undoubtedly furnished the source and inspiration of all that is highest and best in character and conduct, art and literature, culture and civilization—but all that has been merely incidental and secondary to its main purpose of saving men. The angel said to Joseph: "Thou shalt call his name Jesus: for he shall save his people from their sins." Christ defined his own mission, when he said: "The Son of man is come to save that which is lost." Paul expressed it, when he wrote: "Christ Jesus came into the world to save sinners." The cry of a human soul, when brought to a sense of its true condition, is voiced in the anxious and despairing question of the jailer of Philippi: "What must I do to be saved?" The

Bible everywhere bases the whole Gospel system on the lost and helpless condition of the race—sometimes assuming or presupposing it; sometimes emphatically and dogmatically proclaiming it, and again proceeding with irresistible logic to demonstrate it. In short, the Word of God exhausts the power of human language and imagery in presenting the desperate condition of the lost soul out of Christ in this life, and the hopelessness of its destiny in the life to come. In short, sin and death, salvation and life, constitute the marrow of Bible divinity; and outside of and apart from these, the Scriptures have no message that has any great and paramount interest for a human soul. The preaching that leaves out these may just as well cease at once; for its narrowness and shallowness mark it with impotence and foredoom it to failure.

The Church of Christ, as commissioned by Him for saving men, is a spiritual agency. Her supreme task is the salvation of the world—the remaking of men in righteousness, by the power and grace of Christ accompanying and indorsing the commission and message he has given her. The preacher who has not learned this has not learned the alphabet of Christ. He needs to start anew in his work of preparation. His aims, under Christ's commission, are spiritual, not secular. The implements of his warfare are spiritual, not carnal—"the sword of the Spirit" being his chief offensive weapon. He has to bring the world into subjection to Christ—not by benevolence, nor by philanthropy, nor by social reform, but by the Gospel; not by reformation, but by regeneration and salvation from sin.

*A Spiritual Agency.*

## SECTION FIRST.

**Bible Christianity as a Saving Power.**

The preacher's fundamental theme must, therefore, be Christianity as a saving power. The ultimate first principle for him is not that it is the duty of the Church to save the world by reforming it, but that it is her duty to reform the world by saving it. As put in the famous epigram of Bushnell: "The soul of all improvement is the improvement of the soul."

### I. REGENERATING POWER AND GRACE FUNDAMENTAL.

Let it be emphasized that the aim of the preacher is to bring in the new heavens and the new earth, and to inaugurate the reign of Christ, not by reforming men, but by saving them; and that the only effective agency in saving men is Christianity as a regenerating power.

This is undoubtedly the Scriptural view on this subject, as that view is everywhere presented, but especially as it is presented in the one great Bible treatise on the way of salvation, Paul's Epistle to the Romans. To the Roman—the man of power, action, law—Paul wrote: "I am not ashamed of the Gospel of Christ, for it is the power of God unto salvation to every one that believeth." *(Man's Moral Disorder.)*

After making this bold statement the apostle proceeds to show that all men, Jews and Gentiles, are under the condemnation of the law, and that the fact that the Gospel is the power of God to deliver men from this lost condition, through justification by faith in the righteousness of God in Christ, is the ground of his glorying in it.

But it may be taken to be demonstrable, even without recourse to the clear teaching of the Scriptures on the subject—as far as demonstration can be said to be applicable to the region of contingent thought—that the evil condition of human nature without the grace of God, and the resulting evil conditions of society and of politics, are such as can be met by nothing less than divine regeneration. Christianity has shown itself to be the only agency able to remedy the abnormal moral and social condition, and bring about the moral reconstruction of the individual and society. In short, man's natural state is one of moral obliquity and disorder, hopelessly beyond the reach of everything but the religion of Jesus Christ.

Any candid and adequate investigation brings to light abundant evidence that human nature is in such disorder, and that the ideal life of duty, prescribed by God and by conscience, has become impossible to man without moral renovation.

This disorder is apparent in that condition of evil in the nature out of which, as from a fountain, all the evil of human conduct flows. Man's moral judgment is confessedly both weakened and darkened; his moral feelings are both deadened and perverted; his strongest moral impulses are persistently inclined toward evil, so that while his whole being shows, in accordance with the voice of conscience, that he was undoubtedly made for virtue, he is now just as evidently biased toward the morally evil.

This disorder appears, with equal clearness, in the fact that man's moral nature does not work harmoniously under the moral law, either as moral rule or as moral mission. In none of his great relations does he, in a state of nature, fulfil his mission of duty and conform his conduct to the requirements of God's law. It is true of the majority of mankind, even in Christendom, that, while acknowledging their obligation to supreme devotion to God, they yet practically neglect or even reject God; that, while acknowledging their obligation to a proper regard for and care of their own being, they yet in the worst sense neglect or even abuse that being; that, while freely confessing their obligation to do to others as they would that others should do to them, they yet selfishly disregard the well-being of their fellow-men, or even do their utmost to injure them.

Indeed, this is true of men universally, except so far as something extraneous comes in to prevent these results. Positive law and government, using force to restrain evil and to inflict penalty, are necessary for the preservation of the individual and society from destruction; and even these have never been able to preserve either the man or the State from corruption and anarchy and ruin, without the added regenerating power of vital Christianity.

Following upon man's condition of disorder, there is found everywhere the inevitable accompaniment of wreck and wretchedness that attaches to all breaking of law, as at once penalty for transgression and a warning against ruin. Broken law is inexorable to the impenitent. The penalty of immoral conduct is not always immediate, for that might prevent the possibility of morality; but the extreme penalty of moral death is in the end inevitable. "Thou shalt surely die" was the penalty attached to the first transgression, and it is the pen- **Wreck and Wretchedness.**

alty that must follow the moral disorder so manifest and so wide-spread in man's nature and the world. There is neither ultimate secrecy nor impunity for sin in God's moral government. The only escape from the penalty is to be found in removal of the disorder.

The great practical moral question in all ages has therefore been: *Is there any way of escape or of moral restoration?* The answer of the ages, that rings out clearly everywhere, is, that Christianity has proved itself, not only philosophically but also historically, the only effective agency in man's deliverance and moral renovation and reconstruction. The absolute certainty of this conclusion appears from the very conditions of any true solution of the problem involved. (1) Any

**Requirements of the Case.** effective scheme of moral renovation must take into account all the main facts of man's moral nature, moral condition, and moral destiny. (2) It must not overlook the wreck of the moral manhood, nor the failure of the life of man to attain to the moral ideal; but must furnish a power adequate to the reconstruction of the one, and a universal motive and mission equal to the task of lifting up the other to the normal and ideal standard. (3) It must likewise make provision for counteracting the natural forces that are set to work by transgression of law, and that must otherwise doom man to perpetual pain and ruin; and for remaking or reconstructing the human wreck.

Much of the thinking of the ages has been devoted to this problem, and innumerable solutions have been proposed. These solutions, by their failure to meet the conditions of the problem, or requirements of the case, as just stated, have proved themselves worthless. Self-reconstruction has been shown, both philosophically and historically, to be impracticable. The false religions—Confucianism, Brahmanism, Buddhism, and Mohammedanism—have in the same way been proved insufficient. Man's new philosophies all the way up to date—Pantheism, Positivism, Culturism, Secularism—have been shown in the same way to be worthless.

Christianity alone meets the demands legitimately made of any scheme of moral reconstruction that has any right to claim the attention of man- **Christianity's** kind; and it thereby demonstrates itself **Proposals.** to be the only adequate solution of the great moral problem. It takes into account the facts of man's natural condition of moral disorder. It takes full cognizance of the all-important facts of the wreck of the moral manhood and the failure in the moral task. It provides for the restoration of the former by an almighty reconstructing agency, the Holy Spirit; and for the lifting up of the latter by the new and universal motive power of divine faith and love, and by an elevating and everlasting mission for the glory of God. It embodies its perfect system of morality and its marvelous scheme of grace in a person, Jesus Christ, who is at once the perfect example of human right-doing and self-sacrifice, the complete exhibition of divine love for man, and the almighty helper of man in his struggle up toward the right life and manhood. It seats upon the throne of the universe the once crucified but now risen and ascended Savior as Lord, to whom all authority and all power in heaven and earth are given, to save from the bondage and defilement of sin, and from its dreadful consequences, all sinners who repent and believe on him.

Making such provision for human reconstruction, Christianity has shown itself able to make over the individual life, and with equal ease to transform the cultivated Saul of Tarsus and the savage Africaner into ideal men; and to reconstruct the social life, as in the early transformation of the Roman Empire and the savage Anglo-Saxons, and in the later making over of the Sandwich Islanders, Fuegians, and South Sea Islanders.

*Christianity Reconstructs.*

Christianity as a regenerating and saving power is therefore necessarily and essentially the message of the preacher to men, and the only one that has in it any gospel for men.

## II. THE IGNORING OF REGENERATION FATAL.

It follows that any other method than that by the application of the Gospel, with its saving power, even tho that method be presented and advocated by the Church, must inevitably prove a failure in the end. It is a fatal objection to all such methods, by whomsoever suggested, adopted, or advocated, that they deal only with the surface symptoms, and do not touch the deep-lying seat of the fatal moral disease. Those who make use of them must logically be classed with the prophets and priests of old, against whom Jeremiah brought the accusation of the Lord:

"They have healed also the hurt of the daughter of my people slightly, saying, Peace, peace; when there is no peace" (Jer. vi. 14).

### *The Relations of Preaching to Reform.*

It can be made abundantly clear that the multitudinous schemes of reform that have not their root in Christianity must fail of accomplishing the moral results desired and aimed at.

No scheme of government can give permanent of a true elevation to society without the aid of Christianity. Two things are absolutely necessary in order that society may be made what it should be : A standard of absolute right and justice must be furnished and put into the hands and minds of rulers and subjects, to be the perfect guide of both; and a power must be provided to bring men in their conduct up to this standard. Christianity alone furnishes the requisite standard and necessary transforming power. No scheme of philosophy or of moral reform can give permanent elevation to society, except as it adopts the aims and uses the means furnished by the Christian system. In order to the actual removal of the various evils of society, the moral disorder of man's nature in which they have their origin must be removed. The Christian system alone provides the remedy required.

No scheme of education can lead to the permanent elevation of society, except as it is Christian education. Education as divorced from Christianity can only develop what is in the man. As man's nature is in a condition of moral disorder, even education of the most liberal and comprehensive character must fail to purify and transform the man, and may at the highest make no more than a Lord Bacon, or a Byron, or a Burr, or a Stuart Mill. If men are good, education will make them the more powerful for good; if they are bad, it will only make them stronger for evil. Education, transformed, elevated, and controlled by the spirit of Christ, is the only kind that can essentially and permanently elevate society.

These remarks are especially applicable to all such agencies as Mr. Stead's "Civic Church," by which he cultures to elevate the masses, as well as to all the intrices of socialistic secularism. It has no root in Christ, in God's law of right and justice, or in the Word of God; and no motive but a sentimental notion of a brotherhood without a basis in a Divine Fatherhood, and which could not, therefore, prove effective even with regenerate men, much less with a morally corrupt and debased mass of men.

If the preceding observations are well grounded, it follows that the present effort in much of the preaching apparently so popular in many quarters, to subordinate the mission and work of the Church to the various common reform activities, is in the wrong direction, and must ultimately not only fail but also prove most positively harmful. The Gospel is not something merely subsidiary to reform.

*1. The Gospel not Subsidiary to Reform.*

1. This subordination is entirely at variance with the whole method and spirit of Christ and his religion, and with the method of the Apostles. The Duke of Argyll recently brought out this point very clearly in his article on "Christian Socialism" in *The Nineteenth Century* for November, 1894. He writes:

*(1) Not the Method of Christ.*

"It has been well said by a modern philosopher that the whole system of human society rests on a few fundamental conceptions and a few accepted beliefs. And this is exactly what Christianity supplied to a world which had come to believe in nothing. Without condescending to take the least notice of anything that could be connected with the politics of its own early days, without breathing one word which can be construed as taking any side in the great secular contests of men, whether then or since, it did, nevertheless, bring in and establish a few fundamental conceptions and beliefs which have transformed the world. Beyond this it deliberately abstained from going.

"There is nothing more striking, more divine, than its majestic reticence. It made no attack upon anything in the nature of a political institution.

"Although many of the evils under which heathendom was then suffering were undoubtedly and closely connected with bad systems and principles of government, Christianity was silent upon them all. Save in so far as, in its own higher sphere, it implanted some new truth pregnant with new consequences, it left them all to be judged by the more enlightened reason and the gradually awakened conscience of mankind. There is no method of reform so powerful as this. If alongside of any false and corrupt belief, or any vicious and cruel custom, however strong and however deeply rooted these may be, we can succeed in planting successfully some one incompatible idea, then, without the noise of controversy or the clash of battle, those beliefs and customs will wane and die. It was thus that Christianity, without a single word of direct attack, killed off one of the greatest and most universal curses of the pagan world—the ever-deepening curse of slavery. The antagonistic and incompatible truth which had this effect was among the profoundest in the Christian system, namely: the inalienable dignity, value, and responsibility of the individual human soul. But this truth was left to work out its own results without any attempt to anticipate that work in its thousand applications."

This is the rational side of the principle presented by Dr. Chalmers, in his celebrated sermon on "The Expulsive Power of a New Affection." This is undoubtedly the true and effective method of procedure for the preacher of the present day. It is well for him to keep to the great example of Christ and to practise the Apostolic rule. That gives him an immense domain; for those far-reaching moral and spiritual truths that were the only theme of our Lord and his Apostles take in the question as to what extent the evils of the world, social and political, are directly due to the failure of men to come up to Christ's standard of doctrine and of precept; and that is a question of inexhaustible variety and of the widest reach.

The recently proposed method inevitably leads the preacher and the Church out of the sphere of religion into that of the State and of politics, and can only result in the same complications of Church and State that have been the curse of both, and the cause of political and religious oppression and persecution in past ages. The State goes beyond its sphere, and encroaches upon the freedom of the individual, when it says that the church-member shall do this or that, or shall refrain from doing this or that, in matters that have nothing to do with the field of politics as such. The Church takes undue liberties with the rights of conscience when it says that, in the sphere of purely secular or political activity, its members shall do this and shall not do that. The result, in the former case, is always political oppression, and in extreme cases political persecution. In the latter case, it is always religious oppression, or religious ostracism or persecution.

(2) **Trenches upon Politics.**

This new method inevitably leads the preacher and the Church back to the system of self-righteousness and formal and outward works, from the bondage of which the Reformation emancipated Protestant Christendom.

(3) **Leads to Legalism and Formality.**

Human conduct is operated on by two great agencies: by outward rule and by inward principle. The true method of the Christian religion, as has been seen, is to regenerate the man and implant within him the inward principle that shall substantially work itself out in the Christian life. The Romish Church had substituted for this inward principle the outward rule, and its elaborate system of rules, covering all human activities and claiming control over both Church and State, had destroyed the spontaneous activities of the inward principle of faith. It called for work done in conformity with its rules, and that made life a drudgery and a weariness of the flesh. Its morality had become a morality of outward formality and rules. Its system of outward works had usurped the place of the life of faith, and held all the world in absolute bondage. It was from this bondage of outward rule that the Reformers broke loose, in their great movement in the sixteenth century, and sought to carry back the Church to the control of the inner principles of Christian faith.

There are two modes of preaching, in the present age, that are diametrically opposed. The one presses the Gospel upon men as a saving power, aims at regeneration, and encourages spontaneous conformity to Gospel principles, which is the old method. The other dwells constantly upon social and political questions, and attempts to lay down rules that shall govern the entire range of human activity, and to say to men, everywhere and on every occasion, "Thus thou shalt do, and thus." The former is the method of the Reformation, and the true method of Protestant Christendom; the latter, the method of the new reformers and the old Romanism. The one, as Paul teaches, carries back the Church to the covenant "from the Mount Sinai, which gendereth bondage" (Gal. iv. 24) to ritual observance and legal obedience; the other carries her forward to the covenant that is from Mount Zion, from "the Jerusalem above which is free, which is the mother of us all," and tends to free spiritual activity by bringing her members more thoroughly under the influence of love, the higher law of the spirit of liberty. See Rom. viii. and xiii. 8, 10. It is difficult to see how anything can come from this new departure, except the old evil and the old bondage of ritualism and legalism.

The fatal defect of the new method is, that it leads to the neglect of the vital matter of all Christian teaching—the presentation of the saving doctrines of the Gospel—and to the exaltation into its place of social problems, political issues, and minor morals generally.

*(4) Fatal to the Gospel.*

However clearly these ethical and political matters may be presented, in the preaching that dwells extensively or exclusively upon them, such preaching does nothing toward regenerating men, and thereby preparing in them the moral character that would lead them to conform to the requirements laid down. But it will hardly be denied that the average preacher fails to present such matters clearly; for, while he may be most familiar with the fundamental theological and moral principles, and abundantly qualified to present these principles, he is usually—and that justly—looked upon by the mass of intellectual men as the last man to take up and attempt to discuss and settle such industrial, social, and civic problems. As the Duke of Argyll shows, in the article already referred to, even Dr. Chalmers failed, in undertaking to solve the problems of poverty practically, tho perfectly familiar with the conditions involved.

The true vocation of the preacher, in relation to the working out of the social and political problems of the day, may perhaps be summed up in the following particulars:

*2. True Relation of the Preacher to Reform.*

It is the preacher's fundamental and all-important task to bring about, through the preaching of Christianity as a saving power, the regeneration of individual men—that is,

*(1) Regeneration.*

to make Christians of them. That alone makes reform possible, and that makes it practicable, by making Christian conscience and Christian character.

It is his task to indoctrinate the individual members of the Church in the great fundamental principles of Christianity as a system of salvation, and to educate and to inspire individual men, especially men of marked ability and fitness, to become leaders and guides and influential factors of society, along the lines and in the interests of righteousness and of Christian living and self-sacrifice for mankind. It is especially his duty to present and enforce the great principles of the moral law and of Christianity itself, that men are to apply in the practical solution of the problems that are so prominently before the public mind. *(2) To Indoctrinate in Gospel Principles.*

But in these days of so complicated social relations and of such complex social problems, it would be arrant folly for the preacher himself to attempt to make specific and exhaustive application of the Gospel principles to all those relations and problems. The field is too vast; and the man who attempts to cover it in this way will inevitably become involved in the endless unimportant details and lose sight of all-important vital principles. The method of Christ and of the primitive Christianity is the simple and only true and effective method. There are multitudes among the members of the Christian Church—professors, lawyers, physicians, engineers, business men, farmers, artisans, who represent vast practical knowledge along all lines, and immense brain-power—in whose mind the preacher is sent to fix the principles of righteousness and benevolence that should control all the conduct and relations *Agency of Laymen.*

of men. These men have the qualifications—of intimate knowledge of the various spheres of life and activity, industrial, social, political, and moral, and of practical sense and experience in affairs—that the average preacher can not be expected to have, and that are essential to the right application of the principles of the Gospel to the practical solution of all the difficult problems at present demanding solution. It is in this way, through the Gospel message and the Christian inspiration and instruction of the pulpit, that Christianity has in time past revolutionized the world; and in this way it may be expected to bring like results in time to come.

It is the preacher's task, also, to make conscience in society, by persistently pressing upon men the authority of the law of God and of Christ over the public conscience. Without such creation and development of conscience, all attempts at reform must necessarily be evanescent, since they will have no root in the moral convictions and character of the community to support them. But this subject will be treated more fully under the preaching of the law, as a part of the preacher's message.

**(3) To Make Conscience.**

It is the preacher's task, finally, to furnish the moral strength and spirit needed by the varied ministries of help and healing that assist in the work of elevating society. This he can do most efficiently by enlarging the views of men and by exalting their Christian character and ideals. His work is, by the teaching of the Gospel, to lead men to Christian views of benevolence and philanthropy and human brotherhood, and to Christlike self-sacrifice in the interests of humanity and for the glory of God.

**(4) To Give Tone to Society.**

The right kind of preaching unquestionably has an immense moral influence in this direction.

Thomas Chalmers, Scotland's most famous pulpit orator, furnishes a historic example of the worthlessness of the preaching that aims at reform without regeneration. For many years he devoted his splendid eloquence to the task of trying to make men better by secular motives, dilating upon "the meanness of dishonesty, the villainy of falsehood," and kindred subjects. After the regenerating grace of God had transformed the preacher and opened his eyes to divine realities, he summed up the results of his comparatively wasted years when, under stress of conscience—in an address delivered to the inhabitants of Kilmany, Fifeshire, in 1815, the year of his translation to Glasgow—he said: *3. Futility of the Popular Method.*

"I never heard of any such reformation having been effected: if there was anything at all brought about in this way it is more than I ever got any account of. It was not until the free offer of forgiveness through the blood of Christ was urged upon men, that I ever heard of any of those subordinate reformations."

The practical futility of the popular method, of substituting the preaching of morality for that of the Gospel, and of reform for that of regeneration, has had abundant illustration in the struggles for moral, social, and municipal reform, in our cities, in the cases in which the clergy have been the leaders and have applied the new method. The work has been shown by the results to be mere surface work, followed by inevitable reaction and deeper and more widely pervading corruption. The reform, in such instances, is often merely a matter of outward decency in appearance, to be thrown off as *Recent Illustrations.*

soon as the public gaze is withdrawn. It proceeds and returns in spasmodic cycles. When corruption in a great commercial metropolis becomes absolutely unendurable, the public journals set to work to expose it; the preachers join in denouncing it; decent citizens whose comfort or pocket has been seriously affected raise their voices against it; practical politicians, who always know "which way the wind blows," hasten, in the rôle of reformers, to get control of the movement and to profit by it; the corrupt leaders and bosses, against whom public indignation is turned, hide themselves for a time, while some of their miserable and insignificant tools vicariously suffer for them, and the people rejoice over a "glorious revolution!" Soon the waking up comes, when it is found that the great seething heart of corruption, whether designated as Tweedism or as Tammanyism, has not been changed nor affected in the slightest degree, and that the new political bosses are largely men with the same unregenerate hearts as the old, and equally ready to illustrate Vergil's "facilis descensus Averni." Anon the old lethargy returns, and the people once more find themselves helpless in the grip of organized vice; and immorality and crime again hold high carnival. Such is inevitably the last result of even honest, earnest Christian work, that seeks only outward reform and not inward regeneration—a result always conspicuously illustrating, at the same time, both the futility of the new reformer's method, and the absolute necessity for a return to the method of Christ and primitive Christianity. It is thereby demonstrated, for the time being, that no mere thin blanket of decency can cover and smother the deep-burning fires and Titanic forces of a great moral Vesuvius, and insure the safety of those who take refuge upon it. The volcanic fires must first be put out by Almighty Power.

Equally powerless for securing genuine reform is the legal method so often advocated. It is a good thing to have wise and just laws on the statute books. The mere existence of such laws raises a moral presumption against unrighteousness and vice and crime. But no pressure of law, even in a nation with despotic government, can permanently hold down the forces of evil. Much less can it do this in a democratic nation, where the pressure of law decreases as the iniquity increases. Regeneration must go before and make and sustain the law.

*Reformation by Law.*

## SECTION SECOND.

### Both Law and Gospel Essential to the Message.

But to be more specific, the preacher must present with all clearness and fulness the law of God and man's lost condition under it, and the Gospel provision for salvation.

It must go with the saying that the preacher's message, both in its matter and its authority, rests back on the Word of God. It behooves him to inquire diligently and first of all: What has the Divine Word to say on this all-important subject of the way of salvation?

The pages of the Bible obviously abound in incidental presentations, literal and figurative, of the nature and method of salvation. But, as this is the one all-important subject of revelation, it is not left to mere incidental illustration. In the Old Testament, it is the heart of the whole sacrificial and priestly system and ritual, on which the religion of Judaism rested or of which it mainly consisted. In the New Testament, three of the principal Epistles of Paul are devoted to the doctrine of salvation, with the purpose of exhibiting the truth on that subject, and of guarding against the three errors into which Jew, Greek, and Roman—the world-races of that age and the representative and typical men of all time—were peculiarly liable to fall. In the Epistle to the Galatians, it is shown for the Jew, the representative of religious forms and ceremonies, that man is not to be saved by the observances of the ceremonial law, in which the Jew was inclined to trust; but by faith in Christ and "circumcision of the heart." In the Epistles to the Corinthians, it is made clear to the Greek, the representative of reason and philosophy, that salvation is not to be attained by human wisdom, on which he was accustomed to rest his faith; but by faith in "Jesus Christ and him crucified," "who of God is made unto us wisdom and righteousness, and sanctification, and redemption." In the Epistle to the Romans, it is demonstrated for the Roman, the representative of activity and works and law, that salvation can not be secured by any human acts or works in the observance of any law whatsoever; but, that "being justified by faith, we have peace with God through our Lord Jesus Christ," the vicarious sacrifice for sin.

<small>The Bible Text-Books of Salvation.</small>

Of these three Epistles, that to the Romans manifestly approaches nearest to being of universal application, partaking of the character of a systematic treatise, and in its sweep taking in the whole range of law, human and divine. Moreover, it has peculiar applicability to the English-speaking peoples, the modern representatives of *law*, in free governmental institutions and vast extent of rule, and of *works*, in the development and extension of industrial enterprise and the solution of the great industrial and social problems. For us especially, and in this age, the Epistle to the Romans may, therefore, be taken as God's presentation, according to Paul, of the preacher's message, in the business of saving mankind. Preaching that omits any of its great features, or that fails to give prominence to what it emphasizes, must be in so far defective.

In taking this Epistle as a guide and authority in ascertaining what the preacher's message of salvation should be, it is easily to be seen that, in order to completeness, two things must always be presented: the law as exhibiting and enforcing the lost condition of the sinner; and the Gospel as the divine provision for his salvation.

It is not the preaching of the law in itself, or for its own sake, that is to be advocated. There may be much preaching of *law* that does not result in the salvation of sinners; either because it does not so much as suggest either the Gospel or salvation, or because it does not bring men into relation to the Law-giver, so as to bring out the sense of responsibility and of lost condition under the law. There is also assuredly, in this age, much preaching of *love*, that has no tendency to save man; because there is no law-work back of it to bring home to the sinner his lost condition that leaves him in perishing need of the Gospel. Paul said: "When the law came, sin revived and I died;" and that is the condition precedent to salvation.

I. The Law the Starting-point in the Message.

The preacher must lay the foundation for the saving power of the Gospel by presenting the law, in all the length and breadth of its requirement, and in all the solemnity and awfulness of its sanctions; in fact, with the very definiteness and clearness and with the divine authority of the Word of God.

The generation past, in this country, has heard but little of the law of God. "Come to Jesus"; "Come to Jesus"; "Go work"; "Go work"—this has too often been regarded and affirmed as making up the sum of all necessary and helpful theology. It is in fact mere shallow sentimentalism—totally inadequate, either to rouse any one to a sense of his need of salvation, or to develop anything like Christian character.

The result has been an almost universal reign of shallow evangelism, and a rain of superficial evangelists, that have well-nigh killed out the life of the Church. Hence, the conscious impotence of pastors and people, and the meager ingatherings into the Church in connection with the ordinary means of grace. Hence, the periodical sending for the traveling evangelist, the boy-preacher, the student, or the talking layman, or the praying-band; and the introduction of sentimental and mass-meeting methods, in order to enlarge the membership of the churches. Hence, from another side, the universal worldliness and the rage for amusements and follies, and the making of life a time of play, without any aim, rather than a period of earnest work for the accomplishment of a rational mission. Hence, from still another side, or by further evolution, the universal and awful moral corruption, individual, social, and political.

"Back to the law!" should be the cry in this age of every preacher who has any conception of the real situation of things in this land, or any adequate sense of the relations of the divine law to individual and public conscience, character, and life. And the man, assuredly, who has no proper conception of these things, should make haste to get such a conception, for life and death depend upon its being gained quickly.

As in Paul's presentation of the way of salvation to the Romans, so now, in the preaching of Bible Christianity as a saving power, the law of God needs to be presented in various aspects and relations. *[God's Law in Various Aspects.]*

It needs to be presented fundamentally as *the law of God*, binding every moral being in duty *to God* and *to God alone*, and thus furnishing the only basis for sound morality. Any so-called morality that starts from some other foundation is essentially vicious and worthless. *[1. God's Law the Basis of Morality.]*

There are two essentially different theories of morality, the pagan and the Christian. Their basal difference lies in the fact that one is man-centered and the other God-centered. The essence of the pagan morality, whether taught in heathen or in Christian countries, is selfishness, and its results are inevitably demoralizing and destructive. Christian morality, on the other hand, is God-centered. In the Christian dispensation, God becomes Christ in his relation to man in redemption, and Christ is the sovereign or Lord in the Kingdom of Heaven. See Matthew xxviii. 18. In the view of the Word of God, *righteousness*, or conformity to the will of God, or Christ, is the supreme thing to be sought in human conduct. The call of the law, from this point of view, is a call to duty and to obedience. The proper preaching of the law must have this fundamentally in view, and not benevolence, or philanthropy, or happiness. If this is left out of view, the preaching of the law is vitiated and perverted in its whole nature and effect.

In the view of the Word of God—which is directly contrary to the popular view of the day—all duty and morality turn Godward and Christward, rather than manward. Egoism and altruism, as usually understood, are the one immoral and the other non-moral. All duty is owed *to God* and *to him only*. It may be performed, according to his directions—*toward* oneself, in which case it is selfial and moral; toward one's fellows, in which case it is social and moral; or toward God, in which case it is theistic and moral, If not done as *to God*, selfial actions become selfish and immoral; social actions, altruistic merely and non-moral; and all alike are directed to selfish or merely humanitarian ends.

From the general theistic point of view, that alone is morally good which is intentionally conformed to the will of God; from the specific Christian point of view, that alone is morally good which is conformed to the will of Christ the Lord. Failure to recognize and to emphasize this has been the perverting and fatal defect of very much of the moral teaching from the pulpit and in the schools, since Hobbes and the days of the English Restoration. In the last century, Paley crystallized the principles of selfishness for the Church, by making "virtue" "consist in doing the will of God for the sake of everlasting happiness." Others have followed, who have taken out the hypocritical feature of the happiness theory, and, in thereby saving it from being immoral, have left it purely heathen. Sometimes "the dignity of human nature" has taken the place of the will of God, as the ground of moral obligation. Sometimes the principle has appeared as "the greatest good of the greatest number"; sometimes as "the greatest good of the individual himself." Recently it has been exploited as "*altruism*," or as judious advice to man to avoid injuring other people lest they should injure him. And, so far as morality so-called has been preached from the pulpit, for generations it has largely been this heathen so-called morality, which is in fact debasing immorality.

Twenty years ago Bishop Warren, then of Boston University, called attention, in his "Introduction" to the translation of Wuttke's *Christian Ethics*, to the schism between the prevalent dogmatics and ethics. The doctrine he regarded as substantially and prevailingly Scriptural and Christian; the morality as essentially pagan and self-centered.

<small>Schism of Ethics and Dogmatics.</small>

The ethics taught in our schools has been largely paganism, and that not even baptized. Man is made a law and end to himself; his own enjoyment, or dignity, or culture, or blessedness, is kept uppermost, has been kept uppermost for these generations. And so the dogmatics has largely swung loose from the ethics; the creed from the practise.

The legitimate outcome of this ethical system has been manifest in the exaltation of wealth and money-getting, as means to the happiness and culture that are set before men as the great ends; in the underestimate of manhood and character; in the increasing tendency to ignore God and think that "his laws will not work"; in the materialization and brutalization of humanity and civilization. Hence, the great problems of capital and labor; of caste and communism; of the church-going people and the lapsed masses; of public and private corruption everywhere. It is impossible to overstate the fact, that a large portion of the so-called moral teaching is totally and distinctively pagan and immoral; and that, so long as it is continued, the schism in society can only widen and the yawning chasm grow deeper.

The new Dornerism, that has come in from Germany, has introduced into the theology certain erroneous ideas that have helped still further to befog the moral teachings and teachers of this generation. It makes the essence of God, the supreme thing in the divine goodness, to be "love." It analyzes "love" or goodness into three parts: the primary and fundamental, benevolence; the second, sympathy; the third, righteousness. Now this is undoubtedly the natural order on the materialistic basis of sensation, which makes feeling the supreme thing and reduces all feeling to pleasure or pain. But it reverses the order set by God. That makes the fundamental element in God's goodness his infinite desire for the righteousness and purity, or moral well-being, of his creatures, and not for their happiness merely. Unconsciously the preacher, under the guidance of this false theology, finds his way back into the ethical fog of heathenism. The supreme goodness of God becomes his supreme regard for the *well-being* of his creatures; *well-being* becomes *comfortable-being;* and God's supreme goodness becomes his benevolence to his creatures, and is manifested in supreme regard for their happiness. As an ethical basis, this naturally prepares the way for and leads to post-mortem probation, semi-universalism, and universalism, in theology. It deftly puts man in the place of God as the center, by making man's comfort the supreme thing; and so, after having appeared to thrust pagan ethics out of the front door, in the name of Christ and righteousness, it brings them in at the back door, in the name of humanity and happiness. If, on the contrary, the *well-being* becomes the *right-being*, then the supreme goodness of God becomes his righteousness and holiness, and is manifested in his supreme regard for the perfection and righteousness of his creatures. As the true ethical basis, this last necessarily excludes all the previously mentioned errors. Is God first benevolent, and then subordinately righteous? Or is the reverse the case? Is God first a father, and then subordinately a moral governor and law-giver? Or is the reverse the case? These are test questions.

All this false theorizing is in the face of the fact that the law of the universe is a law of righteousness primarily, and of happiness only secondarily; as well as of the fact that conscience never fails to exalt the *right* to the place of supremacy over the *pleasurable.*

On the basis of such false theologizing, eudemonism is the only ethical theory logically possible, and universalism the only ultimate orthodoxy possible. The natural outcome from teaching such so-called morality is immorality on the broadest possible scale, and the perversion of all human and Christian relations. The universal corruption prevalent in this nation to-day, and reaching every phase of life, and every position from the lowest to the highest, is the natural and inevitable product of

*The Moral Results.*

such teaching and preaching. The only remedy is to be found in the call, "Back to the *law*," as the *law of God*—not as the battle-cry of reform merely, but as a call to duty, repentance, and salvation.

The preacher, if his preaching is to meet the needs of the times, must urge the requirements of the law upon the individual, calling for diligent and earnest self-conservation, self-culture, and self-conduct, and all these as the requirements of God. He must thus convince the man that he is not at liberty, as the common notion has it, to use or abuse himself or his powers and possessions as he pleases; but that he has a right to do as he pleases only so far as it pleases him to do right, that is, so far as it pleases him to conform to God's requirements. He must show him as well that he is under the same law with reference to his fellow-men in society. He is not great, nor rich, nor strong, for himself alone. The poor, the ignorant, the low, are not stepping-stones, nor lawful plunder; they are brothers to be respected and helped. His power and position are to be used for the elevation of those below him, and his obligation in this direction is limited only by the extent of his power and opportunity. Paul wrote: "I am debtor both to the Greeks and to the barbarians, both to the wise and to the unwise." That is the law of the Christian life. The duties of social conservation, social improvement, and social direction, are to be pressed upon men as the requirements of God. With equal emphasis must man's theistic duties also be urged upon his attention and his conscience. His duty to study God's manifestation of himself in the system of nature, in the human system, and especially in the system of divine revelation; his

*Preaching the Law to Sinners.*

duty of supreme devotion of the intellect, heart, and will to God; the duties of obedience and worship and service—all these must be enforced as the requirements of God. In no other way can the sinner be made to feel his need of salvation because of his utter, ignominious, and wicked failure to keep the law of God, and to fulfil the divine requirements resting upon him in the conduct of life in all its relations.

In the preaching that makes for righteousness, the law needs to be presented as God's law for all organizations and associations of men—in the family, community, and state; in industrial, commercial, and civic pursuits. It needs to be made eminently clear that there can be no relation, no association, no corporation that is not subject to it.

*2. The Law of Human Societies.*

Men have largely been accustomed to separate their social and business relations from what they consider their moral and religious relations. It has been a common saying that corporations have no conscience. The natural and inevitable result of such a theory, constantly reiterated, is infidelity and corruption in all these social and business relations. To be made aware of the real condition of things, one needs but to run the eye over the issues of the daily press of some metropolitan city, as New York or Chicago, and note the long list of marital and domestic infidelities, infelicities, and scandals; the startling record of peculation and speculation and defalcation, of extortion by trusts and monopolies and syndicates, of legislative and Congressional bribery and corruption, of quarrels and rows and murders; lists and records extended enough on any day of the week, and especially on the Sabbath, to fill any soul with horror.

It is high time for the preacher to call a halt in this mad career of lawlessness. It is high time for him to insist that Christian morality binds all human societies and corporations, in their dealings with mankind, by the same principles that it lays upon the individual in his social duties; that there is required of them the same strict regard for the rights of man to life, liberty, property, truthfulness, and the offices of human brotherhood that binds the individual man in his conduct, and that all this is the requirement of God. Genuine social and political reform can be reached in no other way than by bringing men up to these requirements of God, and making them understand that they are requirements of God, not to be escaped by shrewdness and not to be neglected with impunity.

## Problems of Society.

It is at this point that the preacher comes into connection with the great industrial, social, and civil problems that are so prominently before the public mind, and is called upon to mark out his course in dealing with these problems. There are certain things to which he will do well to attend.

His message will need to guard against the new positivist sociology that has arisen out of the atomism and materialism of the age, and that is everywhere exerting its demoralizing influence upon public opinion and law. The materialistic method, in excluding all rational and moral facts, principles, and considerations, leaves out everything that is of any real importance and scientific value in social science, and shuts out all possibility of human improvement on such a basis. Its affirmation

(1) **To Guard against Positivist Sociology.**

of the absolute heredity of crime; its denial of free will and, consequently, of human responsibility; its assertion that there is no such thing as absolute crime, the so-called crimes being merely infractions of social rules made for convenience or self-preservation in certain conditions of society, and changing with those conditions, so that even chastity may be "an artificial and conventional virtue"; its regarding of crime as a matter of condition and environment rather than of character—and the embodiment of all in a positivist criminology by Lombroso and his school—all this is one of the threatening phenomena of the day. The elaborate fooling indulged in by the disciples of these men, in detecting and classifying criminals by physical marks rather than moral, and in presenting "surer methods of detecting the criminal by the observation of tattooing, anthropometry, physiognomy, the physio-psychic conditions, the data as to sensitiveness, reflex activity, vaso-motor reactions, the extent of the field of vision," etc.; their settled purpose of reconstructing on this basis the whole theory of crime and punishment and the system of law applicable to them; and the palming off of all this as "the latest science" —would be simply laughable were it not that, with materialism in the air, it is ominously threatening and terribly demoralizing.

Yet the professedly positivist sociology is not the form that is most dangerous to the preacher. There is a vast amount of talking and teaching and writing on this subject that professes to be Christian, but is, nevertheless, thoroughly vicious, either *Sociological* from its latent materialism or from its *Fallacies.* utter shallowness, or from its tendency to turn the minds of Christians away from the Gospel, with its regenerating power, to the worthless projects of the faddists.

Such so-called sociology attempts to apply the methods of physical science to what is pre-eminently non-physical in all its most important factors. It practically ignores those important factors. It assumes that society is an *organism*, when, as matter of fact, it is only remotely analogous to an organism. It has no vital arrangement of organized parts, and there is no single structural principle of life evolving all social results. It is biological only in a loose and analogical sense.

It assumes the identity of *social evolution* and *social progress*—whereas the former is only "a reasonable sequence of the unintended"; the latter undoubtedly "a reasonable sequence of the intended."* In the former blind forces, under necessary law, unfold along inevitable lines toward unavoidable results; in the latter, will, mind, man, great men, Divine Providence, all enter in as the essential and controlling factors in a movement that has merely a physical basis. Social progress comes from these elements, and Christianity recognizes as fundamental the truth that God is not only the author of all social laws, but that he also superintends their operation.

The general introduction of the preaching of sociology in the place of the preaching of the Gospel, would thus, at its best, be the substitution of positive

* An exceedingly able and helpful exposure of this and many other current sociological fallacies and unverifiable assumptions may be found in a series of articles on "Physics and Sociology," by Mr. W. H. Mallock, in the *Contemporary Review*, running through the numbers for December, 1895, and January and February, 1896, and yet unfinished.

and fatal error for saving truth. What it would be at its worst will appear when we consider that Christ's method—already shown to be the only effective method of lifting up society—accomplishes its work by infusing into the structure and texture of society the regenerative and formative ideas of the Gospel of salvation, and that anything short of this unity centering in Christ and salvation would hopelessly confuse and distract not only the hearers, but the preachers also. Christ's own direction has the basal wisdom in it for preacher as well as hearer:*

"Seek ye first the kingdom of God and his righteousness, and all these things shall be added unto you."

The Apostle Paul's direction to the Corinthian Christians presents the same principle of unity from another point of view : †

"But covet earnestly the best gifts, and yet show I unto you a more excellent way. Though I speak with the tongues of men and of angels, and have not charity, I am become as sounding brass, or a tinkling cymbal."

It is commendable to covet earnestly the best spiritual gifts and to cultivate assiduously the increased breadth; but the most notable gifts and the greatest breadth, leading to the highest achievements in the Kingdom of God, are to be attained only through becoming saturated and possessed with the overwhelming and all-pervading power of Christian love, working in and out from a divinely renewed soul. While, on the one hand, the turning of the human mind and effort to many things unessential, even tho important, dissipates the energies and prevents the accomplishment

* Matt. vi. 32. † 1 Cor. xii. 31 ; xiii. 1.

of anything worth while in any direction; absolute concentration, on the other hand, on the great germinal principle of Christianity, leads to limitless development and accomplishment along all important and essential lines of endeavor.

It will readily become apparent, therefore, to any thoughtful student of theology and the social sciences, that of the thousand and one proposals of the secularized sociologists very many are likely to prove both unscientific and unpractical.

But it will not be enough to scout all this as unscientific, even tho it be so to the last degree, or even to demonstrate it to be unscientific. The preacher must find the message of the law of God in the Bible with which to meet it. He needs to enforce with renewed distinctness and emphasis the teachings of that Bible concerning man's spiritual nature and his freedom and responsibility; the sacredness and absolute character of right and virtue, and the inherently despicable character of wrong and crime; the dependence of character upon the man himself rather than upon his environment—of all of which, with all the kindred and related principles, innumerable illustrations will be found in the preacher's text-book, the Word of God. If the moral atmosphere that is so hazy with secularism and animalism is to be cleared; if the mad, unprecedented rush of vice and crime that to-day dazes Christendom is to be stayed; and if the mawkish sentimentality in dealing with crimes and criminals—that has reached such a pass that, as Dr. Andrew D. White says, "the only taking of life that Americans object to seems to be that which is done by judicial process"—is to be swept out of existence, these Scriptural principles will need to be persistently presented and enforced after Christ's method of enforcing principles, until something of the old moral foundation is restored, through the quickening of conscience and the enlightening power of Divine truth.

The preacher will also need to understand the situation of the English-speaking, or perhaps Teutonic, races, and their special relation to the problems of the age, and to shape and direct his message accordingly. *(2) To Understand the Situation.*

The fact of the giving of the wealth and commerce of the world, and the power of machine production, into the hands of Protestant Christendom, as represented by the Teutonic peoples, and especially by those of Anglo-Saxon descent, carries with it a vast meaning that has probably attracted the attention of few persons. Cunningham in *Politics and Economics*, a book of rare insight and breadth, has given a glimpse of its meaning in connection with Great Britain. He says:*

" Each great race has made a notable contribution to the development of the civilization of the world ; we owe a debt to Egypt for some measure of skill, to Greece for the triumph of art, to Rome for the vigor of her law. We English, too, have a destiny to fulfil, a duty thrust upon us by him whom we profess to serve, a heritage to bequeath to all future generations and all other races. We are a nation of shopkeepers ; a nation whose triumphs and whose position are inextricably bound up with commercial success. And therefore it is that the problems of industrial and social life lie before us for solution ; that it is in our progress and our poverty, our bitter misery and our struggle with it, that the world may learn about the evils of grinding competition and pitiable luxury, of

---

* *Politics and Economics*, p. 275, by W. Cunningham, B. D., Lecturer and Chaplain of Trinity College, Cambridge. London : Kegan Paul, Trench & Co., 1885.

the race for wealth and failure to enjoy it. These are the questions with which the Sphinx has set us face to face, and by our answers to these will our place as a nation be judged in the ages to come."

In order to get a full conception of the meaning of the fact thus presented, the view and scope of Mr. Cunningham must be somewhat widened, and some new factors in the problem must be taken in. To begin with, "the Anglo-Saxon peoples" needs to be substituted for "we English." Possibly an extension may soon be needed, as already suggested, to take in the Teutonic peoples; but for the present the Anglo-Saxons hold the place of supremacy. The capital factors to be taken in, as furnishing the principles and standard of judgment and adjustment, are the open Bible and free democratic institutions. With this new breadth and light the special mission of the Anglo-Saxon peoples, of which we form a very large element, is to solve for mankind the problems of industrial, social, and civil life, by the aid of Bible Christianity and under free democratic political institutions. The things of special account are essential manhood and free development under the sway of Bible principles. The precepts of the Divine Word must therefore furnish the standard of manhood and Christian character, and the rule for the direction of development and progress.

*The Anglo-Saxon Problem.*

These considerations open the way to an understanding of the preacher's message to men regarding present and pressing problems. They make it plain that manhood and character are the things to be sought and regarded supremely in this world. Not wealth, not commerce, not material progress, not the State, but man with his immortal nature, and character that is to remain his only permanent belonging, are the supreme things from the Bible point of view. The moral and Christian precepts laid down by God and Christ are the governing principles, equally applicable to all spheres and all problems. The preacher to the English-speaking peoples is therefore peculiarly bound to unfold and enforce these in his message.

He is to present the moral law as supreme over all questions of society, and social position and relation. High manhood and womanhood, character, attainment, and achievement in service and self-sacrifice, are to be impressed, by Scriptural precept and illustration, as the only titles of nobility and aristocracy in the Kingdom of God. In the precepts of the Divine Word he is to supply the test and touchstone of all social usages, amusements, entertainments, and the like; ruling out thereby all that is detrimental to true manhood and womanhood, and to the interests of humanity, and seeking to mold everything in accordance with the spirit of Christ and his religion. *Moral Law over Society.*

He is to find in the Divine law the supreme rule of economics, applicable to all industrial questions, whether concerning supply or demand, labor or capital, employee or employer. *Moral Law over Economics.* He will need to make deadly onset with "the sword of the Spirit" upon the "age-temptation," and make it full clear that wealth is not an adequate *summum bonum* for man or for society. He will need to ponder well the real condition of things, until he understands and appreciates the exact dangers that just now threaten the Anglo-Saxon peoples, from their long-continued defiance of the righteous law of the universe. Mr. W. S. Lilly, one of the ablest of British writers, has uttered a note of warning that may give a hint of the foreboding of one clear thinker and seer. He says : *

"The law of the world—whether stated in theological phraseology or not—is justice : yes, *retributive* justice. It rules absolutely throughout the universe, in every sphere of action of all intelligent being. Fraud upon workers, fraud upon buyers, *must*, by the very nature of things, entail the destruction of any society which tolerates it ; nay, which blesses and approves it with the names of competition, supply and demand, the Course of Trade. Who, that has eyes to see, can fail to discern even now the handwriting upon the wall— the Mene, Tekel, Upharsin of this great Babylon which we have built? Socialism, Communism, Nihilism—think you they portend nothing? Do not think it. These should need no Daniel to expound them. Their interpretation is plain enough. Different expressions of one and the same movement, they mean 'red ruin and the breaking up of laws' for a society which has enthroned Mammon as the supreme object of human affection and worship ; which sets up, as the all-sufficient rule of life, the principle of self-interest ; which accounts of man as a mere wealth-producing animal. They mean the negation of country, of history, of liberty, of property ; the destruction of all that constitutes civilization in the highest sense."

In escaping such fate, the preacher will find no help in the materialistic platitudes and mummeries of the Spencerian social science, or in the inane mutterings and babblings of a positivist sociology. He will need to resort for such help to the Word of God; to bring from that the simple principles that fell with the weight of omnipotence from the inspired lips of Moses and Paul and John, and from the divine lips of Christ; and to present these to men for their guidance, and to be applied by them with the united wisdom of the Church of Christ, and the higher and silent wisdom of the Holy Spirit, to the solution of the intricate and perplexing problems now demanding attention.

* *On Shibboleths*, pp. 212, 213.

He is to find in the same law the supreme rule in politics and statesmanship, and to unfold and enforce its principles in all the civil and civic rela- *Moral Law* tions. In this way alone is the remedy *over Politics.* to be found for the slavery that has come from the brutal despot upon a throne in the Old World, and for the slavery and bottomless political corruption combined that have come from the " brutal individualism" of the "sovereign people" in the New World. Necessity will be on him to hold up the divine standard, with absolute clearness and distinctness, until every citizen shall feel the weight of obligation resting upon citizenship and hasten to the performance of his duties, in the primary, in the political meeting, at the polls, in public office and trust, in short, in all his civil relations; until every citizen shall understand that he is individually responsible, and accept the responsibility, for the character of politics and of the legislators, and of public officers and rulers; and until every office-seeker shall be made to understand that, as "public office is a public trust," it should never be committed to a rake or to a drunkard, to a mere politician or to a sheer scoundrel, whether that one is an impecunious lawyer, a fat saloon-keeper, or a multi-millionaire.

As regards the state of things that needs to be remedied in our own country, and that has been so emphasized by the recent Lexow investigations in New York City, and the subsequent political developments, it may be well to look upon American politics through the eyes of the same foreigner just quoted. Mr. Lilly says: *

"In what I am writing, I know that I am but expressing the views of the most highly educated and thoughtful among the inhabitants of

* *On Shibboleths*, p. 93.

the United States, who, undazzled by the immense industries, the colossal capitalism, the magnificent material progress of their Republic, perceive clearly the rottenness of the foundations whereon it rests, but who dare not give utterance to their thoughts. 'America,' wrote Heine, 'that frightful dungeon of freedom, where the invisible chains gall still more painfully than the visible ones at home, and where the most repulsive of all tyrants, the mob, exercises its coarse despotism.'"

So desperate a case as that which confronts him, the messenger of God will never reach by any advocacy of mere reform measures. He will need to summon men to the judgment of the law and the testimony, and then to urge evermore Christianity as a divine saving power, as did the prophet Isaiah of old, in a similar crisis: *

"Therefore, thus saith the Lord God, Behold, I lay in Zion for a foundation stone, a tried stone, a precious corner-stone, a sure foundation; he that believeth shall not make haste. Judgment also will I lay to the line, and righteousness to the plummet, and the hail shall sweep away the refuge of lies, and the waters shall overflow the hiding-place. And your covenant with death shall be disannulled, and your agreement with hell shall not stand; when the overflowing scourge shall pass through, then ye shall be trodden down by it."

In fine, the preacher's message is to bear from the Word of God the appropriate moral principles that are to be applied by the Church to the complicated problem that has been committed to the Anglo-Saxon peoples for solution, and that is clearly insoluble except by the application of Christianity as a divine law and a regenerating power. The other phases of his message will aid him in this task; for if he succeeds in impressing upon the Church her duty in the immediate evangelization of the world; in bringing her to right views regarding this vast

*The Preacher's Duty.*

* Isaiah xxviii. 16-18.

wealth in her possession as given for this end; and in leading her to consecrate her sons and daughters, her untold treasures of silver and gold, and her almost limitless energies and administrative power, to the immediate carrying out of the Great Commission as her one duty—the world will be speedily revolutionized, since the causes of the industrial, social, and political evil and corruption—human greed and ambition—will be swept away by the new spiritual power, or swallowed up in grander hopes and enterprises for the glory of Christ in the salvation of the world.

The preacher needs also to present God's law, in a wise and discriminating manner, as the law of life for man, marking out God's way of blessedness through obedience.

3. The Way of Life.

Quite different should such preaching be from that so common in some quarters, which indiscriminately presents the law of God as if it were simply the divine benevolence toward the sinner; and which encourages transgressors by minimizing or taking out of it the divine justice, which is its essential characteristic, and so lifting from man the obligation to that righteousness in the securing of which in some way is his only safety. The Lord said, through Moses, to the children of Israel of old, as recorded in Deuteronomy: "All these things have I commanded you for your *good* always." That expresses an important truth. The law is the perfect statement by God, of man's way of maintaining righteousness, and securing perfection and blessedness, provided he is not already a lawbreaker and subject to the penalty of the broken law. But from the moment he becomes a sinner, the law has henceforth only wrath, condemnation, terror, and destruction.

In presenting the law as the law of life, the preacher needs to guard against the common sentimentality, the subtle universalism, and the false benevolence of the day; and at the same time to vindicate the divine goodness in connection with the divine justice. He should utter his call to men for loving submission to, and acquiescence in, this law of God, that is not made a barrier and penalty and curse to the righteous, but a good and a blessing; and that becomes a curse only through the perverse wickedness of man himself.

Especially must the preacher present the law of God as the law of judgment, by which the natural man is to be judged here, and by which, if he remain impenitent, he must stand or fall at the bar of the final judgment.

*4. The Standard of Judgment.*

It is in the presentation of this aspect of the law that much of the preaching of the present day is confessedly and peculiarly deficient. Apparently, men have almost ceased to think of the law of God as the standard of judgment for their conduct; and have almost forgotten that there is a judgment to come. They do not willingly listen to the preaching that hales them to the judgment bar. Preachers preach such preaching hesitatingly, if at all. In many so-called revivals, the old stress of a conscience roused by the appeal to the teachings of God's Word concerning the judgment, is no longer deemed a proper way of leading men to repent and accept the Gospel; hence, the demand for the introduction of some outside influence, or the bringing to bear of some new method, so as to accomplish by means of machinery what the message of the preacher and the Spirit of God should bring about.

## THE PREACHER'S MESSAGE.

There is pressing necessity for a return to the old and authoritative preaching of the law of God as the law of judgment. Some years since, in such a revival, in view of the hesitancy of some of the principal members of the community openly to accept Christ and his Gospel, the writer suggested to one of his young men that they needed to have the influence of the law brought to bear. The law presented brought the desired results. Years afterward that young man, now a prominent clergyman in one of our large cities, accompanied his pastor to assist him in a series of revival meetings in a neighboring town. There was much seriousness and solemnity in the audience, but for several days meager practical results were obtained. Half a score of the leading business and professional men of the town were regularly present, and undoubtedly very seriously affected, but they held out against the persuasions of the Gospel, and their influence kept others from salvation. After one of the evening services, the two, pastor and assistant, were consulting together over what seemed to be the almost hopeless outlook. The young man recalled just then the incident of former years, and suggested: "My old professor would say now, as he said then, 'Try the law.'" They determined to do this. The preacher, who was possessed of a remarkable memory, had by him the sermons of Jonathan Edwards. He read and reread and saturated his mind with the sermon entitled, "Sinners in the Hands of an Angry God." The next evening he gave the audience the substance of it. The result was the immediate submission and profession of all those leaders in the community, and a complete and extended work of grace in that town.

*[margin: Condemning Power of Law.]*

The same subtle pride and infidelity, the same supercilious disregard of God's law of judgment, that characterized the age of Edwards, are prevalent in this age; and, if the Gospel is to do its full work now, there is again needed something of the old-fashioned preaching that made men mad and roused conscience and brought the sinner trembling before the bar of God.

Repentance in view of the coming judgment is one of the essentials in all preaching that is to lead souls to Christ. We have almost lost it out of our teachings and of our thought; but note the stress laid upon it in the confessions of the Church, and its prominence in the preparatory preaching of John the Baptist, in Christ's own early teachings, and in the view of the Apostles. Salvation is salvation *from* sin. It can not be had without *turning from* sin. In other words there can be no such thing as salvation *in* sin, that is, without *repentance.* The Bible as law addresses sinners as rebels against God, and calls upon them to throw down the weapons of their rebellion. It was in his taking up of this Bible call to submission and repentance that largely lay the power of Finney's revival preaching, that had such efficiency in bringing strong men to humble themselves before God; in some cases, as in the city of Rochester, completely transforming the professions, by reaching doctors and lawyers and judges alike. Upon this necessity for repentance that great theologian, Dr. Henry B. Smith, was accustomed to lay special stress; and in connection with it he so strongly insisted upon holding up the divine side of this great matter, rather than the merely moral, human side in preaching; the call to the sinner being: "Repent; submit to God;

yield to your rightful sovereign," not, "Come, save yourself from the consequences of sin."

The preacher's call to repentance should always ring out with no uncertain sound. Nothing less than such preaching can furnish a thorough preparation for the saving faith that lays hold upon Christ; and the largest infusion and strongest expression of it are called for in the preaching of the present day. Repentance was always the burden of the New Testament messages to dying men. When John the Baptist, the forerunner of Christ, came preaching in the wilderness, it was with the cry: "Repent ye: for the kingdom of heaven is at hand."* When Christ entered upon his ministry his earliest call was: "Repent: for the kingdom of heaven is at hand."† Later in that ministry, in exhorting the captious Jews "not to lose the short season of grace and salvation," his thrilling and repeated warning was: "Except ye repent, ye shall all likewise perish."‡ After Christ's resurrection, in that rousing sermon at Pentecost, Peter drew to a close with the same peremptory call: "Repent, and be baptized every one of you in the name of Jesus Christ, for the remission of sins, and ye shall receive the gift of the Holy Ghost."§

Such preaching alone will prepare sinful men for the appreciation and reception of the Gospel.

II. THE GOSPEL ESSENTIAL TO THE MESSAGE.

In presenting Bible Christianity as God's saving power, the preacher needs to press upon the lost sinner, with special clearness and power, and as the

\* Matt. iii. 2.   † Matt. iv. 17.   ‡ Luke xiii. 3.   § Acts ii. 38.

complement of the law, the Gospel provision for salvation.

There are two fundamental aspects of the Gospel that are often emphasized : that of a *doctrine*, and that of a *life*. There is a marked tendency in this age to depress or ignore the doctrine, and to exalt or make exclusive the life. The dictum is often put forth, as if it were an axiom or an intuition: " Christianity is not a doctrine, but a life." Never was graver or more fatal error put in human language. Man is a rational being, and his life can only be reached, miracle and supernatural influence excepted, through his reason. The only way for the preacher to appeal to the reason is by doctrine or teaching. Some thought or truth must be presented, in order to lay any reasonable basis for rational or spiritual living. It is absurd, then, this tendency to cast contempt upon the Word of God, by calling its teachings *dogmas*, and then sneering at them or ignoring them in preaching. If man were an ape or an idiot, he could afford to do that; but so long as he remains a rational creature of God, made in the image of God, and brought into internal and inevitable relations to God, he can not afford either to sneer at or to ignore any teachings or dogmas or doctrines it may have pleased God to reveal to him in his Word.

The old truth—the truth that the effective preacher, called of God, needs to present—is that Christianity is a doctrine and a regenerating power on the side of God, to begin with; and a renewed, sanctified, consecrated life, on the side of man, to proceed with. The message that leaves out either of these features is so far deficient, and likely to fail of any spiritual results, or at least of any spiritual results worth the while.

<small>1. Christianity a Doctrine and a Life.</small>

## THE PREACHER'S MESSAGE.

There are two entirely distinct sides to the work of salvation as presented in the Bible: the God-ward side and the man-ward side.

To the jailer's question: "What must I do to be saved?" the answer of Paul and Silas was: "Believe on the Lord Jesus, and thou shalt be saved."* That presents, on the God-ward side, Christ, as "Jesus," or as the atoning sacrifice and Savior; and as the "Lord," who subdues the sinner by renewing him, and then reigns in and over him. On the man-ward side, it presents "belief *on*" the Lord Jesus, or practical faith and trust, on the sinner's part; involving not only the resting of the hopes upon, but also the consecration of the life to the service of Christ.

On its God-ward side, the Bible is full of teaching concerning the work of redemption, as something done by God for man. This is the aspect of redemption that has been emphasized—sometimes doubtless at the expense of other essential features—through the centuries, especially the post-reformation centuries. It is hard to conceive of any folly more monumental than that involved in the present attempt to ignore or deny it, in the newest theology, which would fain make of Christianity a transcendental or mystical superstructure without any foundation. In this matter the preacher can not break with the Christian ages, without breaking with Christ and bankrupting the Christian religion. (1) Redemption on its God-ward Side.

A single passage may be taken, as summing up several of the features of this side of the work of Christ as Redeemer. Paul says: †

"Being justified freely by his grace, through the redemption that is in Christ Jesus: whom God hath set forth to be a propitiation, through

\* Acts xvi. 31. † Rom. iii. 24-26.

faith in his blood, to declare his righteousness for the remission of sins that are past, through the forbearance of God ; to declare, I say, at this time his righteousness : that he might be just, and the justifier of him which believeth in Jesus."

Here is something manifestly quite different and aside from a change in personal behavior or a process by which man grows better. Here are presented justification, propitiation, redemption, as essential elements in salvation; and any explaining away of the plain teachings of this and similar passages, by the hypothesis that they are "accommodations" to Jewish, or Roman, or other notions, is an impossibility in right thinking and in rational interpretation of the Scriptures, and would be scouted as arrant folly or sheer dishonesty, if applied to any other literary production whatsoever. Christ's death is here set forth clearly as penal, vicarious, propitiatory. All this teaching implies law and penalty and justice; and these conceptions carry with them corresponding sets of ideas, that are not peculiar to the Word of God merely, but run through all human laws and institutions, and through all human conduct. The Scriptures are full of these ideas. The whole of the Old Testament system is merely their embodiment in symbols and types and shadows. The Bible presents the lost condition of man, and then, upon that presupposition, insists everywhere on the necessity for atonement, propitiation, and redemption, to meet the requirements of justice. It represents the great problem before the Divine Mind in redemption as being, how to save man from the just penalty of sin, and at the same time preserve God's justice and truth intact. Unquestionably the tendency of the liberalism of these times is to minimize or to explain away this necessary work of God for lost men. This drift has doubtless resulted largely from the ignoring of the divine law, or the lowering of its requirements, or the loss of a sense of its sacredness and inexorableness—due to the failure of preacher and moralist to understand, appreciate, and enforce its nature and scope and claims. As a natural consequence, sin has come to be regarded as a little thing; and man has so lost out the sense of it that he has ceased to feel the need of any great work of atonement, on the part of the God-man, as an essential element in salvation.

Equally important with a return to the appreciation and distinct preaching of the law of God—if not even more important—is a return to the Bible view of the work done by God for man's salvation in redemption. Men are in perishing need of hearing the doctrine of atonement, or of the sacrifice of Christ upon the cross to satisfy the divine justice, and as the sinner's substitute before the law. Not less important than the return to the preaching of repentance toward God is the return to the preaching of the propitiation of God.

On its man-ward side, the Bible is full of doctrine concerning what redemption accomplishes for man and in man, and of which the preacher should make larger use, if the ends of redemption for man and in man are to be attained. (2) **Redemption in its Application.** The Apostle Paul presents this divine work, in connection with his three great "therefores," in the Epistle to the Romans. "*Therefore*, being justified by faith" (Rom. v. 1); "There is *therefore* now no condemnation" (Rom. viii. 1); "I beseech you *therefore*, brethren, by the mercies of God" (Rom. xii. 1).

On the threshold, and prepared for by the preaching of the law and of the atonement by Christ for man, is the doctrine of justification by faith in Jesus Christ, the great test doctrine from the point of view of Protestantism. It is Luther's doctrine of a "standing or falling Church." Paul introduces this point by his first "*therefore.*"

And just here there is need of special caution against confounding justification with sanctification. By confounding the two and giving to the former merely the signification of the latter, the new liberalism is remanding the Church to the bondage to the law from which the Reformation sought to deliver her. Justification is to be regarded as the change in the relation of the sinner to God and his law, made by the grace of God on the ground of faith in a righteousness provided by God. It is not God's making the sinner good or righteous; but his regarding and treating him as righteous, on the ground of what Christ has done for him. Justification is a forensic conception, based upon the sinner's relation to God in law and justice. Romanism and the new liberalism confound this treating of man as righteous, with making him righteous; and so remand the Christian to the old system of law, leaving him to live on in legal bondage, instead of in a condition of grace. In the Bible and Protestant view, justification is the necessary preparation for regeneration and sanctification, and for all that follows them in the Christian life. It introduces the sinner into a state of grace in which, having been justified for Christ's sake, God treats him as tho he were actually righteous; graciously bestowing upon him, in consideration of his acceptance of what Christ has done for him, all that he needs of help and life and saving power. The Roman doctrine, in ignoring this distinction, is fatal to vital Christianity, and, where fully accepted, inevitably leads to dead legalism and formalism, in short, to that whole system of works which makes the righteousness of Christ of none effect.

This justification is by faith. Not that faith is any great thing in itself, or has any merit in itself; but that God has used faith, in accordance with the constitution of man's nature, as the agency for adjusting the relations of the great scheme of redemption. It is the soul's act in receiving the atonement made for it by Christ, and resting upon Christ alone for salvation. It takes in the soul's act of repentance, which is the turning away from sin and wandering, in turning back toward God and fixing its thoughts, feelings, and purposes on God as revealed in Christ its Savior. It is the attitude and drift of the Christian soul God-ward. In its connection with justification, it therefore shapes character and decides the conduct and the life. It is like the key in its adaptation to the adjustments of the lock, insignificant in itself, but great in its accomplishments because of that adaptation.

Justification by faith thus becomes, on the man-ward side, the foundation of the Christian life. It is easy to see, in the light of these relations, why the great reformer of the sixteenth century made so much of it; and why Paul, in the one authoritative treatise in the Bible on the way of salvation, makes so much of it. It is the parting of the way between Romanism and legal liberalism, and genuine evangelical religion. It is the one only and essential basis and starting-point in vital piety and a right religious life. The so-called preaching of Christianity that omits it is necessarily without regenerating and saving efficacy.

Regeneration and sanctification by the Holy Spirit accompany or follow upon justification, being prepared for by it. The doctrines concerning these need to be made especially prominent in the preacher's message in this age. The historic passage on the first of these doctrines is, of course, Christ's teaching to Nicodemus in the third chapter of John. The second doctrine Christ expressed in one of the most intense yearnings in his Intercessory Prayer (John xvii. 18, 19), and the Bible is full of it.

The tendency, as already seen, has been of the strongest to displace regeneration by reformation. But Christ himself taught, with that *double verily* which he never used except in connection with life-and-death doctrines, "Except a man be born again, he can not see the kingdom of God," and again : " Except a man be born of water and of the Spirit, he can not enter into the kingdom of God." Most assuredly, that without which man can neither *see* nor *enter into* the Kingdom of God must be an essential in the Christian religion; and the preaching that ignores it is not the preaching for which the Master commissioned his messengers.

The tendency has been equally marked to ignore or slur over the doctrine of sanctification by the Holy Spirit, and to teach in its place outward, moral reformation. Outward change of conduct that has no root in that truth by which Christ prayed that his followers might be sanctified, and in which the Holy Spirit, the divine author of sanctification, has no part, can not properly claim to have any spiritual value.

A renewed life of righteousness, holiness, and service, on the part of the believer, is the natural and **(3) The New Life in Christ.** necessary outcome of justification, regeneration, and sanctification. This is what the Apostle Paul introduces by his third emphatic "*therefore*" (Rom. xii. 1).

The Christian is saved, not merely for his own sake, nor for his own special comfort and selfish enjoyment,— a conception that would neutralize or nullify salvation itself,—but for the great interests and services of the Kingdom of God, in which he is to be a coworker with Christ and all other Christians, for the glory of God and the salvation of the world—in short, in the carrying out of the Great Commission.

The *inner life* of religion is an essential element in the Bible idea of Christianity, and forms the only adequate basis for the right outward life of Christian activity. The preacher needs to emphasize this feature in the present age. Christians in the past no doubt sometimes gave too exclusive attention to the inner, contemplative life of faith, devoting themselves morbidly to the work of introspection and self-examination; but the tendency of the completed organizations, the vast machinery of the present day, is to sink this element, and keep in view only the outward activity. The true mean is to be found in calling men back to the life of reflection and contemplation, not for its own sake, nor as a means of spiritual comfort, but as furnishing the only living basis for real, genuine spiritual activity in the service of Christ.

Preachers would do well to review their system of fundamental doctrines, from time to time, and, taking a broad view of the field, to complete and round out that system in accordance with the latest illumination of God's truth by the Holy Spirit. Such a review will lead, not to an addition to the doctrines of the Word of God, "The faith *once for all* delivered to the saints," but to a better comprehension of the Scriptural

*Four Fundamental Doctrines.*

doctrines that stand out prominently in the Christian consciousness of the Church of the present day. There are the old doctrines, that have long been recognized as essential by the Church of Christ, and that are still essential: the doctrine of an inspired revelation from God, laying a sure foundation for Christian faith; the doctrine of a vicarious atonement by the active and passive obedience of Christ, presenting a way of salvation indorsed by God himself; and the doctrine of regeneration by the Holy Spirit, furnishing men the needed power for the application of this divinely revealed and divinely wrought atonement. But since the age of the Reformation, through the spiritual awakening of the Church to its great mission of saving the world, a fourth doctrine of the Word of God has been brought into peculiar and appropriate prominence, in the mind of the Christian Church: the doctrine of Christian service for the Master, that makes every saved soul a coworker with Christ, under the Great Commission, in the work of giving the Gospel to all mankind, and that, as already seen, binds every follower of Christ to devote himself, with all his powers and possessions, to that as the supreme end of his life on earth. This new doctrine—not new to the Word of God, nor new to the Christian of missionary spirit in any age, but new in the consciousness of the Church as a whole—needs to be added to the others already emphasized as essentials. If the Gospel structure in the world is to stand out four-square to all the winds of heaven, these four corner-stones must all be laid underneath—Christ with his atonement, the chief corner-stone; the inspired revelation, divine regeneration, and Christian service, the remaining corner-stones.

At the same time, the message of the preacher must take in the truth that redemption is to be regarded as a manifold process, every phase of which should occupy its proportionate part and its appropriate place, in "holding forth the word of life" to lost men. **2. Redemption has Manifold Aspects.** Failures in this regard have always led, not only to seriously defective views, but also to unsatisfactory results. That there have been such failures goes without saying. It seems well-nigh impossible for the preacher with his many distractions, and even for the quiet and contemplative theological thinker without any distractions, to take, and keep always in mind, a broad and comprehensive view of a great subject, with so many prominent factors and features. Yet nothing, except perhaps the doctrine of justification by faith, is more important to be borne in mind by the preacher than that redemption has manifold relations, all of which are essential to its integrity.

It has its legal aspect. It is God's work of freeing the sinner from the bondage and curse of the law. Paul says, in Rom. v. 1, 2: **(1) Legal Aspect.**

"Therefore being justified by faith, we have peace with God, through our Lord Jesus Christ: by whom also we have access by faith into this grace wherein we stand, and rejoice in hope of the glory of God."

Doubtless the perversion of this view has often led to antinomianism, but it is nevertheless an essential part of divine truth.

It has its governmental aspect, as it seeks to bring the sinner into right relations to the divine government, under which he must live whether he will or not. The perversion of this aspect has led to the governmental theory, regarded **(2) Governmental Aspect.**

as a complete theory of redemption. But notwithstanding the error possibly resulting, this too must be retained and presented as essential.

It has its moral aspect, proposing to bring the sinner to a right life before God, and in doing this **(3) Moral Aspect.** bringing to bear upon him the moral influence of all the truths and motives of religion. The perversion of this may have led to the moral influence theory—Bushnellism and all that—a scheme that in its extreme form would make "nature and nurture" adequate to all needed changes in the sinner's character, and would exclude divine, supernatural regeneration, the work of the Holy Spirit "by and with the truth" of the Word of God. But the truth involved in it is an essential element in redemption, and must be enforced, tho always in its proper relation, as such.

It has its dynamic aspect, for Christ on the throne of the universe has become the possessor of all **(4) Dynamic Aspect.** authority and power, to be used in making "all things work together for good" to those who love God. The too common neglect of this has led to mistaken views of the inevitableness of natural consequences following upon all sin. The perversion of it has led men to naturalistic views respecting what redemption can do for man. Such views have regarded the Christian as wholly subject to natural law, and doomed to reap the natural consequences of his sins, despite the grace of salvation. But, while guarding against the error and perversion, the truth must be enforced, that, in the work of redemption, omnipotence, in the person of Christ on the throne, comes in to deliver, as it only can deliver, the penitent from natural retribution.

It has its aspect of self-sacrifice and of service, as illustrated in the lives of the redeemed in following the example of Christ. The perversion of this has led to dead works, to efforts after salvation by works, to legal bondage, and, in this age, to Christian socialism in its extreme forms. The fault has been, not in undue *devotion* to works, but in undue *exaltation* of human works and merit. The office of self-sacrifice and service is to demonstrate the saved condition and exhibit the gratitude of the saved; to give expression to the renewed life, and to push the work of the Great Commission to its consummation—and to this office, as a factor of redemption, the preacher should give all emphasis. *(5) Aspect of Service.*

It has its sacrificial and vicarious aspect—the one upon which the Bible places special emphasis—representing the crucified Christ as the sacrifice for sin, and as the lost sinner's substitute before the law and justice of God. The perversion of this, or its exclusive consideration, even tho it be the most important factor of all, has often led to selfish indolence and carnal security, in connection with a life demonstrating the man not a Christian at all. Oftener, however, its neglect has remanded man to the bondage of law, and left him without any salvation, since "without shedding of blood there is no remission" of sin. This last defect, with its tendency to discredit divine revelation and all Scriptural agencies and influences, is the defect against which the preacher needs most earnestly to set himself in his preaching to the present generation, as this is the most marked current phase of error, and most fatal to the success of Christianity as a saving power. *(6) Sacrificial Aspect.*

All these great truths and phases of the Gospel enter

into the full message of the preacher, and constitute its essentials. So far as that message has been effective in any age, it has been because of their more or less complete, more or less faithful, presentation. There can be no question regarding their importance as factors in the preaching of Biblical Christianity as a saving power. A question that has, however, arisen, in these later days, and that has been prominently before the public, and needs now to be considered, is: Shall this preaching take on a doctrinal form?

## SECTION THIRD.

### Bible Christianity in Doctrinal Form an Essential.

In presenting Bible Christianity as a saving power, the preacher needs, at the present day, to give special attention to the right doctrinal presentation of the great truths that cluster around and center in salvation by the cross of Christ.

We are quite aware that this does not give expression to the tendency of the present day. With a few, the question of abandoning doctrinal teaching and preaching is no longer regarded as an open question. Such teaching and preaching they have already discarded. Very many are sure that the matter has gone much further, and they loudly affirm that only fossils and old fogies think of continuing to give any attention to the great Scriptural doctrines that once constituted the staple of all evangelical preaching. In view of this state of things, the preacher needs to inquire very seriously:

How has this break with past methods come about?

Is it rationally or Biblically justifiable? What is the true method of presenting the message of the Gospel, and does it not require a return to all that was essential in the past methods now partially discredited?

If the reasons for the present tendency to eschew doctrinal teaching and preaching are fairly and candidly weighed, we think that their consideration will not only show clearly, but also emphasize tremendously, the imperative need for a powerful revival of such teaching and preaching.

## I. Change of Method from Erroneous Views.

The reasons for the present tendency are to be looked for in the influence of the current philosophic opinions and of the resulting practical life. The philosophy shapes the conduct; hence, the explanation of the latter is to be found in the former. It will appear, from even a cursory examination, that certain philosophical assumptions, all equally baseless, have resulted in placing a ban upon the preaching of the great Christian doctrines, and in leaving them at a discount in the estimation of the Church of the present day.

A shallow rationalistic transcendentalism has persistently assumed and asserted the supremacy of philosophy over faith and the antagonism of the two, until the mass of mankind almost feel that the great distinctive doctrines of Christianity have been generally discarded as quite obsolete. What ground is there for this?

*1. Influence of Shallow Transcendentalism.*

We have nothing to say against a rational transcendentalism; rather everything in its favor. It has its legitimate sphere, and is the only possible basis of a rational, as distinguished from a purely speculative, philosophy. There is no antagonism between such a system of philosophy and the doctrines of the Christian system. This is made plain by the relations of philosophy and Christian faith.\*

<small>(1) **Rational Transcendentalism Legitimate.**</small>

The sources of the two, philosophy and faith, are entirely different. Philosophy seeks a knowledge of ultimate facts and principles, by studying man, the universe, and God, as revelations of such principles, and verifying these by reason—in order to find the final explanation of all existences. Christianity finds the source of its truth in the Bible, accepted as a revelation from God. The two deal, to a certain extent, with the same themes—man, the universe, and God, and the relations of these; but the starting-points and the modes of procedure are different. Philosophy culminates in these truths as the end of its rational processes; Christianity starts out with them as a direct revelation from God in the Bible. The one depends upon reason, the other upon faith. The one says : " This is intuitive truth "; the other, " This is the testimony of God." The evidence in each sphere is distinct and peculiar. In philosophy, inductive verification is employed, in bringing out rational principles as tested by the canons of intuition—self-evidence, necessity, and catholicity; in our religion,

---

\* The reader will find special help and inspiration on this subject in an article by the late Dr. Henry B. Smith, entitled " the Relations of Faith and Philosophy," in his volume, *Faith and Philosophy*, published by Charles Scribner's Sons, New York.

induction proper is made use of, on the basis of the facts and truths in God's Word written. It is apparent, therefore, that the range of Christian doctrine is vastly more extended than the sphere of philosophy, as the range of revelation is much wider than that of intuition.

Nor is faith in the Christian system simply a blind trust; it is rather a rational belief or conviction. It rests on a revelation historically attested, confirmed by miracle and prophecy, centering in Jesus Christ, and recorded in an inspired book, and proposing and claiming to solve the great problems .of human life and destiny. It has its corresponding subjective evidence, in the profound experiences in which the believer's soul responds to this great divine revelation, and all centering in the same divine person as the historical revelation. This revelation has entered into and controlled the whole course of human history and human thought—the movement of the old world, before Jesus of Nazareth, converging to the cross of Calvary, and the movement of the ages since radiating from that same cross, thus confirming the historical revelation and the experience. The great problems of the universe, the life-and-death questions always pressing upon the human soul, this revelation answers with sublime simplicity, clearness, certainty, and sufficiency in its doctrines of creation, providence, original sin, incarnation, and redemption—making all again center in the person and work of the historical Christ.

Resting, as does the Christian faith, upon such a vast scheme of rational evidence, no weapon forged from so-called reason or intuition has ever been lifted against it to prosper. Indeed, what clear utterance has intuition to make about the Trinity and the nature of God, the origin of sin and evil, the work of redemption, the judgment of man and his final destiny? And, so far as those truths are concerned, concerning which intuition, reason, has something to say, its utterances are in accord with those of revelation. It is only by speculation, and by perversion of principles, that antagonism has been made to appear to exist between the two.

In short, the whole vast fabric of rationalistic philosophy is made up of speculation, based upon assumption and assertion. A single example will illustrate the entire method and scheme. The so-called philosopher affirms that there is no God, and therefore that the Bible revelation of God is baseless, and Christianity the latest and most stupendous of the ancient superstitions. But how does he reach his affirmation? He asserts that there is no such thing as spirit, and no such thing as cause, and therefore no such being as the Infinite Spirit and the First Cause. Now, all this is in the very face of the most certain of our intuitive knowledges. For the most intimate and fundamental knowledge is that of our existence as spiritual personalities, and of our causal agency; since these are involved in all our conscious activity. The philosopher, professing to deal with reason and intuition, and to set these up as authorities against revelation, starts out therefore by assuming the contradictories of the real intuitions, and bases all his speculation upon these fundamental lies. It is all mere brazen assertion. And that is the best that Mill and Spencer, the modern Aristotle and Plato, can do! On such grounds their senseless followers raise the

(2) **Rationalistic Transcendentalism Baseless.**

cry that Christianity is obsolete, and bow down and worship the great philosophers! For a "Thus saith the Lord," they have substituted, "Thus it is written in the books of Mill and Spencer!"

Let it be understood then and affirmed, in the face of this "philosophy falsely so-called," that there is not one fact or doctrine in all the Christian system that a true and rational philosophy has ever done anything else than to confirm. The relation of philosophy and faith is not that of absolute exclusion—philosophy *or* faith; nor that of antagonism—philosophy *versus* faith; but that of harmony and co-operation—philosophy *and* faith. It would be as senseless and irrational to give up the great Scriptural doctrines, because of this persistent and impudent cry of rationalism about the "collapse of the supernatural," as it would be for the world to suspend all its business activities because Vennor predicts a coming cyclone, or, rather, because of the one that he predicted but which did not come.

A still more shallow sensationalism and materialism, culminating in the all-pervasive teaching of Herbert Spencer, has gone far toward muddling the minds of men over the question whether we are anything more than developed brutes, or, worse than that, anything more than mere developments of matter and motion by redistribution. "There is no God, no soul, no freedom, no immortality—at bottom, only matter and motion." This is sensationalism run mad, "the philosophy of dirt" clasping hands with the philosophy of brutality. Animal enjoyment is the great end of existence. Virtue consists in pursuing it under stress of the master instincts of nutrition and reproduction, and is thus merged in pure bestiality. God there is

2. Influence of Shallow Materialism.

none, except perhaps the double, or supposed ghost, of our great-great-grandfather! Of course both religion and virtue are blotted out and men are left to bald animalism and blank despair.

And this is the so-called new philosophy that scouts God and revelation and Christianity! Now philosophy, according to Ueberweg, is "the science of principles";* but this scheme of so-called philosophy has no principles, and its assumptions and assertions fly in the face of all the fundamental truths of reason. Its truth, which its followers boast of as being established, is just as nearly demonstrated, and just as demonstrable, as the proposition that "the moon is made of green cheese"; and it has just as much philosophical basis as that proposition. It is high time that thinking men should wake up to this fact of the essentially irrational character of this pretentious system, and estimate it at its real, rational value, which is mathematically expressed by zero. It is a "bugaboo," and not a philosophy.

But perhaps the chief force militating against doctrinal teaching and preaching is the indefinite thinking, or no-thinking, embodied in so much of what is furnished for popular reading. It commonly takes on a highly rhetorical form.

3. Influence of Indefinite Thinking.

These false philosophies, in connection with others of kindred nature inherited from the past, with the aid of all the indefinite theological thinking, have resulted in the prevalence of a heathen and immoral morality that has led to the divorce of Christian doctrine from Christian ethics, thus fossilizing the former and annihilating the latter.

* *History of Philosophy*, vol. i. p. 1.

Now, if this be so, it is certainly a very serious state of things. The Fathers said : "Truth is in order to holiness." Christian doctrine was evidently intended to be the foundation of Christian ethics—*i. e.*, of an ethics whose essential elements are self-renunciation and self-sacrifice in devotion to Christ, and that leads to a heroism that crucifies self and scorns all ends centering merely in man, whether in his happiness, his culture, or his dignity. The great Christian doctrines, rightly presented, imperatively demand, and by the grace of God surely lead to, such Christian morality.

But the false and heathen philosophy, new and old, has introduced the new morality, so-called, of egoism, selfishness and mere humanitarianism, **Ethics of Selfishness.** which bids man get the best and the most for his own enjoyment, and perhaps for the enjoyment of his fellows, so far as that promotes his own. This unchristian, heathen, unmoral, or rather immoral, morality, based on the ethics of animalism, has, as has been already indicated, largely supplanted Christian morality as a theory of life. It answers the first question of the catechism, What is the chief end of man? in its own peculiar style: "To have a good time and come out *number one!*" The view of practical life is thus revolutionized. There is no room for the old doctrines. They only make men uncomfortable; and as comfort is the chief end of man, the preacher who in this day would preach those doctrines is regarded as a brute. Said a lady to another in a fashionable congregation recently: "How did you like Dr. V.?" The reply was : "Ah! the vulgar man! Why, he said, 'You sinners!'" And so, if they are to be preached at all, the practical bearings, the force and fire, must be taken out of them. A congregation thoroughly enlightened (?) by the new ethics, does not and will not hear of a just God, sin, the judgment, hell, and everlasting punishment; and therefore has no conscious need to hear of Christ as the incarnate Son of God, the sacrifice for sin, the atonement, and no disposition to hear of him as Lord and Master. They say to the preacher, as Israel of old said to the prophets: "Prophesy unto us smooth things." They tell him blandly—echoing Mr. Greg and that style of essayist—that there is no possibility of the old kind of Christian life; that no man in this age can live the life required of the primitive Christians; and that Christ in the very requirement showed the narrowness of his age and of himself, and proved that his religion was not the absolute religion!

As a natural consequence, the systems of the theologians have tended more and more to become dry, mathematical, barren statements—mere dogmas divorced from all the great practical Christian ends which God contemplated in the Gospel revelation—and often, as one has remarked, "about as fit to nourish the soul as sawdust would be to nourish the body." So there has been some reason for the cry of even good Christians: "Don't give us any of your dry, dead theology!"

**Dead Orthodoxy.**

Even where the old truth has been preached with freshness and living, practical power, the hearers, under control of the new ethics, have come to cry out: "Away with it! Away with it! It is gloomy and morose, and belongs to the Dark Ages! We will have none of it! Give us something abreast of the times. Your doctrine is a 'back number.'" To meet this popular demand the truth has been minimized, until there is little left of doctrine

**Distaste for Sound Doctrine.**

but the "Fatherhood of God" and "Come to Jesus!" in short, nothing but semi-universalism; and nothing left of ethics but heathen and minor morals, summed up in the various maxims of the lowest epicureanism or utilitarianism.

To vary and add spice to this gospel of twaddle, which is essentially commonplace and monotonous, the preacher who is "abreast of the times," your Rev. Shallow Æstheticus, must add the gospel of clap-trap, of vinegar, and wormwood (applicable to the sinners not present), and of art and esthetics, until the perfection of the new state of things is reached in some ideal "Church of the Holy Oriflamme." The multitudes must have a "smart gospel," and prefer the "gospel of smartness" even to that.

In fine, the question: "Shall we give up doctrine in our teaching and preaching?" really means, "Shall we, under stress of a false and heathen view of life—called Christian, but without a single Christian element in it—give up Christianity?" The demand is infinitely unreasonable.

## II. Return to Doctrine a Necessity.

The genesis of the present and prevailing treatment of doctrines in preaching would be enough, even were there nothing else to be said, to stamp it as not the treatment needed in the preaching that is to save the world. But, besides and beyond all this, the very nature and aim of Gospel message make doctrinal preaching a necessity. And in view of the defect and failure, the preacher should understand, and the Church should be made to understand, that the one great and absolutely imperative need of the present day is a powerful revival of the right kind of doctrinal teaching and preaching.

This is not the place to discuss the need for the revival of such teaching in the training of the ministry. That is, doubtless, a matter of vital import to the Church. The fact is well known that the study of theology has been reduced to a minimum, other subjects having absorbed nearly all the time once given to it. Moreover, it is easy to see that a homeopathic dose of theological lore, administered once a week, through two years of the course, by means of written lectures smoked and dried a generation ago, is not likely to result in any theological plethora. And there is undoubtedly a growing feeling among competent judges that there must be a great revolution in present methods, if the Church is not to perish of theological inanity and emptiness.

But apart from the question of theological training, it is easily shown that the teaching and preaching of the great Christian doctrines, in their practical bearings, is the only possible way of accomplishing the ends sought in Christ's Kingdom. The end to be attained, in Gospel teaching and preaching, is ultimately the glory of God. But, proximately and directly, it is to save sinners, and to develop them in Christian character and power, so as to make them strong and intelligent coworkers with Christ in bringing the world back to God. No one will deny this.

*1. Doctrines Essential to Preaching.*

It can not be reasonably denied that the first aim of Gospel teaching and preaching is to save sinners, or make them Christians. That end can not ordinarily be attained except through the fundamental Christian doctrines. In becoming a

*(1) Doctrine and Salvation*

Christian two things are implied : the reception of the Christian system as the creed, and the conforming of the inward and outward life to its teachings. There is the acceptance of Christ, first, as Savior, the sacrificial atonement ; and, secondly, as Lord, the Divine Master, to whom the life is given up in obedience and devotion. The method of the Christian life is that of faith working by love. Christ and the great doctrines of revelation centering in him are presented to the sinner in the Divine Word on the testimony of God. Upon them he lays hold by faith, which thus becomes the inspiration of love and devotion. The entire process is properly a rational one, proceeding on the basis of intelligent instruction in essential truth.

From another point of view, the three R's are at the foundation of the transformation from death to life : Ruin, Redemption, and Regeneration. The sinner's conception and appreciation of his own *ruin* and lost condition must depend upon his understanding of the doctrine concerning God, against whom he has sinned; of the nature and heinousness of sin, as transgression of the holy law of God ; of his own depravity and corruption ; of the powerful foes within and without who are seeking his destruction; and of the utter hopelessness of his case, as a sinner hastening to the bar of God. But this involves all the great doctrines of theology proper and of anthropology. His conception and appreciation of *redemption* must depend upon his knowledge of the doctrines of the everlasting love of the Father for a lost world ; of the incarnation, humiliation, vicarious obedience and sacrifice, the resurrection, ascension, intercession, and universal and everlasting kingdom of the Son of God as the Redeemer. His conception and appreciation of *regen-*

*eration* must depend upon his knowledge of the condition and needs of his own heart; of the person, character, and mission of the Holy Spirit, as the applier of redemption; and of the nature of holiness, and its necessity before God, in order to peace and eternal life. But this involves the doctrines of soteriology, as well as those centering in the Trinity. In fine, the preaching of Christian doctrine, under the stress of a divine call, must necessarily be the only intelligent way of seeking to save sinners, so long as man remains a rational being. As Paul phrases it:

"How shall they believe except they hear? And how shall they hear without a preacher? And how can they preach except they be sent?"

But the doctrinal instruction is just as essential to the attainment of the second aim of Gospel preaching. (2) **Doctrine and Christian Life.** The saved sinner cannot be developed into a strong and efficient coworker with Christ, in the work of conquering the world, without intelligently grasping, in their practical Christian bearings, the divine teachings involved in the Christian life and work.

Paul devotes the Epistle to the Philippians to the unfolding of the ideal Christian life, as having its **Paul's Ideal Christian.** ground and root in the knowledge and acceptance of the atonement of Christ, and its model and standard in the self-sacrifice and self-denying career of Christ—in fine, as having its beginning, middle, and end in Christ. It has its root in the "knowledge" of Christ as furnishing the basis of "love." He presents his aim and theme at the opening of the Epistle:

"And this I pray, that your love may abound yet more and more in knowledge and all discernment, so that ye may approve the things that are excellent ; that ye may be sincere and void of offense unto the day of Christ, being filled with the fruits of righteousness, which are through Jesus Christ, unto the glory and praise of God."

But the wonderful presentation in brief, of the aim of the Gospel in Christian character and activity, is that made by Peter in the opening of his second Epistle : * {Peter's Ideal Christian.}

"Grace to you and peace be multiplied in the knowledge of God and of Jesus our Lord, seeing that his divine power hath granted unto us all things that pertain unto life and godliness, through the knowledge of him that called us by his own glory and virtue, whereby he hath granted unto us his precious and exceeding great promises ; that through these ye may become partakers of the divine nature, having escaped from the corruption that is in the world by lust. Yea, and for this very cause adding on your part diligence, in your faith supply virtue, and in your virtue knowledge, and in your knowledge temperance, and in your temperance patience, and in your patience godliness, and in your godliness love of the brethren, and in your love of the brethren love. For if these things are yours and abound, they make you to be not idle nor unfruitful unto the knowledge of our Lord Jesus Christ."

After laying the foundation of the "precious faith" "through the righteousness of God and our Savior Jesus Christ," the Apostle unfolds the Christian character and career for the sake of which this foundation is laid. It is "in the knowledge" of the doctrines "of God and of Jesus our Lord"—that is, in experimental acquaintance with these—that grace and peace are multiplied. Having his call "to glory and strength," the Christian, resting on God's promised power and grace, is to lead out the chorus of Christian graces—faith,

* 2 Peter i. 2-8 (Revised Version).

virtue, knowledge, temperance, patience, godliness, brotherly love, love—each clasping the hand of the one that goes before, in making up the circle of spiritual completeness. And the end of all is that, through the abounding of these, the Christian man may be "neither workless nor fruitless in advancing to the knowledge of our Lord Jesus Christ"—that is, that there may be developed in him an intelligent activity leading to abundant practical results in the Kingdom of Christ for the glory of God.

Every sentence in these remarkable passages is bristling with demand for large intelligence concerning all the great doctrines that center in God and Christ and the cross, and culminate in the ideal Christian life. It would be hard to state more distinctly, or to emphasize more strongly, the call for doctrinal knowledge as a foundation for Christian character and Christian activity.

And this emphatic requirement is a most natural one; for the rational spirit finds its appropriate aliment in truth, and its religious aliment in the truth of the Word of God. To make a strong Christian there needs to be developed that powerful character which finds a sufficient basis only in the grand doctrines of the Word of God. As the historian Froude has shown in his *Short Studies*,* Calvinism, which he hates, has in all ages furnished the substantial backbone of the moral universe, and the pith and puissance of the world's heroism. His friends may question whether it has been because it is Calvinism, or because of the great essential truths involved, but they can not question the fact. The

**Froude's View.**

* *Short Studies on Great Subjects*, Second Series, Article "Calvinism."

strong character must be bottomed in great principles, and the requisite principles have been furnished only by the doctrines that Christianity has formulated in answer to the life-and-death questions of the human soul. It is these truths alone that link the Christian with God and with his sublime and eternal plan. A strong, heroic, godlike Christian character, such as Christ wants in his work, can find no other adequate basis. There is no other possible way for the development of genuine Christian power.

However little truth may be sufficient to maintain in the pulpit the clap-trap and fustian that claim to be the Gospel; and to keep up the life of shocking selfishness and silliness and indifference to the demands of Christ and the needs of a lost world, that too often passes in this age for Christian; it must be clear as sunlight, to any man taught of God and in sympathy with Christ, that this is not adequate to make of a saved sinner such a coworker with Christ as can be used for the speedy evangelization of the world. That can be done only by bringing him to a comprehension of the situation; in short, leading him to understand something of the terrible struggle in which the Captain of our salvation is engaged with Satan and his hosts; something of the lost and ruined condition of the world of sinners hastening to eternal perdition; something of his own personal responsibility for the soul of his brother-man all over the world; something of his obligation as a steward of Christ to use all his powers and possessions in the service of Christ in saving men by the Gospel; something of the presence of Omniscience taking note of every idle word and deed and extending perpetual inspiration and hope and help; and some-

*Great Truths and Powerful Life.*

thing of the absolute worthlessness of a whole universe of worldly treasures when balanced against even one human soul. Who does not see that the divine hopes and enterprises revealed in these doctrines of the Bible are just what are needed to make men efficient coworkers with Christ—furnishing them all-powerful motives, and lifting them up to the sublimest heights of their possibilities of effort and achievement?

And if this be so, it can not but be reasonably clear that nothing but the renewed and powerful preaching of these doctrines can remedy the defects in the type of piety too largely prevailing in the Church and hindering its efficiency—the want of singleness of aim; of a just measure of consecration; of self-denial for Christ; of Scriptural faith; of earnestness of life; of a sense of individual responsibility to the Master. Nothing else can be expected to revolutionize the so-called ethics of the age, and lead to the substitution of Christian ethics for a heathen and brutish—putting in the place of baptized selfishness and greed the law of self-sacrifice and devotion to Christ.

It follows, therefore, from the very ends contemplated by the Gospel, that the needs of this age, so far from calling for an abandonment of doctrinal teaching and preaching, imperatively demand a powerful revival of such teaching and preaching.

*2. Doctrine the Special Requirement.*

There are vastly greater things waiting for accomplishment by the Christian Church in this age than in any preceding age, and, as surely as God lives and his Word is true, they can not be compassed in any selfish and lazy way, nor by any ignorant and half-hearted work.

There are the multitudes to be saved. There is need that the Church and the world should be roused and stirred, as in the "Great Awakening" of a century and a half ago, only on a vastly wider scale and to profounder depths. The preaching of Edwards, Whitefield, and their colaborers of that day, was the preaching of doctrine in its powerful, practical bearings, and that whether men would hear or whether they would forbear. God, in his being and attributes; his absolute sovereignty in salvation; his "just liberty with regard to answering the prayers or succeeding the pains of mere natural men, continuing such"; the helplessness and hopelessness of "sinners in the hands of an angry God"; justification by faith alone; the necessity for the new birth or of a transformation of nature by the Spirit of God—all these, and the whole range of rousing and quickening doctrine, were burned into the souls of the men of that age. The fruits were seen in a revolution in life, individual, domestic, and social; in the organizations for pushing the work of missions; and in the vastly enlarged sphere and activity of the Church. Who will say that there is not greater need to-day? Who will show us any other and better way?

With the whole world waiting for the Gospel, and Christ calling his followers to the task of giving it to all, the Christian worker must be taught, in the light of God's Word, just what the world needs and God requires, and how the needs and requirements are to be met. *The Preacher's Duty in the Crisis.* He will find the requisite light in the doctrines of the Divine Word. He may find help toward the light, and impulse to a better life, in works like Fish's *Primitive Piety Revived*, which had such influence in the revival of a third of a century ago; but they will help him chiefly by leading him back to the essential

Christian doctrines of the Word. The work has become so much broader that the pressing home of the doctrines must be all the mightier and more persistent, if a life powerful enough to meet the needs of the age is to be the result. The hosts of evil are so marshaled and panoplied that only a truer and stronger presentation of vital Christian doctrine can gird the Church with the power to accomplish their overthrow. The Christian may find some of the facts concerning the evil with which he is to cope, in such works as Strong's *Our Country*, or Pierson's *Crisis of Missions;* he may find the defects of the Christianity of the age set forth in such works as Fish's *Primitive Piety Revived*, and the needs of the ministry in Horatius Bonar's *Words to the Winners of Souls;* but the needed power must come out of the practical doctrines of the Christian revelation.

In fine, nothing short of the message of the preacher, as given him by Christ himself,—the Gospel as a regenerating and saving power,—embracing all the essential factors and truths already noted in sketching that message, and presented to men as rational and religious beings, in the form of rational instruction, *i. e.*, as *doctrine*, in its rational relations and connections, *i. e.*, in coherent *doctrinal system*, can meet the needs of the present hour. A rational spiritual life can not be developed in an irrational way, nor by an irrational method. The preacher must press home his message with the tongue of fire—until God and the unseen world, the lost soul and its condemnation to everlasting wo, Christ and his redemption, the judgment and eternity, become living realities, and the theology of the Church a living theology—if the coming of Christ's Kingdom is to be hastened. He needs to lift up the standard of the cross anew, and to rally the Church around it for the conquest of the world for Christ, and to proclaim his message to that Church, as an official instructor, with an energy born of the Holy Spirit. With a minister in the lead bearing such a message, girded with divine power, with a single aim for Christ, a complete consecration to him, entire self-sacrifice for his cause, absolute faith in him as Savior and Lord, and a holy earnestness in his service; with a Church understanding its mission for the world, and inspired with such principles and such self-sacrifice in the Master's service—the requirement which the Great Commission makes of the preacher and the Church, for the immediate evangelization of all the world, is far within the possibilities of accomplishment for the present generation.

But if the possible is to become the actual, the preacher will need, in bearing his message and rousing men, to give supreme heed and supreme emphasis to *God's manifest call* for the immediate evangelization of the world, and to press that call upon the Church, with all the energy and enthusiasm that its paramount importance can inspire, with all the solemnity he can draw from the consciousness of his own overwhelming responsibility, with all the weight and authority of the divine command of Christ, and with all the fiery earnestness that can blaze forth from a tongue touched and kindled by the Holy Spirit.

# CHAPTER III.

## THE PREACHER AND HIS FURNISHING.

HAVING such a commission and such a message for mankind, the question naturally arises : What manner of man should the preacher be, and what furnishing will best fit him for the special work of this generation ? We answer :

*He needs to be a man who has complete mastery of himself, of the situation, and of his Bible message.*

This is an age of Sphinx riddles, of which the Gospel furnishes the only possible solution. The modern Sphinx—our boasted and boastful material civilization, with its godless principles and equally godless practise—is plying her vocation and working her destruction among us, on a scale far grander than Greek ever imagined. Her riddles are : the political economy riddle—how to prevent the destruction and demoralization resulting from the frequent alternation of inflation and prostration in the national industries; the social riddle—how to eliminate the caste system generated by the separation of labor and capital; the political riddle—how to get rid of demagogism and official corruption; the scientific riddle—how to stay the force of the materialism "that is sapping the genius and spiritual aspirations of many of our best minds, and which shows its disastrous effects even in the sacred desk." And we may rest

*Sphinx Riddles.*

assured that this modern Sphinx will not fail to destroy—as did the ancient Sphinx, in the days of Œdipus—those who can not answer her riddles.

But the riddle of riddles is the one propounded to the Church of this age, the one pressing especially upon the ministry, and perhaps most of all upon the men who are to-day making their way into the ministry—the Sphinx riddle of religion: how to bring the ministry up to the extraordinary demands of these times, and give it larger measure of power, as God's agency, through the Gospel, for regenerating and purifying society and saving the world. That is the riddle pressing upon us to-day, and destruction—industrial, social, political, moral, and spiritual—will be the inevitable penalty of failure to solve it speedily, correctly, and completely.

Seven centuries and a half before the coming of Christ, in the year that Rome was founded, the prophet Isaiah had his wonderful vision of Jehovah in the Temple, as recorded in the sixth chapter of his prophecies. It was then that the prophet was called and set apart by God—amid surroundings at once magnificent and awful—to meet a great crisis in the history of God's chosen people. That call and crisis suggest the crisis that is upon us in this day, and the preparation of the prophet for his work suggests the preparation that the preacher needs, if he is to meet successfully the demands of the present crisis.

It is difficult to present the real state of the case clearly, so as to enforce adequately the preacher's duty, and yet escape the danger of being misunderstood. We hear much of the decline of the power of the Church. Has there been such a decline? We hear equally often of the progress and requirements of this age of culture. Has there been such progress as to outstrip the Gospel? It is not necessary to decide whether either, or neither, or both, of these things be true. However it may have arisen, he must be blind who does not see that there is certainly a tremendous gap between the power and work of the ministry and the present demand of God, in his providence, for the immediate giving of the Gospel to all the world. Comparing this extraordinary providential call with what we are accomplishing, it becomes manifest that the Church is nowhere doing all that needs to be done. Is not the insufficiency of the power and work for the needs only too obvious?

But, taking the facts as they appear, is this condition of things inevitable and irremediable? Or is there a cause that may be pointed out and a remedy that may be applied: a *cause* which it is the preacher's first duty to understand and appreciate; and a *remedy* which it is his special mission to apply?

The fact presupposes and proves a cause. That a remedy may be found is the belief of all who are not pessimists. There is need to point out the cause and the remedy, and to show what is the present duty of the ministry in the premises. In doing this, some preliminary observations, touching the characteristics of the age, as affecting the world, the Church, and the minister himself, will bring us upon the profitable consideration of the kind of preacher and the character of the furnishing called for.

## SECTION FIRST.

**The Cause of the Present Inadequacy of the Ministry.**

The cause of the present inadequacy of the ministry to the work to be done is doubtless to be found in the materialistic and secular spirit of the age, which is at once most powerful in resisting the influence of the Church and most dangerous and harmful in molding the Church and the ministry.

"Because ye are not of the world, . . . therefore the world hateth you,"—so taught the Master.* There is an essential and eternal hostility between the spirit of worldliness and the spirit of Christ. An age in which the world wields the Church influence is an age of evil. An age in which the Church and ministry are either in accord with the world or molded by it must be an age of religious degeneracy and godlessness and spiritual inefficiency—and these always indicate the highroad to destruction.

### I. AN AGE OF INTENSE SECULARISM.

No preacher can fail to be made aware of the fact that secularism, which is, literally, *this-world-ism*, is to-day assuredly at the front. Note that we are not emphasizing here the practical tendencies and social customs that grow out of the secular spirit, and that have revolutionized the preaching and pastoral work; but the intellectual tendencies, the spirit of the age, the *zeitgeist*, that controls and molds man, both in the pulpit and out of it.

* John xv. 19.

The age, through the influence of Mill and Darwin and Spencer and Huxley, and such as they, has come **Materialistic Scientism.** largely under control of a materialistic scientism, tending toward atomism, and on the verge of culminating in organized socialistic secularism.

What is here objected to is not science, but the vast mass of superficial imagination, assumption, and assertion, that is decked out in imposing verbiage and palmed off upon men as science. No one is disposed to ignore or underrate the great achievements of genuine science in this age. As Christians we are thankful for them. They are our heritage. All true science is for us. Every great scientist of the land will be found on the side of God and Christianity—President Hitchcock, Professors Silliman, Agassiz, Henry, Guyot, Dana, Dawson—all along the line. The mighty thinkers and philosophers will be found in the same ranks—Professors Tayler Lewis and Bowen, and Presidents Woolsey, McCosh, Porter, Anderson—all along the line again. It is much the same across the water. But the strange thing about it all is that a superficial scientism has the ear of the public, rather than this profound science; that a shallow and baseless atomism molds society, rather than a deep and well-founded theism.

Preachers are especially familiar with the "progress" of "advanced science," from the old-fashioned Bible notion of a personal, spiritual God, infinite, eternal, and unchangeable in his being and attributes, to the new God of the atomist; which is neither personal nor spiritual, which is without either quantitative or qualitative attributes, and which is changeable at the will of every wiseacre. The noise of it has gone out into all the world. Popular Science magazines and Popular Science series have borne the new doctrine everywhere, asserting its truth with a boldness and impudence equaled only by its shallowness and want of scientific basis. It is all around us, in the atmosphere, so that men take it in at every breath.

The men who advocate these new views arrogate to themselves the right of eminent domain in the region of science; and tho the grand men of science all repudiate their doctrines, yet so confident has been the tone of the quasi-scientists that they have made the world abjure faith in God and then receive their teachings on faith, and so are claiming to have it all their own way.

The natural result is the reign of a shallow and boastful egotism, that does not hesitate to put forward the wildest and most irrational speculations as truths fit to take the place of the grand and eternal verities of the Word of God. "There is no God." "Or, if there be a God, he must forever remain unknown and unknowable." "Or, if he can be known, it is only as an impersonal, blind force." Atheism, pantheism, know-nothingism, pessimism, have flooded the world. The same spirit of egotism and shallowness and dogmatism that marked their original authors and advocates has been reproduced in the hosts outside the Church, and drifting farther and farther away from it, that need to be reached by the ministry of this age if Christianity is to prevail.

*Shallow Philosophy.*

The world is filled with doubt and neglect, or with despair and hatred, of God and religion, of morality and immortality. This blighting materialism and atheism have not only made logical wreck of the world's thinking, but are making wreck of all the highest feelings, grandest motives, and sublimest possibilities to which Christianity would exalt humanity. The present, the fleeting, the tangible, is all that is left to man, the blind infant of father Chance and mother Matter and Must-be. The invisible and eternal personal God has been pushed from his throne because, forsooth, no man has seen nor can see him, and the atom which no man hath seen nor can see, and to whose existence no one can hold with any clear scientific reason, has been enthroned in his place; and Professor Clifford even proceeded so far as to replace his worship by "cosmic emotion"!

All this has made the world a hard world to reach with the Gospel. It is not inclined to listen to what the messenger of God has to say from the pulpit. It has drifted away from the Church. It is scarcely more inclined to listen to what he may have to say outside of the pulpit, for it confidently assumes, on the worst of hearsay, that the Bible is an obsolete book, and that Christianity has nothing in it really worthy the belief of reasonable men, and especially of the men of this highly educated and intelligent age! In truth, in its opinion, the scientific *zeitgeist* has breathed upon the religion of Christ and straightway resolved it into shadowy, unsubstantial, mythical elements and dissipated it forever!

Nor is this the worst. It is impossible to escape the conviction that this flood of materialistic atheism has **Influence upon the Church.** come in upon the Church, and is perceptibly molding and modifying it in creed and practise. Almost everywhere one can see a growing want of faith in the grand doctrines of the Bible. There is a tendency to estimate all things invisible and spiritual according to the standard of this quasi-scientific atheism. We hear science and art and literature, physiology and biology, cried up, and psychology and metaphysics, philosophy and theology, cried down. In many quarters there is a manifest weakening in the hold of even the great essential doctrines, upon laymen and ministers, upon churches and conferences and councils. Dogmas and creeds are at a discount in too many pulpits, in too many pews, in too much of the literature of the Church. Who could not point to instances illustrating the giving way of the old-fashioned, permanent, every-day religion of principle, before the new-fashioned, intermittent, midwinter religion of feeling and excitement? And here is evidently a new element of difficulty in the work of the minister of the present period.

But even this is not the worst. "Like priest like people" was the old half-truth. "Like people like priest" is the new complementary half-truth of this age. Is it any wonder that these evil tendencies have had large influence in molding the ministry? It is doubtful if any of us have wholly escaped the baleful influence of this rationalism and materialism.

We recognize in ourselves, in spite of ourselves, a prevailing want of faith in the reality of God and heaven and hell, of the judgment and eternity. The veil of the seen hides from our eyes the glory of the unseen. Recall how an overwhelming sense of the invisible made Luther hurl his inkstand at the devil; and then imagine such a sense of reality taking possession of some learned and eminent preacher at the present day! With a scientific curl of the lip we complacently say: "Luther lived in an age of darkness!" Imagine such a sense of the worth of souls as made

Paul weep night and day for three years, over the perishing sinners at Ephesus, taking possession of some of our ministers in New York or Chicago! "Ah, well!" we would be ready to say, "he is a weak brother, doubtless a little beside himself!" Imagine such a sense of the power of prayer as moved the souls of martyrs and confessors, taking possession of one of ourselves in this age of the supremacy of "things seen"! Why, the rest of us would think him insane! Who does not feel that the faith and fire with which Christ and the Apostles inspired the first believers, the faith and fire that were rekindled in the Reformation and in the later times under Whitefield and the Wesleys, have well-nigh gone out of us under the blighting influence of this modern materialism?

But it is to be feared that even this is not the worst. The spirit of secularism has followed the skepticism of secularism into the Church. The same standards for the measurement of the man are too often applied there. There is a wide-reaching tendency to break with the poor and ignorant. Several years before his death, Dr. Charles Hodge wrote in a careful paper on "Preaching the Gospel to the Poor":*

<small>Dr. Charles Hodge's View.</small>

> "It is with great reluctance that we are constrained to acknowledge that the Presbyterian Church of this country is not the Church for the poor. . . We, as a church, are not doing, and never have done, what we were bound to do in order to secure the preaching of the Gospel to the poor."

And what if it be true, as Dr. Hodge says, that "the Church which fails to bring the Gospel to bear upon the poor, fails in its duty to Christ"? What if it be

* *Princeton Review*, January, 1871, p. 86.

true that "it refuses or neglects to do what he has specially commanded; and sooner or later its candlestick will be removed out of its place"? And what if all the Church so fail, and the poor drift away to perdition?

All unconsciously to themselves, some of the best men in the Church are influenced by this spirit of caste. The writer well remembers once hearing an officer in his church—and a good man he was, too—complaining of the sexton: "He is unfit for his office. He doesn't know broadcloth." The sexton had seated a plain person in an eligible pew in the center of the church. Now, that man never for one moment dreamed that he was manifesting the same spirit against which the Apostle James brings that most terrible charge in his Epistle, when he writes of the man with the gold ring and the goodly apparel!* The consequences of all this may be seen in the "lapsed masses," or the immense non-church-going multitude, and in the growing spirit of communism and hostility to religion among the poor and debased.

Nor will it escape any observing man that there is a tendency in the Church to apply the worldly standard, so far as may be, in the choice of its ministry and in its forms of worship. It is assumed that in this age, if men are to go to church on the Sabbath, they must be entertained, and must get the worth of their money as the world judges. We are in danger of having interesting "entertainment" set above "spiritual religion"; "eloquence," above "soul-saving"; "culture," above "Christ."

Could the ministry possibly escape being molded by these forces of secularism? Have not questions of

* James ii. 1-9.

position and salary been made far more prominent than is warranted by the Word of God? Has not the Christ-idea of preaching the Gospel to the poor, and lifting up the low and debased, largely given way to the new-fashioned theory that men must be reached from above down, so that the preaching must be primarily for the refined and cultivated if we would reach and influence the masses? Are there not terrible forces of evil at work tending to transform the man who, as God's messenger, should be on fire of the Holy Ghost, into the lion of social occasions, the man of elegant manners, attainments, and leisure? Do not our own hearts assure us that few, if any, of us have escaped without some taint of secularism?

## II. An Age of Socialistic Secularism.

But the tide of secularism, that in this age threatens to leave helpless or to sweep away preacher and Church alike, is not merely that of the old-fashioned secularism, based upon *disbelief*, but that of the new secularism that takes on the sociological form and bases itself on the *discontent* and *unrest* abroad among men the world over—the tide of *socialistic secularism.*

<small>The New Secularism.</small>

The extreme positive pole of churchism may be the *other-worldliness*, at which George Eliot sneers; the extreme negative pole of materialism is the *this-worldliness*, that has come in upon Christendom like a vast electric wave, infolding and enswathing everything. Of this new phase, Mr. Walter Walsh writes ably, in an article in the *Contemporary Review*, for January, 1895. He says:

" The old secularism is dead. Peripatetic lecturers may still, in dingy halls and before dingier audiences, galvanize the thing into some convulsive mimicry of life. But Higher Criticism and the New Theology have taken the wind out of the sails of Ingersoll and Foote, while a thousand pulpits are engaged in showing that faith and worship may exist and flourish anew on the 'fairy tales of science and the long results of time.'

" The new secularism comes fifty years after the old and, like it, is the child of the age. Fifty years ago the splendid audacities of physical science dazzled the eye of faith, and ever since a few men have lived who could not see heaven or the sun. To-day, however, it is the sociological question that engages the deepest attention and attracts the fondest hopes, and it is from this the new secularism springs. The likeness and the difference between the old and the new are apparent at a glance. Both concern themselves primarily with physical conditions,—a planet, a human body,—but the latter lends itself more freely to the world of sentiment and aspiration. To what extent the new is a development of the old is a question which would lead us too far afield. But assuredly as the older secularism claimed to be a gospel for the whole man, physically considered, it begins to find that it can only fulfil its prophecy through modern socialistic materialism. Man is not all brain, and the bald rationalism of the Hall of Science fails before the positive demands of modern humanitarianism. The age is impatient of mere negations. It has discovered that man has a back and a belly as well as a brain, and the question how to clothe the one and fill the other has eclipsed public interest in Cain's wife and the mistakes of Moses."

The older secularism threatened the Church merely; the new menaces the existence of the State also. It links itself with the popular reform movement, enters into the domain of practical politics and seeks to control it, and ultimately attempts to enlist religion on the side of revolution.

" It tries to float the political economy of Marx upon the religious sentiment of Mazzini, and with this twofold appeal to the lower and the higher moves forward to the capture of the modern world."\*

\* *Contemporary Review*, January, 1895, p. 118.

This new form of secularism is the child of the times, as was the old—the natural evolution from the materialistic scientism of the day.

It has its wide-spread manifestations outside the Church, everywhere at bottom and essentially antag-onistic to the principles, methods, and spirit of Christianity. Christianity, as has already been seen, assumes the absolute obligation of man to supreme devotion to God, in all the relations of life, and the moral disorder of man's nature, called in theological phrase *original sin;* and insists upon regeneration as the only remedy for the evil condition of mankind. With the new secularism, God having been reduced to the almighty atom, or to a minimum, or eliminated from the universe, he may be practically left out of the account. The present life, on its material side, in the supreme importance assigned to it, crowds out the higher life, and immortality becomes an imagination, or a guess, or at best a dim hope or irrational wish. It makes evil the result of condition or environment, and ignores its moral taint and hereditary sweep; and it proposes its removal, not by regeneration or a change of nature, but by reformation, or a change of condition, or by modification of environment. Christianity regards character as the supreme thing, and starts its work, in reforming and elevating, by making character in the new birth by the power of the Spirit of God, as the only basis and spring of reform in the present condition of man; the new secularism, reversing the order of things, starts with condition and attempts to struggle back to improved character. The new teaching is : "Man is not essentially bad; he is the victim of environment. Give him plenty to eat and to drink,

[sidenote: Antagonistic to Christianity.]

and he will be all right." "Treat the tramp and thief kindly," is the reasoning of the good French rural bishop, in *Les Misérables* of Victor Hugo—the reasoning of the new socialism, the skepticism in philosophy and morality, that has morally wrecked France—"and he will become a holy man and will steal no more." But the tramp disappears all the same, despite the reasoning, and the bishop's silver candlesticks disappear with him! That is the new method, by which it is proposed to deal with a world made up of such natures—they are to be made over morally from the outside, through the skin and the stomach!

Christianity, as has been seen, places upon man the obligations of the moral law, making him responsible to God for all his conduct toward himself, his fellow-man, and the Moral Governor. The new secularism practically reduces the moral law to the customs of society, cuts everything loose from God, and devotes itself to what it terms "the economic laws of God," that is, to the socialistic scheme by which the millennium of plenty for all men to eat and to drink is to be realized. It advocates and pushes social reforms and political reforms, and is the perennial spring of anarchism.

Christianity recognizes man's sin as the source of evil, and sends forth the preacher to proclaim the message of salvation : as law, calling to repentance and a right life before God ; and as Gospel, promising and furnishing the power needed to make over man in righteousness and holiness. The new secularism recognizes the facts—so prominent at the present time—of universal discontent and unrest, and, looking upon unequal industrial, social, and political conditions as the cause of these, it sends out as its apostles and canonized saints the walking delegate, the social reformer, and the religious agitator.

Christ commands men : *

"Seek ye first the kingdom of God and his righteousness, and all these [other and temporal] things shall be added unto you."

The secularist apostle reverses the order, and bids men to seek the other things—food and drink and clothing—first, and assures them that then the Kingdom of Heaven, which is after all only the kingdom of this world, will be theirs also.

The "Labor Church" is the beginning of the crystallizing of the new secularism, the evolution from it. Writes Mr. Walter Walsh: *

**The "Labor Church."**

"This is the distinguishing and specific mark of the whole movement. Looking round upon the waste waters of the modern deluge for some landmark, we fix upon the 'Labor Church' as the most prominent and the most expressive sign of the times. The 'Labor Church' is far from covering the whole area of the new secularism. On the contrary, it numbers but a few hundreds of people, scattered over about a score of centers, tho it claims to be a growing movement. It is not its size, but its significance that concerns us. It is typical of much. It is the prominent and outstanding feature of a wide-spread materialism ; the highest, and furthest, and clearest-defined guide-post of the great army marching forward to possess the kingdom of this world ; the topmost wave of the vast sea of social discontent which surges forward to become the hope and the fear of a new century. . . Every appeal of historic Christianity is reversed by the new Church of Socialism. It speaks, not about sin, but about sociology ; not of penitence, but of reform ; of economics, but not of faith ; it aspires to satisfy the body rather than the soul, aims at *goods* rather than goodness, and denounces ill conditions rather than vicious inclinations. Its devil is not evil personified, but

---

* Matthew vi. 33.—"The New Secularism," *Contemporary Review*, January, 1895, pp. 121, 124.

an economic specter called capitalism; and the devil's wife is not Sin, as Milton thought, but competition. No reversal could be more complete. The pendulum has swung the other way with a vengeance!"

The new socialism has no fatherhood of God on which to base a brotherhood of man. It has no Bible and no divine basis on which to rest. It cuts loose from the great human and religious needs and faiths and hopes that have inspired, sustained, and shaped history in all the ages, and demonstrates itself ephemeral, a thing of the hour, by planting itself on modern life and modern necessities merely. It furnishes no hint of any agency for the remedy or the moral reconstruction that the existing moral disorder has been shown to make imperative, and for which Christianity makes such ample provision. It rules out with equal imperiousness the Christian triad, faith, hope, and charity, and the Pagan triad, the true, the beautiful, and the good. In making man supreme and the service of man the *summum bonum*, it depresses, or ignores, or denies God. In exalting the social and minor moralities—generosity, honesty, courage, comraderie, manliness, and the like—it minimizes, or scouts, or repudiates the personal and Christian virtues—faith, patience, meekness, purity, holiness, and all the rest. In short, it is the embodiment, the incarnation, the completer evolution, of materialism and atomism; and, in seeking the life of the body only, it has doomed its adherents to destruction of both body and soul.

These considerations cast light upon the influences and forces that are shown, in the course of this discussion, to be at work in the Church, in revolutionizing and disintegrating Christian doctrine and faith, and in cutting the nerve of Christian effort.

But this new secularism has almost as varied manifestations within the Church as outside of it, in the pulpit and in manifold reform movements.

*Manifestations in the Church.*

It is at the bottom of the turning away from the preaching of Bible Christianity, as a divine regenerating and saving power, to the preaching of the social moralities and amenities. It brings tremendous pressure to bear upon the pulpit through the newspapers and magazines; reporters and journalists being absolutely saturated with the new views. By way of illustration, one takes up his morning paper, and reads, in bold head-lines : " Why don't young men go to church?" Then follows the reason, that "out of thirty sermons to young men, fourteen had for the text the story of the Prodigal Son." Then it is added :

"Young men who go to city churches habitually are not of the stuff of which this wicked Scriptural prodigal was made. What they want of a minister is, not doctrine, but direction ; not exhortation to prepare for a successful death, but inspiration for a consistent life. Only a few clergymen and women understand how hard it is for man to be good. These few, however, of both classes exercise great and lasting influence. I am speaking of the ordinary, temperate, industrious, self-respecting young man, who wants to lead a decent life, make as much money as he can, and get all the fun out of both which the law and his own conscience allow. . . That's why such men as Robert Collyer, who know these things, talk to more men every Sunday than their churches can comfortably hold [a statement contrary to fact]."

All of which the reporter brought, not from his own observation as he professed to do, but from the columns of a cheap, secular magazine ; to which it had just as manifestly been contributed without personal observation, and without knowledge of either the young men or the ministers concerned.

In its better manifestation it has crystallized, in this country, in the new doctrine concerning the Kingdom of God, which teaches, that "competition is not law but anarchy," and that the cure of all the present troubles and discontent in the world is to be found in right views concerning property and in its right use, and that the main thing in the preaching of the Church should be, not sin and salvation by the atonement wrought by Christ, in the old sense, but self-sacrifice for man, and the social influences and duties that have to do with restoring to the poor the kingdom of this world with abundance of its meat and drink. There is thus, in the Church itself, a powerful cooperative influence in aid of the social secularism that is leavening the world outside the Church.

*New Doctrine of "the Kingdom of God."*

### III. AN AGE OF ANARCHISM.

The materialism and secularism have naturally culminated in an age of anarchism, or of revolt against all authority and all law, human and divine. The Electric Age is passing into the Age of Anarchism. As, according to these theories, all so-called authority and law are merely the expression of the will of the stronger, having no root in God or in the nature of things or in justice, but arising out of the brute instincts of self-preservation and reproduction of the species, and intended merely for the continuance of the supremacy of the strongest in the struggle for existence, what reason is there for their continuance? What binding power have they, except the law of the strongest? Are they not at once unnecessary and necessarily evil? Such is the theory, and such are the conclusions drawn from it. The

*Revolt against all Authority.*

most unfortunate feature of the situation is that there is so much in the character of existing laws—especially of the laws governing economic and other purely material and selfish interests—to give coloring of truth and logic to both the theory and the inferences from it. But however it has come about, the fact is indisputable that anarchism—the breaking with all authority, law, and obligation—is in the social atmosphere of the day, and must be reckoned with.

The "bankruptcy of science," which Carlyle announced, on the threshold of the Mechanical Era, almost three quarters of a century ago, has reached its complete results, in its general influence on literature, art, and life. Materialistic science, mere mechanism, in the full consciousness of its new powers, promised to bring success, and plenty, and comfort to all men— in short, promised to regenerate the world. Its triumphs have certainly been immense and amazing; but, whatever it may have done for the "sovereign minority," it has done nothing of what it promised to do for the great majority. Its promise to reconstruct and glorify the social order, on a basis of mechanism, instead of religious faith, loyalty, and individual worth, has proved a disastrous and dismal failure, resulting in world-wide discontent and unrest.

As an able writer in the *Quarterly Review*, for January, 1894, phrases it, "'Science' has brought forth anarchy; and anarchy is the 'reduction to the absurd' of those principles on which its reasoning in the province of the supernatural has been founded." The same writer, following the lead of Max Nordau's book on *Degeneration*, shows how the "discontent and sense of failure in modern life" have transformed and degraded European literature,—as seen in the works of Swinburne, Oscar Wilde, M. Zola, Tolstoi, Ibsen, and their kind,—leading it to break with all authority, and with all the recognized principles and rules of art, manners, and morals.* The generalization might have been carried out into all spheres of art and life; for the same deleterious influences are everywhere pervasive and operative.

Even more marked have been the results of anarchism, in the removal of the old restraints upon selfishness in all its forms. Unbridled appetite and passion, unlimited self-indulgence, are the order of the day. **Unbridled Selfishness.** Intemperance, the monster curse of the age, has intrenched itself in the saloon system, and is doing its utmost, on the plea of "personal liberty," to transform the nations of the earth into nations of drunkards. Licentiousness—while by the pen of Tolstoi, in *The Kreutzer Sonata*, condemning the institution of marriage as "a crime and contrary to natural law"; and, in the great reviews, denouncing marriage as "an evil with which we are *cursed*," and pleading for a solution of "the sexual problem," by a legalized system of "concubinage for married men";* and in the world's legislatures seeking to legalize and regulate "the social evil"—is fast intrenching itself everywhere, destroying the foundations of the home by its subtle insinuation, dishonoring public life with its disgusting and horrifying exhibitions, demoralizing the young by its fascinating allurements open or disguised, and disintegrating society itself by its influences of corruption and moral death. Self-indulgence is likewise working

* *Quarterly Review*, January, 1894, article "Anarchist Literature," p. 4.—"The Sexual Problem," *Westminster Review*, February, 1895, p. 171.

itself out, in the rage for entertainment and amusement, in theater and social function and every other form, especially in forms made questionable or damnable by satire upon virtue or by touch or even broad smirch of licentiousness, as in the "ballet" and the "living picture" show, and apparently hastening on to still more flagrant and immoral manifestations, until life, already with vast numbers merely a play, threatens to become a "dance of death." The picture presented by the age is one of vast wealth used in extravagant outlay for selfish enjoyment and show, and contributing to little else than the sweeping tide of intemperance, licentiousness, and moral worthlessness and ruin.

Even more marked is the development of anarchism, in the criminal disregard, so widely exhibited, for the feelings and rights and personality of others. The rich, in the enjoyment of unstinted indulgence in the Christian palace, laugh lightly at, or think not at all of, the starving poor, in the Christian hovel hard by. Selfishness and greed have organized themselves in giant corporations and trusts, that are simply combinations for robbing the masses of mankind, under guise of law or in spite of law, for the benefit of the few; so that the great wealth heaped upon us by Providence for the ends of the Gospel is being turned instead into a means of oppression and into a curse. The lawlessness has culminated in that condition of things that marks this age as the Age of Murder in all Christendom. The astonishing disregard of that most sacred possession, human life—a disregard to which attention is now being aroused—may well amaze men. All who are interested in the welfare of humanity will do well to consider

*The Age of Murder.*

thoughtfully the statistics on the subject, furnished by Mr. Henry C. Lea, in *The Forum*, of August, 1894. The record of homicides has gone on swelling in numbers, until the annual tale in Europe has reached 15,000, and in America 10,000,—in the United States alone averaging from 3000 to 5000. The record of 20,000 to 25,000 murders annually, in the so-called Christian nations—surpassing the death-roll of most of the great decisive battles of the world, and rolling up a hundred Waterloos or Gettysburgs of death in a century—is assuredly frightful to contemplate, while horribly emphasizing the age as the Age of Anarchism!

And what of the task of the preacher in reaching such a world with his message? What of the hopefulness of it? What of the message he is sent to deliver to it? If there be nothing but reform forces; if there be no divine, regenerating power to transform men and remedy the existing state of things,—then the task of the preacher— judged by the *zeitgeist*, or by the drift of the century even—is a hopeless one.

*The Preacher's Task.*

The preacher will find such a world hard to reach with the Gospel. Law is the only preparation for Gospel, the only thing that brings home the need of it. He who blots out the law-giver, or gives the relation to him a subordinate place, discounts and minimizes the Gospel. The world of to-day hates all law, and has no care for the Gospel. The people in the Church do not listen to it willingly. A practical protest comes up from multitudes whenever opportunity offers. The recent wide discussion of the doctrine of "future punishment," and of "post-mortem probation," is absolute proof of the dislike of the law of God and of the drift toward semi-universalism. Men do not like even to be called "sinners." They resent it.

The *zeitgeist* has no doubt gone further and done a large work in molding the ministry and their preaching. Where such tremendous pressure is brought to bear against the strong truths of the Word of God, and against the awful sanctions of the law, the unconscious drift of the minister is, at the outset, from the messenger toward the advocate and apologist. Instead of boldly proclaiming God's truth, and thus holding firmly his high vantage ground, he gives himself to the useless work of defending God, or to the mean work of apologizing for God. And, when he has descended to that, he is likely soon to be found teaching restorationism, repentance in a future world, preaching to the lost spirits in prison, or uttering any other sentimental twaddle men may desire to hear.

Innumerable examples could be given of the working of these things. As a typical case, a thoroughly godly man was, not long since, driven out of a New England parish by the influence of one rich Universalist pew-holder, just because he ventured mildly to affirm his belief in future punishment. The writer recalls an examination for ordination, at which he himself was present, several years since. In the course of the examination, the candidate was asked: "What does the Bible teach on the subject of future punishment?" He leaned back in his seat, and, with half-closed eyes, toyed with his pet mustache for a moment, and then answered, with evident satisfaction and profound confidence of superior wisdom: "I have not made up my mind on that point." He was ordained! Naturally, he long since drifted out of the evangelical ministry.

To sum up the condition of things: the world of to-day, with its atomism and its secularism, presents the most tremendous obstacles to the work of the ministry. The Church of God, with its shattered sense of the invisible and eternal, with its low estimate of character and souls, and with its practical dislike of these life-and-death truths of God's Word, furnishes but little of that earnestness and inspiration that would lead her membership to overtake this vast work of salvation—for the lapsed masses, for the Greek and Roman Churches, and for the dying heathen—a vast work which, as has been seen, God calls upon her to do without delay. We of the ministry—without the overwhelming sense of the presence of God and the call from God; without the profound conviction of the infinite value of souls; and without the unfaltering faith in the grand and terrible truths that make the work of salvation matter of infinite urgency—have not the elements of power necessary to inspire and lead men, to mold society, and save a lost world. We are manifestly at one of these crises in the history of the Church, where there is imperative and supreme need for the interposition of the Spirit of God.

*Summary of Difficulties.*

## SECTION SECOND.

### The Remedy in the Preacher and his Furnishing.

The remedy for this evil condition is to be found in such a mighty outpouring of the Holy Spirit upon the Church as this age needs, and as the signs of the times seem to indicate to be imminent, and, in connection with and as the outcome of this, in a new order of preachers, who shall be so prepared for their work, and so divinely girded, as to be able to mold the Church and the world, rather than be molded by the Church and the world. Besides these general requirements, there is need to emphasize some of the special needs of the preacher.

## I. Intellectual Mastery of the Situation.

The preacher who would belong to this order will need to begin with surveying carefully and mastering the existing situation, in its relations to the development and progress of Christianity. He will need to study and ascertain the origin and causes of the present crisis in Christendom. He will find, by such study, that the state of things is the result of perversions of the fundamental principles of Protestant Christianity. The Reformation of the sixteenth century undertook the task of freeing man from slavery to the Roman hierarchy, with its unhistorical traditions and its usurped authority over the human soul and the Church. Its fundamental principles may be summed up as embracing:

**Perversions of Protestantism.**

*First.* The Bible, as the Word of God, the only authoritative rule of faith and practise, and Christ the sole Head of the Church.

*Second.* Justification by faith the only way of salvation.

*Third.* The right of private judgment, under the authority of the Bible, in matters of religion—involving religious responsibility and liberty.

He will find marked perversions, especially in the making of one of these principles supreme. The

Bible and Christ as sole rule and Head have been displaced by State-Church and decrees of ecclesiastical councils and assemblies, and by the assumed authority of secular and theological schools, and secular scholars, critics, and philosophers. Every one knows the results. Christianity as a saving power, working through justification by faith and regeneration, has given place to merely formal religion, seeking at best nothing above rites and ceremonies with outward morality, and, at worst, permitting all immorality. Reform and decency have been substituted for regeneration and holiness.

The power of godliness at the foundation having been thus removed, the principle of individual freedom has been pushed to the extreme, until men have repudiated, not only all illegitimate authority, but all authority of whatever kind, human and divine. Individualism has reached egoism pure and simple, which makes the essence of life thinking of oneself only, living for oneself only—in short, has reached Mr. Spencer's complete morality, in the working out of the two basal brute instincts of self-preservation and the reproduction of the species. Those who have thrown off the authority of the Bible and the Church, elevated bodily comfort and interests to the chief places, and come to think the enjoyment of plenty to eat and drink in this world the only Kingdom of Heaven, have naturally developed into modern democracy, inspired with the hope of bringing in their Kingdom of Heaven by political means and forces.

It can hardly be doubted that democratic principle is in the line of normal Protestant development; but always in due subordination to the authority of God and his Word, and of law divine and human. It may have been necessary in the working out of the best final results, in the present evil condition of humanity, that this development should pass through certain perversions and extremes. But, however that may be, the extreme development of democracy has apparently been reached, throughout Christendom. In 1894, in Europe, $5,500,000,000 was added to the national debts in sustaining the militarism necessary to hold down the masses; and the nations are thereby rapidly drifting, under stress of the democratic forces, into the national bankruptcy that must wreck that militarism and revolutionize society. In this country the destiny of the nation has seemed to be quite as rapidly drifting under the control of a bloated plutocracy—more dangerous and demoralizing than the militarism—built upon a basis of gigantic frauds and robberies, in railway wreckings and Black Fridays, and of robber trade-combinations and trusts, holding monopoly of everything used by the people—from sugar and oil to quinine and coffins—a plutocracy that has debauched the legislatures, the national congress, and the courts of justice, and is doing its best to corrupt popular sentiment by aping the manners and morals of the effete European aristocracy or seeking alliances with it, and lowering the tone of Christian sentiment by its efforts to purchase churchly respectability and a reputation for Christian charity. The phenomenal development of populism and socialism, and the frequent recurrence of strikes and riots, show that the masses in this country are becoming quite as desperate as in Europe, and the situation almost as threatening.

It is the perverted democratic principle against the world and everything else. Everywhere the human tiger—the fiercest of all beasts when driven to the wall—has evidently almost reached the point of desperation—as is shown in the anarchism of the age that is so portentous of coming anarchy.

The preacher will also note, in his study, that leading economists and publicists are everywhere anticipating as possible—nay, as probable, if not inevitable—in the near future, great and radical changes in society and politics; perhaps absolute and world-wide upheaval and revolution. As Mr. W. S. Lilly has so strikingly said : *

"Assuredly, if morality be the life of nations, these ominous symptoms might lead us to anticipate a social cataclysm ; a breaking up of civilization more terrible and complete than that which Europe witnessed fourteen hundred years ago ; for the destroyers would not be simple and uncorrupted races, with strong, broad notions of right and wrong, with keen susceptibility to the influences of religion, but decivilized men, emancipated from moral and civil restraints, and ruled solely by brute instincts and passions."

He will also be convinced by his study that were there nothing more or stronger, in modern society, to counteract these destructive tendencies than the moral forces of the old Roman world, the outlook would certainly be hopeless. *Christianity a Principle of Recovery.* But he will find Christianity is in the world as an immense recuperative and reconstructive force. The extreme developments of individualism, while they are the perversion of a principle of the Reformation, are proof of an immense advance in "the apprehension of the transcendent worth of human personality." The Church is in the world and yet not of it—the Church invisible, the Church "against which the gates of hell shall not prevail,"—

* *On Shibboleths*, pp. 36, 37.

containing in it a "principle of recovery" unknown to the ancient world. The moral advance of the ages through her influence has been immense. The silent influence she wields is incalculable. The principles that she has wrought into law, into the higher elements of society, into great permanent institutions, show themselves to be dominant when great crises come. A divine life and power are in her. While the trend of a generation may seem to be away from the right : the trend of the ages under Christian forces is upward and God-ward. The purpose of God in the Gospel moves majestically on. James Russell Lowell has justly contrasted the seeming and the reality, and his contrast answers to history :

"Careless seems the Great Avenger ; History's pages but record
One death-grapple in the darkness 'twixt old systems and the Word ;
Truth forever on the scaffold, Wrong forever on the throne—
Yet that scaffold sways the future and, behind the dim unknown,
Standeth God within the shadow, keeping watch above his own."

The investigator will likwise see how this perverted individualism has carried with it elevated conceptions, before undreamed of in history, of the dignity of manhood and of human responsibility, freedom, and power. And the survey will help him to see clearly that Christianity as a saving power—in the vital principles that made the Reformation—has the principles that can shape and direct aright the destiny of Christendom in this time of so grave contingencies; that, as the present condition has resulted from their perversion, and carries elements of vast progress along with the elements of evil; so the remedy indicated for the correction of the evil is the reaffirmation and the vigorous pushing of those principles in their correct form, especially in its formal principle, of the Bible as the Word of God, and in its material principle, of justification by faith. The coming upheavals and revolutions may thus be made the means of progress in saving the world.

The preacher of to-day, as the leader of the Church and the representative and expounder of her mission, who thus masters the situation, will understand that the saving efficacy of his message will depend, so far as truth is concerned, upon the emphasizing of the discredited truths of Protestantism that must go to correct the spurious individualism and bring men back to God and the Bible. He will be prepared to fill men's minds with the words of deliverance and salvation, and of true freedom that, with the blessing of God, will silently master and transform the forces of evil and reconstruct society when the breaking up comes, on the principles of a genuine Christianity. *The Preacher's Timely Message.*

In addition to calling attention to the general and fundamental truths of Protestantism, it is proposed to emphasize some special characteristics required in the typical preacher, for whom the Church of this age has such urgent need, and for whom Christ so urgently calls.

## II. A More Scriptural Working-Theory.

The preacher for these times needs to adopt, at the outset, a more Scriptural working-theory of the ministry—one that will give him such a sense of the truth that he is the representative of God in the world, the embassador of God to lost souls, that his very personal presence shall bring God down into the world as a reality again.

Let it be understood that, in all that is to be said on this subject, piety is presupposed. Without that there can be no minister of God; but presupposing that, there are certain special requirements.

The preacher needs to have an unmistakable call from God. The only warrant for any man's entrance upon the ministry is such a divine call. An uncalled ministry must be an unqualified and an unsent ministry; for God only qualifies and sends whom he calls. "I have not sent these prophets, yet they ran; I have not spoken to them, yet they prophesied." "Wo be to the pastors that destroy and scatter the sheep of my pasture! saith the Lord." A man who has simply gone through the training-school, and been licensed and ordained by the Presbytery or Consociation or Council, is not necessarily a minister of the Gospel in the sight of God. No mere human training and setting apart can make him such. God only can call to the sacred office, and the one who enters uncalled helps to "overstock" the ministry, and becomes the cause, perhaps unwitting and unwilling, of innumerable and grievous evils, even tho it still be true that there is need of a hundred ministers where there is but one. No man can speak or act with the authority with which men must speak and act in this day, to be heard above the thunder of the world's traffic, and heeded, unless he has a call as real, if not as articulate, as had the prophets in the olden times.

There is special need to remember, in this day, that the ministry is not simply a *profession*, like medicine or law, in which a man is to make a living and gain a

1. A Call from God.

position. We have known men to enter it as a profession, by a syllogism, instead of by a call from God. It may have been by a syllogism in everybody's mouth: "A Christian man can accomplish more good in the ministry than in any other work in life; therefore, I am bound to enter the ministry." It may have been by a syllogism from a Secretary of some Board of Education : "Every pious young man is bound to enter the ministry, unless he can demonstrate that he is not." If one will look into them, he will see that both of these syllogisms are sheer fallacies. Take the first. There is many a Christian man who would accomplish a hundred-fold more for God as a plowman, or a carpenter, or a merchant, than as a minister. Take the last. Its major premise would be nearer Scripture, if it read: "Every pious young man is bound to stay out of the ministry, unless he can demonstrate the contrary."

If a man is to be worth the most in the ministry, he must go into it in answer to that prayer which Christ taught his disciples, when he said : "Pray, ye, therefore, the Lord of the harvest that he will send forth laborers into the harvest." The word is *send, hurl, drive forth!* The ministry needed is a ministry sent, hurled, driven, into the work by stress of conscience and divine command; a ministry with the urgency of God himself back of them, so that they can sympathize with Paul, when he said, "Wo is me if I preach not the Gospel," and with John Knox, when he tried to hide himself from God and his call.

Said a brilliant preacher to the writer, not long since, "I entered the ministry as a profession. I have never been conscious of anything like a call to preach the Gospel, and wonder if any such thing is necessary." He had been a brilliant sermonizer, had ministered to rich, cultivated, and fashionable churches, had won a large circle of admirers; but he had become soured and misanthropic, had become conscious that even his success had been failure. The fruits of his ministry in saved souls, in noble Christian characters, and in energetic spiritual workers for Christ, had been wanting. He acknowledged with sadness that his was an uncalled ministry.

The preacher must find his one message in the Word of God. "Go preach my Gospel" is the commission. "Preach the Word" is the command. Bible Christianity as a saving power is the message. Men in this rapid age have tried many ways of reaching the busy and absorbed world. They have tried the Gospel of philosophy and esthetics, the Gospel of science and art; they have tried the Gospel of sensation, clap-trap, and twaddle; the gospel of scolding, of denunciation and abuse, of vinegar and wormwood; but the masses have been steadily drifting away from the Church in spite of them. The philosophers and scientists can beat the pulpit at the first; the theatrical managers can distance it at the second; and the Daily Heralds and Times can place themselves beyond its competition at the third. No message has been found to take the place of the Word of God; no keenness of speculation, no profundity of philosophy, no polish of learning. There is nothing but God's eternal Word, uttered from a heart and lips touched and fired by a call from God, brought to bear upon the sins and evils of the time, and driven home upon the conscience with a voice of divine authority—there is nothing but this that can reach and hold the attention of this modern world.

*2. The Message from God.*

The preacher must have as his grand aim the saving of souls. It is not, as too many seem to think, the mission of the preacher to deliver two polished orations weekly to applauding audiences. It is something higher by all the spaces than that. Dr. Gardiner Spring remarks, in his *Autobiography*,* that laborious ministers generally gain their object. "If it is to write *elegant* sermons, they write them, and gain their object. If it is to write *learned* sermons, they write them, and gain their object. If it is to *enrich their discourses* with the pithy and concentrated sentences of other days, and great men, they do it and gain their object. If it is to be *popular*, they are popular, and there the matter ends. They look no further. They gain their object, and have never thought of anything beyond it. It was not the conversion of sinners they were aiming at, and therefore they never attained it. I know a most worthy minister who preached more than a year to the same people, and his preaching was sound in doctrine, logical, and able; but during that whole period I have yet to learn that a single sinner was alarmed, convinced, or converted to God. And the reason is, that was not his object. He did not study for it, nor pray for it, nor preach for it. He gained his object most effectually, but it was not the conversion of men." The preacher will be tested before God, by his aim in the work.

3. **The Aim of Saving Souls.**

An aged minister—we suspect it was Dr. Spring—once put the pointed question to Dr. William M. Paxton, then of New York: "When you prepare a sermon, what are you in favor of?" In explaining his meaning he added: "Some ministers are in favor of

* *Autobiography*, vol. i., p. 107.

preparing a discourse; some of discussing a subject before the public; and some of saving souls. What are you in favor of?" There is only one thing that one can be in favor of, and be in sympathy with Him who called him to the sacred office. He sent his Son into the world to save sinners; and he sends men, if he sends them at all, on a mission of soul-seeking to lost sinners, and with no other aim can they overtake and rescue this world of lost souls, hastening on the wings of steam and electricity to perdition.

To the call from God, the message from him, and the single aim of saving souls, there must be added the quickening power of the Holy Ghost. In that sublime vision of the Prophet in the temple, before God called from his throne, "Who will go for us?" and the trembling prophet responded, "Here am I. Send me," one of the seraphim flew with a live coal, which he had taken from off the altar, and laid it upon the prophet's mouth, and said, "Lo, this hath touched thy lips; and thine iniquity is taken away and thy sin purged." So the fire from the Holy Ghost must needs touch the lips, before the message will avail.

*4. The Quickening of the Spirit.*

In the New Testament the central point of power was revealed at Pentecost. The command to the Apostles was, not to go out and enter upon the work of evangelizing the world, without any special preparation for this, but, "Tarry ye at Jerusalem until ye shall be endued with power from on high." There was given them the promise of the outpouring of the Holy Spirit. That promise was fulfilled at Pentecost, when the Christian Church was born and the Apostles girded for their work for mankind. The sermon by Peter, the preacher on that

*Pentecostal Power.*

day, gifted with the tongue of fire, was the means of saving thousands of souls.

No preacher can expect to reach the world with a sermon that is not prepared by the aid of the Holy Ghost, delivered under his quickening and inspiring influence, and carried home to the hearer by his illumining and saving power. This is true, too, of the Word of God spoken by the way. The preacher must everywhere and always exalt and lean upon the power of the Holy Ghost, the Spirit who can alone "reprove the world of sin, of righteousness, and of judgment."* His polished rhetoric will fail, his profoundest learning prove impotent, his sublimest eloquence be but as the "sounding brass and tinkling cymbal," without this supreme and only saving power.

Now all this sense of the call and presence of the living God must somehow be embodied in the working-theory of the ministry that is to speak for God to this self-indulgent, utilitarian, God-neglecting, and God-defying age, with any saving efficacy. Let every servant of Christ be urged and warned, in the Master's name, if his working-theory be wrong or defective in any one of these points, to lay not his hand upon the sacred things until he has made it right. Let the word go out to the ministry, in Christ's name : "Tarry at your Jerusalem till you have heard the call, received the message, been inspired with the aim—till ye be endued with power from on high."

### III. A Different and Better Training.

The preacher who would succeed in the highest sense in these times requires a different and better training of his various powers for the work in which he is engaged.

It may seem quite obvious, yet it needs to be especially emphasized, that a better and different training of the logical faculty is indispensable in the present age.

**1. Better Logical Training.**

The bane of the age is the indefinite, indistinct, incoherent thinking that is kept so constantly before the public through all the popular channels of intelligence, and made so prominent, imposing, and fascinating as to shut out of view or obscure all the higher and exact thinking, and cause itself to be regarded as the sum of all truth and wisdom. We refer to the indefinite thinking, or no-thinking, that has come to the present generation, as a special infliction, from those loosest of all modern so-called thinkers, John Stuart Mill and Herbert Spencer, and their friends and disciples, and that has been embodied in so much of what has been furnished for popular reading. It commonly takes on a highly rhetorical form, and delights to explain away, or envelop in haziness or mysticism, the plain doctrines of the Bible, so that they come from its touch so transformed as not to be recognizable by those familiar with the ordinary use of language. Theological weaklings and literary Miss Nancys devote themselves to translating Scriptural truth into popular twaddle, and succeed to perfection. The love of God becomes sentimental gush; the sacrifice of Christ on the cross, a mere exhibition of sentimental sympathy; and the divine retributive justice of God, merely an aspect of his love hitherto obscured by hard-hearted and perverse theologians. They attempt to translate common-sense Bible and Christian thought in terms of Spencerian evolution, and the crowd become wild over it; altho, when competent critics examine the product of their labors, the skilled theologian rejects it as bad theology, and the exact scientist spews it out as pseudo-science. They nod wisely and talk learnedly of "environment" in the Kingdom of God, of "survival of the fittest," of "persistence of force," and all that; and are spoken of as being "abreast of the age." Definition, clear statement, old-fashioned phrase, are the special aversion of these inventors or mongers of the undefined. Appearance of originality, of freshness, of rhetorical finish, of flavor of learning and literary culture, is their peculiar ambition. What with the intellectual thimble-rigging and general sleight-of-hand, supplemented by unlimited assertion and so-called reasoning, the great facts of the Bible dissolve and disappear, under their handling, as readily as do the doctrines. One takes up one of the great foreign reviews, and is entertained by some professor of imposing name and fame, but without scientific knowledge of geology, theology, or Scriptures, with a breezy essay going to show that the Noachic deluge, or the miracle of the destruction of the swine, is a mere myth, if not a fraudulent invention. One opens his American religious paper, and finds a leading clerical writer represented as saying, "Genesis on the fall of man is an ancient legend, which a great writer took, as Tennyson took the Arthurian legends, and rewrote it in order that he might write a moral and spiritual lesson. I think that the Hebrew people believed the fall of man affected the whole human race. I think Paul believed so." And so, with one flourish of the tongue, the entire foundation of the Bible and its theology, of incarnation and redemption, is swept away. These men write and speak patronizingly of Moses and of Christ. Ingersoll talks bluntly of "the mistakes of Moses"; these men talk of "the legends" or "myths" of Moses, with a begging-your-pardon air for using language that might seem to imply that there was a Moses and that he possibly wrote something!

Perhaps the assumption and assertion of these spirits of indefiniteness have done more than anything else to discredit clear thinking and Bible truth, and sound doctrine as resting upon these. And on how slender a capital have they carried on their immense business! It has been brazen impudence—sometimes under the guise of modesty, sometimes not. Every one who knows them knows that they are not acquainted with the principles of scientific method, and that they have neither real theological learning nor logical acumen. Most of them show, in every sentence, that they are incapable of logical and clear thinking, innocent of knowledge of Bible truth, and out of sympathy with earnest, evangelical religion. Their strongest hand with the masses is in the rôle of modesty. They barely suggest that "the old theologians were too confident. They knew too much. Paul's statements were doubtless accommodated to Jewish or Greek, or Roman prejudices. It will not do to take him too literally when he writes of salvation, of propitiation, of vicarious atonement, and all that. The Apostles thought and believed so and so; but they, like ourselves, were under the influence of the popular beliefs of the age. It is better to recognize our limitations, the limitations common to humanity. The region of religion is a mysterious region, and we should not attempt to take the mystery out of it by our too definite dogmatic statements." And on hearing them, in this rôle of the modest theologian, Mr. Hardcastle would no doubt exclaim: "This may be modern modesty, but I never saw anything look so like old-fashioned impudence!" As if the world had just come to itself, and come to know something, in the muddled religious consciousness of these dwarfs and pygmies, the laughing-stock of the thinking men of their own generation even; so that, at their beck and nod, at the wag of their tongue, or the scratch of their pen, all the giants of the ages— Moses and Isaiah, and John and Paul, and even Jesus himself, and all the great theologians of the Christian ages besides—were to be discredited and set aside!

Now no man is in a position to exert so powerful an influence, either for or against the continuance of such thinking, as the preacher of the Gospel. By a gospel of indefiniteness and inconsistency, he can help continue the muddle, in which so many find themselves, regarding the truths of Christianity; by a clear, distinct, and consistent presentation of the truth, he can help them out of this condition.

Owing to many and various influences, besides this drift of the times, chief of which is perhaps the fact that the courses of study are too full of other things to admit of any adequate study of the nature of the human mind and of human thought, the average man gets, in his course of training, by his own confession, next to nothing on these important subjects. Said a young professor, who had been the honor-man in one of the great colleges: "I studied mental philosophy, moral philosophy, and logic, under that distinguished scholar, Professor So and So, but they made no impression whatever on my mind, and I have now no definite theories on those subjects." That is a typical case.

Before the preacher is ready to deal with any subject of discourse that is worth presenting to a people, he needs to lay the proper foundation for it by gaining the power of forming correct conceptions, on the basis of reality and fact; and then to acquire the power of bringing out the essence of these conceptions in exact definitions, and of accurately distributing their elements by means of logical division and partition. He needs to do his thinking in such a way that, when he reaches his conceptions and notions, they shall be *knowledge* to him, and something that he can set before the people as *knowledge*.

"What do you mean by that term?" was asked of a somewhat brilliant young professor. "Define the term." "I cannot define it," was the reply; "this thing of definition is a great hindrance to thought and to progress in attainments." "It is impossible to know," said another. "What do you mean by *know?*" was asked him. The reply was: "It can not be defined. The limitations of knowledge are such that it can not be known what it is to know." The natural response was: "How do you *know* that?"

To the preacher the power of distinct thinking is fundamental, even more clearly so than to the mere teacher. He needs most of all, and first of all, to gain definite, clear, and distinct views of things, so that he shall be able to say, on this point or that, "I *know.*" "This is *truth.*"

He needs to study with equal care the process of forming correct judgments, by comparing and combining the conceptions he has formed, defined to himself, and verified. "Man is intelligent;" "Man is round—square." Are these both judgments? If not, why not? What are the intuitive and natural relations by which conceptions are so bound together in judgments that one can say of such a combination: "This is true." "This is not true." The formation of correct inferences or conclusions from assured judgments, by the process of reasoning, should equally be mastered; so that a man can say of a conclusion reached by such a process: "This is *truth*, and can not be gainsaid." It is simple matter of fact that very few have any clear conviction that there are such things as these to be done; and that fewer still have any distinct idea of how they are to be done.

Especially is there requisite for the preacher a better knowledge and training of the constructive faculty, by which conceptions, judgments, and reasonings are gathered into systems of scientific, artistic, or practical thought. **Training of Constructive Faculty.** From the intellectual side, the construction of such systems is the great work of life; this form of intellectual activity, the form for which all the other and lower forms exist. And yet, how often is this power left without any training or intelligent development! Indeed, the theories of psychology, and the books on that subject, do not even recognize it, except incidentally; so that it is natural that educational methods should ignore it.

In this age, when so much is heard about science, and so much that has no science in it claims to be science, there is peculiar need for a better training to the knowledge and use of scientific methods. **Scientific Method.** What is science? What are its materials? What are its methods? These are fundamental questions. In these days, when both inductive and deductive logic are so travestied, and when speculation and imagination and guess-work are palmed off upon men in the name of science, and especially in the name of Biblical learning and Christian theology, it is of momentous importance that the preacher should be be master of these subjects.

**2. A Better Theological Training.** The preacher needs a different and better theological training to fit him for his work in this age, in which the old truths have so many new bearings, and when so many new doctrinal issues are raised.

The purpose for which theological seminaries were established was the preparation of the preacher for carrying out his divine commission, in proclaiming the salvation of the Gospel to the world. They are religious and Christian institutions, for a particular end; not educational and scholastic institutions, to make scholars in religious or technical specialties. Failure to keep these things in mind has, in some instances, led to tendencies to departure from their original idea and purpose.

There has been in some quarters a marked tendency to Germanize the seminaries, on the assumption that **Germanizing Theological Seminaries.** all scholarship is German, and that mere scholarship is the end of the work in the institution. The essential things in a thelogical school are, on the contrary, evangelical learning and the development of pious activities in connection with the principles of Christianity, and along with this the power to get the message out of the Word of God and to put it in the best shape for reaching and saving men.

Now, if there is one thing manifest in the view of common sense it is, that Continental, and especially German, theological institutions can not be safely made the models for our seminaries, in spirit, method, or ideas. Those institutions are State institutions. The appointments to them are political. The man does not need to be a Christian in order to become either student or professor in one of them. He may

## THE PREACHER AND HIS FURNISHING. 173

even be a pronounced atheist, as Kuenen was, and devote himself to showing that there is no supernatural, and that the so-called supernatural in the Bible is without any foundation in fact or truth. At best, he is required to know only a formal and perfunctory State-Church religion. Ordinarily he has never known anything of vital piety, even by observation. Often he hates evangelical religion and God and earnest Christians, because they are a perpetual rebuke to the corrupt and immoral life he leads. If he fills a professor's chair in such a theological institution—where drunken brawls are not unknown, and where licentiousness is rife and often open—to attract attention, he must have something striking to present in his teaching. Hence, the theological vagaries and speculations, the neologisms and rationalistic hypotheses and assumptions and assertions, to which each generation gives birth.

It would be as reasonable to expect the appointees of the Government in Washington, who owe their places to family relationship, political favoritism, or ability to do "fine work" in politics, to evolve on short notice into pattern saints with rapidly sprouting wings, as it would be to expect the appointees in Continental theological schools to develop into lovers of God's Word and preachers of evangelical truth; or into leaders in evangelistic and Salvation Army work. Such institutions are certainly not the models for Christian theological seminaries.

And when the advocates of rationalistic laxness in this country claim all the Continental leaders in the seminaries as advocates of skeptical and destructive rationalistic criticism, the weight of all that authority, even if the claim be allowed to be correct, should not be regarded by evangelical thinkers and preachers as being very great. But the claims are certainly to be regarded as extravagant, when we find such men as Köhler of Erlangen and Professor Nösgen setting their faces against so many of the critical vagaries and absolutely refuting them. While there has been a long line of rationalistic and atheistic teachers, and while it is true that an orthodox theologian may have been an accident, and an exception to the general rule; still, by the grace of God, Germany has produced such stanch defenders of the faith as Neander, Tholuck, Hengstenberg, Keil, and many others like them in spirit and attainments. And there is at present peculiar reason for gratification and hope, in the fact that the vast majority of the preachers and churches are soundly evangelical, and arrayed in open antagonism and hostility against a comparatively few teachers in the universities who have set themselves to corrupt religion and to destroy the faith they were appointed to teach and are paid to defend.*

This tendency to import Germany and German methods and theological ideas into this country; to push the great mass of skeptical and irreligious criticism and speculation as the sum of all wisdom in theology, and to make use of the impious laxness in unchristian and State institutions there as a reason for the same thing here, is absurdly indefensible. The fact that a young man has studied in Germany or Holland, so far from being a recommendation for a professorship in one of our American theological schools, ought, therefore, to go far toward barring him from such a place, at least until his fitness has been proved

---

* See *Homiletic Review* for February, 1896, article on "Theological Thought in Germany," by Dr. Geo. P. Schodde.

by other methods and tests. A training under even the best of the German unchristian specialists, in the midst of unchristian or anti-christian environment, is not the training that is needed to fit men to prepare young men to preach the Gospel. The introduction of such men and methods into the Church seminaries is simply the planting of the rationalistic and infidel spirit and method and idea right in the heart of the Church. The glorification of the learning and work of these men, when we have in our seminaries such Christian scholars as Dr. Howard Osgood and Dr. William Henry Green, is in the highest degree absurd.

There has been an equally marked tendency toward the introduction of mere specialists as teachers of the great Biblical, theological, and philosophical essentials that constitute the prime requisite in the student's theological furnishing. *Tendency to Mere Specialism.* Mere specialism is, from its very nature, both narrow and superficial. In many instances the ground for the choice of such specialism as a subject of study is to be found in the egotism of the young man and his ambition to occupy a position for which he has not the breadth to qualify him, and which he can only gain through some specialty. Such men, outside their specialties, are mere novices, and are sure speedily to become vain and puffed up by comparison of themselves with others who have not given attention to these specialties, which to them constitute all scientific knowledge. Trained in this way in a mere specialty, perhaps in a secularized German institution, the man enters upon his work without any logical, philosophical, or theological knowledge or perspective ; without any conception, adequate or inadequate, of the nature and aim of the sacred calling of the preacher; with incorrect notions of the objects for which theological seminaries were founded, and without anything of the strong man or the Christian manhood back of the specialist that is absolutely necessary to give proper aim and direction and moral and spiritual weight to his teachings.

Such men form a striking contrast with the broad-minded, evangelical men—like Henry B. Smith and Charles Hodge and Alvah Hovey, and the many others —who have graced and honored such positions in the past history of the Church. All that is necessary to make a theological seminary utterly worthless for the main purpose—perhaps we ought to say for the *one* purpose—of its existence, is to fill its chairs with such exclusive specialists.

Along with the other two features already noticed, there seems to be a tendency to an increasing neglect of that constructive work and training that should be a constant aim in institutions for the training of preachers.

**Neglect of Constructive Thinking.**

The chief work, intellectual and practical, of the preacher must always be constructive work. The disposition to exhaust the time of study in barren critical work, often purely destructive—in short, in all kinds of work that cultivates merely the perceptive powers in gathering minutiæ, and the memory in retaining them—has been the bane of our educational system in these recent times, and is largely the product of the specialism and Germanism already considered. In our public-school system, the introduction of innumerable subjects into the course of study, and the requirement of a smattering of knowledge of each, have already gone far toward transforming the schools into dull, dead machines, and have called forth the reprobation of the best educators. The same thing can not fail to be noted in the curriculum of some of the theological schools. So many subsidiary branches have been added that only the minimum of time is left for study and mental effort upon the great subjects of the Bible and theology in their relations to preaching. And in many cases, because of their newness, and because of the lack of perspective in the view of those who represent them, these purely subordinate topics have been made to overshadow and almost to eliminate from the course, in the case of many a student, the great and all-important ones.

Apart from all its other defects, this method is educationally most vicious; unfitting rather than fitting the theological student for the work of the preacher. It is true, no doubt, that there should be men and instructors who have been specially trained in these subordinate subjects; for, so far as they are involved in the apologetic work of the Church, they must be understood. But it is true also that such men are not needed in great numbers, since the questions to be settled, in connection with such departments, do not turn upon the mere knowledge of the specialists, but upon the great principles of logic, and especially of inductive logic, of which the specialists are often quite as innocent as new-born babes. It is also true that such specialties can only be studied, with safety to the man and profit to the Church, after a broad foundation in logic and philosophy and theology, and in the methods of scientific construction; and we are inclined to think that they should be provided for in a *theological university*.

*Constructive Training Essential.*

The one great need, intellectually, in theological training is manifestly the constructive study and work that lead the man to grasp things in their broad relations and prepare the preacher to present them to men in such relations. In short, the practical training of the constructive faculty of the preacher is the supreme thing for him intellectually.

Now, the rational method of training the constructive faculty is the same as that of training any other power—that is, by intelligently, systematically, and abundantly exercising that power. The exercise must be intelligent; for this infinite beating about the bush in the dark and for nothing, is worse than useless; it is positively harmful. The teacher must know the power and its possibilities and laws, and direct his work accordingly. It must be systematic, for only by system can the maximum of results be reached with the minimum of effort. The procedure must be from the simple to the complex, from the lower part to the higher part, until the whole field is intelligently compassed, and that completeness must be the goal clearly in view from the beginning. The exercise must be abundant, taking in the whole work and period of education. The bee, building his cell by instinct, reaches perfection unconsciously on the first trial; the man, building his structures by reason, must make progress through many attempts and failures, and approximate perfection only as the result of innumerable repetitions.

Moreover the constructive or creative method must proceed in the usual twofold rational way: first, by direction in studying the constructions of others as constructions; secondly, by training the student to construct for himself, and both these educative processes must be pushed along the three lines of scientific, artistic, and practical system.

The starting-point in this training is in the study of the constructions of others as constructions. This should always be accompanied with constant exercises in construction. Just here is where much of our educational work, especially in our higher institutions, utterly fails. There is an infinite difference between the critical, microscopic, and painful study that characterizes the present methods, in which there is nothing educative in any high sense; and the large-minded study of constructions, as such, that is needed if the results are to be educative. In short, a radical change of the methods in vogue, especially in literary and scientific study, is demanded, if they are to be made the means of securing the best educational results. This is peculiarly called for in theological training, which should intelligently aim at grasping each book in the Bible as a whole, in the light of the principle that Genesis or Job or Matthew is infinitely more than the simple sum of all its parts, and with a full understanding of the relation of all the parts to each other, and to the one central theme of the book as a whole; while it aims at like comprehension of the theological system involved in "the faith once delivered to the saints."

The completion of the work of developing the constructive faculty requires the constant exercise of that faculty in the actual work of construction. Every recitation, and every exercise in a course of study, may be made an exercise of this power; and only as they are so made is study transformed, from a dead, dull drudgery, in the use of the senses or memory, or the mere logical faculty, into a joyous and free activity that leads on to higher effort and encourages in such effort.

There is no comprehension of any great subject to be had without such constructive study and training. Without it there can be no preparation to handle such subjects. But such constructive study and exercise are peculiarly essential in training the preacher to preach the Gospel. Nothing short of this will prepare men for the direct, free, and effective preaching so essential for reaching the masses. The increase in the number of studies and of side issues in our seminary work has doubtless strongly tended to the elimination of that constructive work, once a somewhat prominent factor in those institutions. Correct educational method requires that there should be a return to it—nay more, that the chief intellectual energy of the student in his work should be made to take this direction.

If that better preparation, needed by the new order of the ministry called for in the present crisis, is to be had by the Church, it must be by securing a training better than the present and different from it mainly in the respects that have just been emphasized.

### IV. A More Complete Special Furnishing in Knowledge and Oratorical Skill.

It is equally true that the preacher in this age has need of a more complete furnishing in the special knowledge and qualifications required in carrying out his commission.

Such discussions as the present always presuppose general scholarship, knowledge of the original Scriptures, acquaintance with literature, general science, etc. But the preacher needs, besides these, such a thorough furnishing for the work, especially with the material of that field of truth with which he has chiefly to do, as shall force the world to cease its scoffing at the Bible as obsolete, and at the utterances of the pulpit as weak and worthless.

There is undoubtedly demanded of the preacher of the present day, especially of the preacher who addresses the more intelligent audiences in the great centers of thought, a thorough furnishing in the great principles of science and philosophy.  *In Science and Philosophy.*  These subjects are obviously connected most intimately with the great Biblical and religious problems that are common to the pulpit in all ages. Moreover, the present evil condition of the world, which the preacher is called upon to remedy,—the abounding secularism and anarchism,—is the result of false teaching in science and philosophy that he can not hope to counteract without first understanding it. The air is so full of it, literature is so saturated with it, life so pervaded by it, and all industrial, social, and political problems so bound up with it, that he can scarcely come in contact with a human being on the street, or broach a subject in familiar conversation, or deal with a common issue in the pulpit, without having the results of such false teaching forced upon his attention and consideration, by finding that it has prejudiced men against his message, or incapacitated them mentally for understanding the truth of God.

Written sermons, with frequent changes of parish and reversals of the barrel, have, as we take it, often been destructive of intellectual life and activity among the clergy, in these later times, and in the various denominations. There is at present a reasonable and just demand, on the part of the Church, for an increase in substantial breadth and vigor of manhood, in mental acuteness and grasp, and in alertness and enterprise in action, in those who claim the leading places as the teachers and molders of society. Other men are everywhere awake and alive, full of activity and enterprise, in science, in philosophy, in business, in pleasure-seeking ; this is no time for the man in the pulpit to sleep. He needs to keep abreast of the age on all the grand issues, and to be able to measure strength with the strongest, knowledge with the profoundest, wisdom with the wisest, if need be, on all the great theoretical and practical questions, if he is to hold his place for God and truth.

And be it said without fear of contradiction, there is no position or calling so favorable as the ministry for grappling with and mastering the great fundamental doctrines of science and philosophy. There is no place in modern life where there is such constant call for a thorough acquaintance with these principles. True, the preacher is not to preach science or philosophy ; but he must have a large and firm grasp of their principles, if he is to deal successfully with the men whom he meets on the streets every day, to whom he preaches on the Sabbath, and for whose souls he is responsible. He will find that erroneous views regarding both science and philosophy, and most of the questions connected with them, have found their way into all the forms and phases of modern thought, literature, and life. He will have opinions of John Stuart Mill, of Herbert Spencer, of Matthew Arnold, of Professor Tyndall, thrust at him every day, with confident assurance, by those who will take it for granted that the assertions of these scientific dogmatists are unanswerable and boast that they are so, unless they are fairly brought to book and answered.

Let the man of God present these modern apostles and their new gospel in all their shallowness, and faith in them will die.

Mr. Mill wrote with amazing confidence, and with an appearance of candor that enabled him to rule the opinions of vast numbers of so-called educated men in the last generation with absolute tyranny. It may become necessary for the preacher to show, as Professor Jevons has shown it, that, in one way or another, the intellect of this modern Sir Oracle was wrecked; that his mind was essentially illogical ; that his text can never be safely interpreted by the context, because there is no certainty that in his writings the same line of thought will be maintained for two consecutive sentences ; that there is nothing in logic that he has not touched, and that he has touched nothing without confusing it; that he has never advocated any false principles in his works which he has not himself either amply refuted or furnished the materials for refuting, and that without knowing it. Let this be shown to the men who worship Mill instead of the only true God, and they will speedily be silenced, and become agnostics or skeptics on the point of Mill's deity !

He will hear Herbert Spencer called by his admirers the "Apostle of the Understanding," and exalted above Aristotle. It may be necessary to show up the beauties of this apostle. It is an easy matter. He is a very acrobat of logic. In the opening of his *First Principles* he demonstrates, to his own satisfaction, the impossibility of the theistic theory of the universe, of the theory of self-creation, and of that of eternal existence, because they involve the idea of self-existence, which is unthinkable as implying infinity; in the concluding portions of the same discussion, he teaches that "the fundamental verity," whatever that may be, which is to take the place of God, involves the same unthinkable idea of self-existence, and yet is not only possible but actual, and the basis of all philosophy. In his writings on general philosophy, he scouts all intuitions, all necessary truths, as absurdities ; and yet, in his subsequent writings, proceeds to build his Special Philosophy upon these very intuitions! Or let the preacher show up—as may easily be done—Mr. Spencer's latest feat in reducing all ethics to the ethics of bestiality, having no foundation but the two animal instincts of self-preservation and reproduction of the species. Something of this kind, in the way of clear thinking and accurate definition, assuredly needs to be done by the pulpit, at proper times and places, to stay the Spencerian and evolution craze that has swept even such a man as Professor Drummond into the quagmire of materialism, unconsciously to himself, while leading him to pose, and Christian assemblies to let him pose, as the lion of the day.

It is easy to show, and has been abundantly shown by the ablest men in Great Britain, that when that apostle of the new science, Professor Tyndall, attempted anything outside of his own narrow sphere of experimental physics, there is no end to the absurdities into which he rushed. Nothing, for example, could be more absurd than his famous demand made some years ago at Belfast. While insisting upon the experimental method, and making *experience* the only source of knowledge and its limit, he was able to perform that astonishing scientific feat of prolonging his vision *by experience* infinitely *beyond the bounds of experience*, and to *discern* in what he called matter the promise and potency of all life—a feat compared with which seeing through a mill-stone is mere child's play! And immediately following this came his demand, that theologians and philosophers should submit all their

> "religious theories, schemes, and systems, that embrace notions of cosmogony, or that otherwise reach into its domains, . . . to the control of science, and relinquish all thought of controlling it."

How monumentally arrogant all this, and yet how absurdly innocent of the relations of science and philosophy!

The preacher will have Huxley's great accomplishments and victories paraded before him, and will be helped by a knowledge of his defects and limitations. Many accidents favored his quest for fame, but certain essential drawbacks prevented him from attaining a high place in either exact science or philosophy. Like Spencer and Tyndall, he did not receive in his early years a liberal education, and the conditions of his later life were such as to preclude his remedying this defect; so that he had only a showy, superficial, "pick-up" knowledge of theology, philosophy, literature, in fact of the whole broad range of special knowledge opened to the scholar by such a liberal education. Like Darwin and Spencer and Tyndall, he was lacking in real logical acumen, and had no command of that exact logical and scientific method for which the higher spheres of science and philosophy call. His brilliant literary qualities of which so much has been made, and his absolute mastery of the sneer and of brazen assertion, certainly do not entitle the opinions of the inventor and populizer of the term "agnostic" to weigh very heavily at the bar of reason.

The truth is, these men, by starting out with the fundamental denial of what we know best of all things,—

the existence and living activity of the thinking spirit, —and by making all possible shifts to maintain this utterly unreasonable denial, stultified themselves, and committed logical *hari kari.* Or, if anything more is wanting, their advance to the denial of the Supreme Mind—to be seen working everywhere around us, and for believing in which we have the same logical reason that we have for believing that our neighbor exists, and no more reason for denying or doubting than we have for denying or doubting our neighbor's spirituality and personality—completes the stultification and the self-destruction. By the time the man reaches that point there is no logic left in him, as there is none to begin with in the men who blindly follow him.

The preacher who, in the great centers of intelligence, is to stem this tide of egotism and shallowness, that is bearing such multitudes to perdition, needs to understand the foundations of things, the principles of things, and to be a master in them, for the truth's sake and for humanity's sake. Without this he can not succeed.

<small>Must Know Principles.</small>

A firm grasp also of the main principles of exact science will aid the preacher greatly in his interpretation of the Scripture, so far as their teachings are related to the sciences. The unfolding and illustration of the principles of geology, by such men as Hugh Miller, Edward Hitchcock, Arnold Guyot, James D. Dana, and Principal Dawson, will make marvelously luminous important portions of the Word of God that would otherwise be misunderstood or only partially understood; as, for example, the opening portions of the Book of Genesis. Such knowledge will, at the same time, guard the messenger of God against the assumptions and assertions of "science falsely so called."

A better and firmer grasp of the fundamentals of psychology and philosophy is even more important to the preacher. His view of the will, for example, must decide his view of morality and virtue, and the nature of regeneration and conversion, and it will determine the general type of his theology. His ethical views will shape his theological tendencies, decide whether they shall be in the direction of eudemonism and universalism, or in the direction of essential morality and particularism. In short, no theology is possible without its underlying and molding theories of psychology and philosophy. If the preacher has accurate views on these subjects, they will furnish him a solid basis for correct thinking and sound teaching, and they will put him on his guard against the innumerable popular and delusive errors of the day.

If his view of the fundamentals regarding the nature of man, of the universe, and of God, is correct, he will be in no danger of being carried away by the *zeitgeist*, or popular drift of the hour, and of ignoring the *ewig-zeitgeist*, or the eternal and unchangeable trend of things. Without such view, even if he has a theology based upon the plain language of the Scriptures, that theology is liable to be merely a misinterpretation of Scriptures, absurdly false and utterly harmful.

There is, therefore, scarcely anything more essential, by way of preliminary furnishing to the preacher of this age, than a firmer mental grip on a common-sense and natural psychology and philosophy. And this is especially true in the American Church, in which the theological views and discussions have always had their root, so largely, in the views of human nature and its workings and of the principles that transcend human experience.

The minister called and sent of God should see to it that he is thoroughly furnished for this aspect of his work. He is called to save the world from this shallow atheistic scientism and skepticism, and this can not be done without special furnishing for the work.

A demand, certainly no less pressing, is made upon the preacher of to-day, for a more thorough Biblical furnishing, to help him stem the tide of unbelief and scoffing, so far as that is directed against the Word of God.

*2. Special Biblical Knowledge.*

There are three points of view from which the minister of the present and the future must be master of the Bible, in order to attain to any such success as is demanded by the commission Christ has given him, and to any such efficiency as is required by the difficult conditions under which his work as a preacher must be done.

*Three Points of View.*

He must master the Bible as the Book of God, having essential unity of theme, of aim, of trend, and of plan. Men often object to the Bible, or neglect it, because the pulpit has given them so little real knowledge of it. The method, so long and widely in vogue among preachers, of taking a single verse or clause from the Scriptures, severed from all its connections with the context, and then drawing from it a topic even more remote from Scriptural connection, and often indeed having nothing to do with the Scriptures, is obviously not fitted to give the hearers very much knowledge of the Bible. Ten thousand such sermons may be listened to, and yet the listener gain

*(1) The Bible as the Book of God.*

from them no conception whatever of the Book or God. But even if the theme drawn from the text is a Scriptural theme, and its treatment a Scriptural treatment, the knowledge of the Bible given by it may still be exceedingly limited and superficial. The book or literary production that has any unity and breadth of thought in it expresses, as a whole, vastly more than is expressed by all its fragments considered apart from their connection as a whole. The Books of Scriptures have each of them their plan and their unity of truth and thought. Archdeacon Farrar recently said:*

> "Out of the many thousands of sermons which are weekly and sometimes even daily delivered in England, it is I think very desirable that some should be devoted to the scope and meaning of the Books of Scripture, rather than to its separate texts. By thus doing we can as it were kneel down to drink of the pure stream as it bursts from the living rock. The Bible teaches us its best lessons when we search its teachings as wise and humble learners ; when we judge of it by the truths which we learn from it, not by the prejudices and prepossessions which we bring to it ; when we seek in it the elements and bases, not when we go to it for proof-texts of doctrines which we already hold."

The preacher should be master of the Books of the Bible, as they appear in their completeness on the sacred pages. He should also be master of the Bible as a whole, as the Book of God, the one complete, consistent revelation of God's plan of redemption for a lost world. It is not enough that he should understand the original languages, and be able to read the Bible fluently in those languages; not enough that he should study all about the Bible, all around the Bible, or all through the Bible, creeping on his way through the verses, as the worm creeps blindly on its way

* *The Message of the Books.*

through the grass and tangle. He should study the Bible itself, as one great complete thought of God. He should study it and grasp it as a whole, in relation to its great center. He should master it in its every book, until every book is understood in itself and in its relation to the whole Bible. He should study it throughout grammatically, logically, prayerfully, by the help of the Holy Spirit, until it becomes a living book, quick and powerful in all its range of revealed truth and fact.

Such study has its place above all mere human theology. It is infinitely more important than all our mere philosophy. It will help the preacher more in his work of answering objections than all his knowledge of science and of human investigations and speculations. In truth, to most of the objections brought against it and its religion, the Bible is its own best answer. Such objections are largely based upon misconceptions of its character or its teachings. The preacher, in such cases, has only to let its light shine and the darkness will be dissipated. His supreme aim in this regard should be *to help his hearers to come to see the Word of God as it is in itself.* When he has succeeded in doing this, God may be trusted to take care of the ordinary objections, and to make the Word by his Holy Spirit a saving power.

The second point of view, from which the preacher of this age needs to grasp the Word of God, is as (2) **The Bible** a theological system. The Bible teach-**Theology.** ing should be grasped, by the preacher, in a living system of theology that, in its naturalness and completeness, shall confound the skeptic and the scoffer. Doubtless one of the reasons for the cry of the age against theology is that the preachers and the people have had so little living theology from the Bible. The result of the attempt in our theological seminaries to get everything into three so-called years, each of which is only half a year long, has been that men inevitably get next to nothing on any of all the almost innumerable subjects presented. Probably not even a quarter of the time once devoted to theology is now devoted to that subject. Often the number of theologians, that is, of those who take some special interest in theology, in a class of fifty young men, may be counted on the fingers of one hand; and sometimes the number is even less than that. The result is that the preacher, in his training period, fails to get such grasp of this greatest of sciences as will give it an interest to himself; and so he must of course fail of the ability to infuse into it any interest for his hearers. Having failed to grasp the great system of divine truth, in its relations and harmonies, it can be to him only a skeleton of dry bones, which, like the bones in the prophet's vision, are "very dry." No wonder that when the attempt is made to present the- **"Dry Theology."** ology on such a basis of knowledge—or rather of ignorance—men cry out against "dry theology," and insist that they want no more of it! It is the lack of theology that is the matter with the preaching, and against which the people protest, and against which they are right in protesting. One of the most popular preachers in America to-day, for intelligent people, is a man who deals exclusively in the great theological themes, and whose sermons never weary his hearers, even tho they reach into the second hour. The preacher of the present time needs especially a living system of theology. The preacher who is able to marshal a system of Bible truth about Christ crucified, so as to find a place for everything and so as to let everything fall into its place, will have a system full of interest for men and mighty in its saving power over men.

The third point of view, from which the preacher needs to master the Word of God, is that of the practical bearing of its doctrines upon human interests and upon the great questions of human life and conduct and destiny. He needs to master it as practical truth, in all its relations to time and to eternity.

<small>(3) The Bible as Practical Truth.</small>

Doubtless one reason for the outcry against theology, from the pew and from the pulpit, is to be found in the unpractical method of presenting the doctrines of the Word of God. The starting-point in the preacher's working-system should be found in something that comes home to men and lays hold upon them with power. Theological truth is essentially practical truth. Practical truth is truth that has relation to man's feelings and desires, and through these lays hold upon his will and calls him to choice, purpose, and action. The great doctrines of the Word of God have this practical bearing, when properly presented. They are not like mere mathematical axioms or formulas. The omniscience of God may be presented in such abstract way that a man may never think of it in its relation to himself; but that is not the Biblical way, nor the practical theological way of presenting it. Properly viewed, the doctrine brings the sinner into the very presence of Jehovah, and opens all his soul and life to the God with whom he has to do in this world and before whom he must stand at the judgment bar. It is this practical relation and bearing that give to theology its living and unfailing interest to men. Especially is this true of its relation to salvation.

In short, the Bible, which furnishes all valuable theology that has any bearing upon salvation, is an intensely practical book. Its doctrines of creation, providence, original sin, incarnation, and redemption are—as elsewhere indicated—the divine answers to the great questions that no man can fail to ask himself: Whence came I? Upon whom can I depend? Whence the evil in the world? Is there any way of escape? What is that way? These questions have to do principally, not with man's imaginations, not with his logic good or bad, not with his taste rude or cultivated, but with life and death eternal. The Bible appeals to practical instincts, is adapted to practical needs, appeals to practical issues, puts its truths in concrete, practical shape. Preaching that does not appeal to such practical instincts, that does not supply such pressing needs, that does not meet such living issues, that does not put itself into such direct and forceful shape, can not be according to the standard of God's Word. The truth of that Word is no dead orthodoxy, but a living and life-giving thing. *The Bible Practical.*

The preacher needs to seize with special clearness and firmness upon the broader and more quickening views of the lost world and salvation, as presented in the Bible. There are a few grand truths that stand out above the rest. The preacher's conviction of these will in large measure decide his efficiency in the service of God. They are such truths as these: the lost condition and eternal condemnation of man; the vicarious death of the God- *Vital Truths.*

man for his salvation; the mission of the Holy Ghost to apply the provisions of that salvation; the Great Commission to the lost world; the stewardship of all Christians under God for the ends of redemption; a free Gospel for the masses of mankind; the tremendous earnestness and urgency of the work, while a soul perishes with every throb of the heart. If these momentous divine conceptions could be burned into the soul of every preacher, there would speedily result a tide of holy influence, inspired of the Bible, that would sweep back with resistless energy the swift and strong floods of godless self-indulgence and worldliness.

Let it then be emphasized to the utmost—a knowledge of the Bible is what is supremely needed in the ministry of the present day—a firm grasp of its divine structure and unity; a fast hold upon its theology viewed from the cross; a quickening sense of its living, practical doctrines. That, and that alone, will save the ministry from the laxity in doctrine and the maudlin sentiment that come to us from so many "prominent and progressive pulpits," and from the often-recurring blush for the easy-fitting virtue and criminal neglect of souls that are so certain to accompany such doctrine and sentiment.

There is likewise an increasing demand upon the preacher of this age for a better oratorical furnishing for his work, especially for the power of direct and extemporaneous preaching of the Word—in short, for a better knowledge of, and skill in, preaching.

**3. Special Power to Preach.**

There is doubtless a deepening and widening conviction on this point among those who have to do with the practical work of reaching men, especially of reaching the masses. Let not those who press the claim be misunderstood. For the work of saving souls they have no faith in the mere practise of rhetoric and elocution; none in the "start and stare theatric." But they are convinced that there is a power of free speech, that may be given to the messenger of God, and that they verily believe should be given him. They are not inclined to deny that there may possibly be those who can not acquire this power of speech, or that circumstances may arise in which it may be better for the preacher to use the manuscript sermon.

But the command of the Master was, "Go *preach* my Gospel." The Apostles obeyed it and *preached*, as did the Master himself. The primitive Christians obeyed it. The great reform- **Preaching and Reading.** ers in all ages have obeyed it. In seasons of awakened interest men who are trained to *read the Gospel* obey the command of Christ and *preach* it. In all ages in which the power of Christianity has been dominant, preaching has come to the front. It is by the "foolishness of preaching" that the world is to be saved.

Perhaps none can appreciate so well as those who have been trained to *read the Gospel* the infinite difference between that and *preaching* it. But the conviction is certainly rising everywhere of the necessity of direct speech, soul to soul, eye to eye, if the world is to be saved. The men who have the power to reach the masses are the trained and skilful preachers, the Beechers, the Spurgeons, the Moodys, the Newman Halls. Such being the case, it should be one of the foremost aims of all our institutions of learning—while seeking to open the intellects of the rising ministry and fill them with Biblical truths, and while training them to practical power in managing affairs and men in prosecuting great enterprises—to train them also to the ready command of clear, powerful, and polished speech, to be used in a hand-to-hand conflict for the rescue of souls.  And there is little doubt that to the average preacher such training can be given, if the proper constructive and creative method of study and discipline is made use of in such institutions.

But whatever may be said of reading the Gospel for preachers and communities made up of intelligent Christian people, nothing is clearer than that the poor and the ignorant can not be reached with a *read Gospel* in any age.  A clear-minded, unprejudiced man must see that cumbrous written forms are never suited to minds of this class, and that they are peculiarly unsuited to the minds of this age.  Dr. William M. Paxton was right when he said : *

*Preaching, for the Masses.*

"The long, prolix, syllogistic statements of the schoolmen are surely not adapted to an age of telegrams.  The mental conditions of a people who travel in a stage-coach at the rate of five miles an hour must differ greatly from those of a people who travel in a railroad car at a speed of forty miles.  In an age when mind is intensely active and all other ideas come to men on the wing, it will not do for the truth of God to crawl like a snail, or slumber like a crow.  It must fly with the celerity of a carrier-pigeon to bring its messages to men in the thick of life's battle, or it must mount like an eagle to command attention and to carry its glad tidings upon swift wings to every corner of the earth."

It can hardly be doubted that, with the better furnishing, in the directions already considered, the ministry will feel more and more constrained to acquire this power of free and direct speech, to be used as

* " Address at the inauguration of Archibald Alexander Hodge as professor of theology, in Princeton Theological Seminary."

the most effective instrument in carrying out their commission.

Without such thorough furnishing for the work the preacher may not expect to overtake this age of steam and lightning ; with it, with God's help and inspiration, we have the means suited—rationally at least— to the end of bringing the world to heed the Gospel. Given this better intellectual and scholarly equipment, this firmer grip of the Bible with its glorious living theology and practical life-and-death truth, and given this command of the power to bear the message of God right home to men by living speech—and there may be expected, with the divine quickening and a new consecration, and devotion, the speedy hushing and confounding of all the boastful and scoffing secularism and atheism, and a new and healthful atmosphere in which the coming generation may live and accomplish its task.

## V. A More Complete Consecration.

It is preeminently true that in this age the preacher needs a more complete consecration to the work for which he holds his commission. That work is the saving of souls, the speedy conquest of the whole world for Christ, incomparably greater than all other human enterprises.

In order to the accomplishment of this there is needed an awakened sense of responsibility, leading to new devotion, such as the professional preacher has never dreamed of, and resulting in spiritual efforts and enterprises such as the most consecrated has not thought to be within the reach of possibility.

1. Quickened Sense of Responsibility.

The world too often makes mock of the lack of devotion in the ministry of the day. It is justified in doing so. It is a fact established by history that, from time to time the ministry, along with the Church, falls into spiritual decline, needs to be roused anew to a sense of its solemn mission. From time to time God sends his special messengers to rouse them anew. So Gildas came to our forefathers in Britain, in the fifth and sixth centuries; so Wyclif, in the fourteenth century; so John Knox, in the sixteenth; so Baxter and Owen and Bunyan, in the seventeenth; so Whitefield and Wesley and Edwards and Brainerd, in the eighteenth; and so came the noble men, who pushed the revival and Bible and mission work at the beginning of the present century, and who have been its later representatives, the Paysons and Judsons and Duffs and Livingstones. So now there is a pressing need of some messenger of God to awaken and renew a sense of the preacher's responsibility.

In 1651 the Church of Scotland, feeling in regard to her ministers "how deep their hand was in the transgression, and that ministers had no small occasion to the drawing on of the judgments that were upon the land," drew up what was called a complete account of the sins of the ministry. The document is a searching one, and has been pronounced "one of the fullest, most faithful and impartial confessions of sins ever made."

*Confession of Church of Scotland.*

In his *Words to the Winners of Souls*, Horatius Bonar has called this age to substantially the same confession. The confession comes home to all the ministry. It runs thus:

"We have been unfaithful." "We have been carnal

and unspiritual." "We have been selfish." "We have been slothful." "We have been cold." "We have been timid." "We have been wanting in solemnity." "We have been preaching ourselves, not Christ." "We have used words of man's wisdom." "We have not fully preached a free Gospel." "We have not duly studied the Word and honored the Spirit of God." "We have had little of the mind of Christ."

These are confessions drawn from the communion of the mightiest souls with God—the confessions of Archbishop Usher and Jonathan Edwards and Rowland Hill, of Howe and Baxter and Brainerd and Payson, yea, of Paul and Augustine. How much more then should the rest of us make them, with our faces in the dust before God!

There is need of a new life in the ministry, if the preacher is to command the respect of this godless, scoffing age, and to have power with it. There is call for the renunciation of self and the putting on of Christ. There is demand for a singleness of purpose, a consecration to God, a spiritual faith, a self-denial for Christ, such as we of this age have, it is to be feared, scarcely yet a faint conception of. It is recorded that, when the people of Collatia were stipulating about their surrender to the authority and protection of Rome, they were asked: "Do you deliver up yourselves and the Collatine people, your city, your fields, your water, your bounds, your temples, your utensils, all things that are yours, both human and divine, into the hand of the people of Rome?" and when they replied: "We deliver up all," they were received.

God makes loud demand, in this age, for such complete surrender and entire consecration of every Christian; but he most imperatively makes that demand of every one whom he calls into that new order of the ministry that, from this time forth, should be the only order—the *wholly consecrated ministry.* When the prophet was calling Israel to repentance, God commanded him to cry: "Wo be unto the pastors that destroy and scatter the sheep of my pastures."\* Will there not be ten thousand woes for such teachers, living on these heights of time? It is true always, and especially true to-day, that an unconsecrated, worldly, lukewarm, faithless ministry is the worst of blights and curses to the Church!

<small>God's Call to Consecration.</small>

Who does not agree with Bonar, concerning the need for the infusion of new life into the ministry? This he voices, when he says, that this

<small>"ought to be the object of more direct and special effort, as well as of more united and fervent prayer. To the students, and preachers, the ministers of the Christian Church, the prayers of Christians ought more largely to be directed. It is a living ministry that our country needs, and without such a ministry it can not long expect to escape the judgments of God. We need men that will spend and be spent—that will labor and pray—that will watch and wait for souls."†</small>

Nothing but such new life will give the preacher the tremendous power needed for the work of God, in overtaking this whirling, business-driven, materialistic, self-indulgent world.

There is need, too, of such a sublime enthusiasm and holy boldness for God as will lead the preacher to throw himself into his work with all his powers, and make him speak out for God just what needs to be spoken to check the tide of evil and to win victory for the Kingdom of God.

<small>2. Sublime Enthusiasm and Holy Boldness.</small>

\* Jeremiah xxiii. i.    † *Words to the Winners of Souls.*

We have had too much of half-hearted, selfish, ill-directed work, or rather, *play*. The man who is called of God, guided of God, sent of God to speak for God, and upon whom the destiny of the world hangs—what manner of man should he be? Verily, an intense divine enthusiasm ought to fill his soul. Half-hearted work can never succeed, where the preacher has all the forces of nature, and all the adverse forces of his own being and of society, to contend with, master, and turn to account—can never succeed with the world, the flesh, and the devil all combined against him. One who saw Michelangelo engaged at his work, says that he wrought with fearful energy and earnestness, and accomplished many times as much as other men. Every stroke was so with all his soul that the observer, as he saw the huge fragments fly from the rapid blows, trembled lest the statue should be ruined. But the enthusiastic worker held ceaselessly on, cutting and filing, until the once shapeless block took shape and polish and beauty, and stood forth the finished work of his hand, his brain, his soul, his life, and the perfect embodiment of his idea. So needs the servant of God to work for God, in the greater task assigned him, with a boundless enthusiasm, and with all his mind, heart, soul, and strength.

And he should speak for God, with the holy boldness of one who fears Him only who can cast both soul and body into hell; he should speak out to the Church and the world, to the unbelief and covetousness and lawlessness of this age, just the Word of God that is needed. With divine authority he should convict men of the criminal unbelief that is entailing spiritual weakness and will bring eternal ruin. With divine authority he should convict them of robbing God of his tithes, in building up personal fortunes and increasing the glitter and vanity of this godless, material civilization, and should show that these terrible financial reverses, that blot out the property of individuals and of the nation, are but the breath of the God who has been robbed, but who will always have his own. With divine authority and fearlessness he should bring home to the conscience of this law-despising and corrupt age God's own holy law, in its grandeur and its strictness, sparing not until men cry out in agony, as they cried out under the message of an Edwards or a Rowland; and should summon them to view the judgment and the awful penalty of sin, until, in terror and remorse and repentance, they flee from their sins and from the wrath to come.

Without this sublime enthusiasm and this holy boldness, the preacher may not expect to be heard and heeded by this sinful and mad world of to-day.

The preacher needs most of all, in that new order of the ministry, for which God calls in his Word and by the signs of the times, an intense earnestness and energy in rescuing souls from the sin that enthralls them, and from the perdition which they are so recklessly daring.

<small>3. Intense Earnestness in Rescuing Souls.</small>

When Francis Xavier was about to depart on his mission to India, his friend Rodriguez, who shared his room in the Hospital at Rome, was awakened by the exclamations of the dreaming man, and heard from his lips the earnest appeal: "Yet more, O my God! yet more!"

Many months afterward, Xavier revealed the vision. He had seen, in his slumber, the wild and terrible future of his career spread out before him. There were barbarous regions, islands, and continents, and mighty empires, which he was to win to his faith. Storms, indeed, swept around him, and hunger and thirst were everywhere, and death in many a fearful form; yet he shrank not back. He was willing to dare the peril, if he could but win the prize. Nay, he yearned for still wider fields of labor, and with an absorbing passion, that filled every faculty, and haunted him even in his slumber, he exclaimed: "Yet more, O my God! yet more!"

That may furnish the preacher of this age a worthy example. Or, rather, he may find a better example still in that three years of Paul's ministry, recorded in the twentieth chapter of the Acts of the Apostles, in view of which he could say to the Ephesian Church, on his departure from it: "Therefore watch, and remember, that by the space of three years I ceased not to warn every one night and day with tears."* That is what is especially needed in the minister of to-day—a mighty yearning for souls that will not let him rest. With that he will preach the Word, expecting results. With that he will find the way open to the godless souls that have been overtaken by the blighting skepticism and secularism. That will make him watch for souls as those who must give account. That will lead to the awakening and quickening of the Church, and to the speedy carrying out of the commission Christ has given the preacher in sending him with his message to a lost world.

These may seem plain and strong words; but nothing less plain and strong will meet the case. God, by his Word and providence, has put his *now* into the commission of the preacher and Church for the conquest of the world. The embattled hosts of sin and

\* Acts xx. 31.

Satan, in fulfilment of prophecy, are gathered in imposing array. Nothing but a Church aroused and quickened and led by such a ministry can hope for speedy victory, or for victory at all. These may seem heaven-high requirements, but they are assuredly not too high for the needs of the hour, and, by help of the grace of God in the gift of the Holy Spirit, not too high to be met by the ministry of whom they are made.

With Christ's requirements understood and Christ's call heeded, there is no reason why the Church, under the leadership of such a ministry, should not carry out the Great Commission in the present generation.

# CHAPTER IV.

## THE PREACHING FOR THESE TIMES.

THE topics already treated—the Commission of the Preacher, his Message, and the Preacher himself, with his Furnishing—have prepared for the consideration of the question: What is the character of the preaching demanded by the times in which we live? The answer must be:

*Direct and effective Gospel preaching for the immediate salvation of a lost world.*

Before that question can be answered intelligently and satisfactorily, there must come in the preliminary inquiries: What are the characteristics of these times? What special influences and forces are at work in the world?

### SECTION FIRST.

**The Times as a Factor in Preaching.**

Clearly everything depends upon the answers to these interrogations. In the grand problem, How is the Gospel to be brought home to men? we are to look upon "the times," as constituting the one variable quantity. Man remains essentially the same—spiritual, immortal, yet sinning and perishing in his rebellion against God. The Gospel remains essentially the same—the Son of God incarnate, obeying, suffering, dying as the sinner's substitute, freely offered of God to man's faith, as the way of salvation. The times, with their influences and circumstances, change daily in slighter degree, and, in the course of generations, often, if not ordinarily, change essentially. While, therefore, acknowledging the sole efficiency of the Holy Spirit, it must yet be admitted, as in accordance with the Divine method, that a message to men, to be heard and heeded of men, must recognize their altered circumstances. In order to make way for the presentation of the true Bible remedy, it, therefore, becomes necessary to ask:

What are some of the practical characteristics of these times that have special bearing upon preaching?

What have been or should be their effects upon the preaching?

I. PRACTICAL CHARACTERISTICS OF THE TIMES.

The trend toward materialism and secularism that has been seen to mark the present age has naturally resulted in certain practical characteristics, running through all our civilization and demanding to be reckoned with specifically in all the theory and practise of the pulpit. It is necessary for the preacher to understand and appreciate the most important of these.

A glance, even the most superficial, can not fail to fix upon the extraordinary activity of what may be **1. Activity of the** called the scientific spirit, as a marked **Scientific Spirit.** feature of this age with its civilization. This activity, in its special modern manifestation, began more than a century ago, in the realm of physical nature. During all this period, until the present day, the process of correcting and defining the ideas of men touching the outer world has gone on with accelerated speed, until, out of the once chaotic mass of fact and truth, order and system have everywhere been evoked, and the domain of science has been extended to the whole sphere of terrestrial existence and to the material aspects of the starry heavens. From the ice-rivers of Greenland to the fiery mountains of the Antarctic Continent—from the grain of sand at one's feet to the nebulæ in the outer depths of space—from the fuchsia that blooms in the greenhouse of to-day to the tree ferns of the geologic periods of a thousand ages gone—science has pushed her investigations, everywhere recording, arranging, classifying, systematizing, until, to the thinking, intelligent man, the world of nature is a different world from what it was to the man of like mind a century ago—different in its rocks and plants, in its clouds and lightnings, and tempests and rainbows—different, in short, in everything, from the mystic dance of the atoms to the sublimer dance of the stars.

Nor has this scientific spirit of the age confined itself exclusively to the physical world; it has overleaped all such bounds and pushed its inquiries into the regions bordering upon the grossly material in which work the forces that have to do with the increase of wealth and the progress of nations, and on into the province of the more subtile spiritual forces that appear in the human soul and in human history—until, in the work of its masters, political economy has almost taken its place among the exact sciences; until, in the hands of such men as Hamilton and Green, McCosh and Mivart, the graver questions of metaphysics and logic, even where not answered, have become as clearly defined in statement as problems in geometry; and until, in the hands of those whose coming we wait, a philosophy of history, already foreshadowed and outlined in the work of Professor Robert Flint\* of Edinburgh, will no longer be reckoned among the impossibilities.

As this work of the century in its more palpable forms approached completion, the same processes began to be applied to literature and art. Criticism began striving to take on the scientific form. Men were no longer satisfied with a few empirical rules, reverenced and applied simply because an Aristotle or a Blair, some giant or some pygmy, had pronounced them truth. The power that had accomplished so much in behalf of order in other departments led men, in its workings in this sphere, to conclude, by an iron logic, that every art must have its basis of principles, that may, at least in measure, be ascertained and scientifically arranged, and by which one can judge correctly of its products. As a result, we have had a new class of writings, which the seventeenth century or even the eighteenth could not have produced; comprising, in the field of general literature, the works of such men as Goethe and Schiller, Hazlitt and Coleridge, and the whole line of modern British essayists; and in the field of special art, such elaborate criticisms as those of Hermann Ulrici and Gervinus on the plays of Shakespeare, and the *Modern Painters* and kindred works of John Ruskin.

To the man of intelligence and thought, the world of art is not the same as it was to one of like power of a century ago. Not that great art is at all different now from what it was then; not that a man can be taught now by rule to write a great poem, or paint a great picture, or improvise a sublime song, or extem-

\* *The Philosophy of History in France and Germany.*

porize a masterly oration, any more than a lark can be taught to flap its wings by instruction out of Whewell or the Duke of Argyll, or a nightingale to sing according to the musical grammar of Calcott; not, above everything else, that any other than God can make the great artist, and not that any other than a great artist can produce a grand poem, or painting, or song, or oration; but that, given the great artist, made of God and clothed of him with his mission, there is all this new knowledge to aid him in his work, and, given the man of common sense and culture, with the discerning eye, he has all this knowledge at his command to enable him to study, understand, and give intelligent judgment concerning the artist's great productions. The two men, of the past and of the present, brought side by side, look upon essentially the same thing, but he of the present with different and vastly clearer vision.

This restless scientific activity thus reaches and employs itself in every department of thought. The educated, thinking men in every community are under its dominant influence, and, tho not with the masses the chief molding force, it yet exerts more or less power of restraint and control far down among them. There is, consequently, everywhere a demand, within certain limits, for the philosophic and the artistic in the method and form of whatever aspires to be considered a literary production, before it can gain the attention of men.

As a second feature of the times, one can not but note the rage for novelty that so possesses the masses, and shapes literature, art, and life, in all their departments.

2. The Rage for Novelty.

As a fact, the world, in so far as our knowledge of its occurrences is concerned, is another world from what it was a century since. Then the news came from a region comparatively narrow, traveling at the slow pace of the stage-coach, the mounted post, or the sailing vessel, and was narrowly diffused by a few weekly journals. It furnished but little of the novel to excite men. The progress of science and art has latterly brought the world in its vast regions into intimate intercommunion and union of parts. With steam and electricity at his service, the professional man, the merchant, or the mechanic, has for years been able to read in his daily paper, before breakfast, of all the chief events, and especially every startling event, of the past night, occurring in all Christendom and in a large part of heathendom. Circumstances seem thus providentially arranged, if not to develop, at least to meet, the craving for the new and exciting. But however developed, the fact of such a craving is beyond dispute. It is very marked in the reading of the masses of the present day.

This may well be styled the era of novels, and of base and worthless novels at that. Solid literature does not furnish enough of excitement. All through the range of reading, in papers, magazines, and books, to meet the demands of multitudinous readers, we have the descending scale all the way to the bottom, from the weekly sheet of sensational tales, that, after its brazen manner, insists on pressing its way up into good society, to the despicable page that knows its friends too well to think of any such aim; from the pretentious magazine, that, while seeking to exalt itself to the chief literary seat, scarcely dares to tell the truth lest it should not be new, to the yellow-covered pamphlet that is so irredeemably base as never to attempt anything better

*The Era of Novels.*

than a bald lie; from the portly volume that aspires to a place in the Church library, to the unbound ten-cent sheet, that never comes to the light of day and upon which the eyes of the man of virtue never fall.

The descent began with the portrayal by writers of what was simply worthless, and its endurance and acceptance by readers; it has reached the bottom of the downward grade, in the later portrayals by the artists, of positive error, infidelity, vice, and crime, and their eager acceptance by the public—in such books as *Robert Elsmere*, with its weak rehash of stale infidel objections to the Bible and Christianity, already a thousand times exploded, and never having had any better basis than the shallow conceit of their originators or their virulent hatred of God and vital religion; in such sentimental romance as *Anna Karenina* and its fellows, in which the authors at the same time paint vice in glowing colors and inculcate the destructive principles of anarchism that are sapping the foundations of human society; and in such realistic fiction as that in which M. Zola depicts French vice and licentiousness in such cold-blooded style that, altho the depraved masses run wild over it, it is too gross to admit of the indorsement of his genius by the atheistic French Academy. And so immense has been the deterioration of the moral sense of the Christian public, in connection with this literary descent from mere worthlessness to positive irreligion and vice, that the pulpit and the religious press have not hesitated to be among the most prominent agencies in giving publicity to such productions, and thereby adding vastly to their circulation and power for evil.

Public lectures and amusements have moved in the same direction, until in their downward reach there is scarcely anything, however offensive to sound sense, cultivated taste, correct morals, and right religious feeling, that fails to find a place to exhibit itself and an audience to witness the exhibition, provided only that it be novel. The legitimate culmination has been reached in forms indefensibly vicious, in the latest developments, in nude art, the variety show and ballet dance, and in "living pictures," over which eager crowds gloat.

Nor has this tendency left the religion in the Church untouched and uninfluenced. No thinking man has failed to mark its presence in the work of the Sabbath-school—in changing the character of the instruction, until we hear too little of the solid portions of the Scripture, while pointless stories are often substituted for God's truth; in transforming the addresses, until, in some regions, one who is not equal to Gough as a mimic, to Blondin as a rope-walker, and to Punch as a punster, is hardly thought to be fitted to speak to an audience of children; in metamorphosing the library, until it often happens that there is little left to be read but vapid, so-called religious novels, which, in spite of all their pretensions and of all the puffing of the religious press, are, in fact, in their own essential nature, at war with common sense, morality, and religion, and, in their necessary influence, irretrievably, we had almost said, infinitely bad.

The same spirit has not hesitated to invade and desecrate even the pulpit with its unseemly ways. **Novelty in the Pulpit.** Tradition has it that, at a certain stage in their progress, Dr. Archibald Alexander used to address his classes in Princeton Theological Seminary on the subject of popularity as preachers somewhat on this wise: "Why, young gentlemen, you can be popular as preachers. It's the easiest thing in the world. It does not require any genius, or common sense, or study, or culture. Get access to the columns of the newspaper, and advertise that on Sunday, at the usual hours of service, you will preach standing on your head, and the house will be crowded. It's easy to be popular in that way if you want to be." In the present day one could bring from the Saturday and Sunday dailies of many a city advertisements in which clergymen propose in all soberness to perform for the public entertainment feats quite as absurd as that suggested by the great educator of ministers.

It would need no prophet to predict the results of all this, even were they yet in the far future; and since they are here in the present, it takes no seer to discern what they are. This is not the place to demonstrate what must be the logical result of reading novels only, and only poor ones at that. The man who thinks and reasons for himself knows what it must be. We have come, in fact, upon a public with one of its great elements in such a condition that it has no mental muscle with which to lay hold of truth; cares nothing for the standard English literature; takes no interest in theology or the truth of God, and goes to church, if at all, to be entertained rather than instructed. We have trained up a generation of men by the reading of books filled with pretended facts that are yet contrary to the nature of things, of man and of God—that is controlled by a morality not of God, a religion not of Christ, and a spirit infused of Mammon and Fashion, rather than of the Holy Ghost; and in so training them we have substantially destroyed all taste for that which is true and Christ-like, and almost barred the possibility of their becoming the powerful thinkers and the earnest practical workers that the exigencies of the Church demand for its mission.

The day may not yet have come when the people of God are ready to enter their solemn protest, and to sweep all such trash out of church, Sabbath-school, and family; but it must come sooner or later, for God's government is so ordered that it never suffers a foolish, a base, or an evil thing to perpetuate its existence in his Church forever. But, however that may be, there is no disputing the fact of this morbid tendency to novelty, and that is all that need be contended for now and here. It manifests itself everywhere, reaching to some extent all classes. The cultivated and refined are not wholly free from it; with the masses it is the molding, ruling tendency. We are almost repeating the experience of the old Athenians, in the decline of the Greek nation, in the time of Paul, with whom the one all-absorbing question was: "What is there new?"* It need hardly be said that in consequence of this the demand for the novel, the unusual, the startling, is brought to bear upon everything that aspires to the dignity of literature in its higher artistic forms, and almost made a condition of its gaining access to men.

A third feature of the age, and the last we shall enumerate, is the prevalence of the utilitarian spirit, coexisting with the tendencies already noted. "Cui bono?" is the universal cry. Men hurry—we shall not stop to inquire whether consistently or inconsistently—from their scientific investigations, from their art-worship, and from their novel-reading and sight-seeing, to join in that common cry. This we believe an admitted fact.

3. **The Rage for Utility.**

* Acts xvii. 21.

There is doubtless a true and right noble sense of the word "useful." Ruskin has well affirmed that as man's chief use is to be "the witness of the glory of God, and to advance that glory by his reasonable obedience and resultant happiness, whatever enables him to fulfil this function is in the noblest and truest sense of the word useful to him"; but there is a meaner sense as well. "Things that help us to exist are, in a secondary and mean sense, useful; or rather, if they be looked for alone, they are useless and worse, for it would be better that we should not exist than that we should guiltily disappoint the purposes of existence."* And the present is admitted to be one of those periods when men gravitate toward this lower utility.

Taking up this baser sense of utility, we are ready in this age to ask of everything, What is it worth? Wherein will it aid us? Will it make business easier? Will it help us to run our factories, and dig our canals, and build our railroads, and bridge our rivers, and tunnel our mountains? What will its value be, estimated in "greenbacks" or in gold? Even religion can not escape the influence, tho in its case that influence has doubtless been elevating, in producing a reaction against practical worthlessness. We are acquiring a habit of asking, even of religion, What is its value? Will it make better merchants, scholars, and mechanics? Will it make truer husbands and wives, better sons and daughters, more faithful friends and neighbors, happier homes and communities? What is it as a working power, affecting the business and bosoms of men? What profit is it? Everywhere in everything we may note this third tendency, ruling multitudes and influencing all. It demands and exacts of everything literary, even to the poem and the novel, that it submit to an infusion, in seeming at least, of this demonstrable utility, before it can secure the ear of the great public.

## II. The Results of these Characteristics upon the Preaching of the Present Day.

In any ordinary audience these three tendencies are represented, and a corresponding threefold require-
*Threefold Requirement and Tendency.* ment is consequently made of the ministrations of the pulpit: first, for philosophic and artistic form; secondly, for originality and vividness in presenting God's truth; and thirdly, for an intense practicality. Accordingly, the exactions of this age are undoubtedly greater than any ever before made of God's messengers. Humanly speaking, if a mass of men so constituted is to be reached, molded, and controlled, the canons of art must not be violated; God's plain truth must be made more telling than man's most highly wrought fiction, and the Gospel must somehow be made more deeply and attractively practical than stock speculation, banking, and building, and costly and luxurious eating and living. Admitting and insisting upon the mission of the Holy Ghost, still the appalling demand is enough to make the bravest, who at all appreciates it, quail before it, and declare with that wonderfully gifted preacher, F. W. Robertson, "I would rather lead a forlorn hope than mount the pulpit stairs." Yet he who bears his message in God's name may not shrink from meeting the responsibility, whatever trial or effort it may entail. How, then, shall the task be accomplished?

## THE PREACHING FOR THESE TIMES. 217

If we examine their working-schemes, as distinguished from their rhetorical theories, men, in attempting this task, have made trial of three methods, each of which has been determined by predominant or exclusive regard to some one of the three great tendencies of the times—a regard resulting sometimes from eccentricity of temperament, sometimes from peculiarity in circumstances, and sometimes from defective logic. Sincere and in earnest they have doubtless been in the trial, but the result has been admitted failure, for the simple reason that God's world is so made that no half-truth can win and wield permanent influence over all classes in a community.

Men under the influence of the scientific tendency have reasoned thus : "This is the noblest of these prevailing influences of the age. Special heed to it will give us control over the highest class of hearers. We must bring the masses up to our standpoint, rather than descend to theirs." And so, as one-sided things naturally run into extremes, we have had metaphysical disquisitions, and splendid essays, and prose-poems—often profound and elaborate indeed, but quickening the plain man with no new and telling truth, and making no common heart beat faster by laying magic touch on earnest and noble practical instincts; in short, we have had our gospel of philosophy and esthetics. Its theory may be very fine; but it has swept the masses out of the church by a logic inevitable as fate : "If that be the Gospel, it is incomprehensible and worthless to us; we don't see how it can elevate or save us; we may as well stay at home"—and so they have stayed at home, as the complaints and wails of the day attest. Nor has that been all, for this style of presenting

*1. The Scientific and Esthetic Gospel.*

God's message has weakened the sense of obligation even in the higher classes to whom it has been directed. They have reasoned thus : "If the Gospel be only a beautiful thing, with nothing living and practical, it is not worth much to us"—and so they too have stayed at home.

Another class, under the influence of the thirst for novelty, has made chief or exclusive use of that tendency, in seeking to accomplish the great task of securing and holding the attention of men. "Here is the way"—so they have reasoned—"of reaching the masses, and of saving the most souls; anything is right in so noble a work; we must go down to men and take advantage of everything that is in them." And so again, by the common tendency to extremes, we have had our gospel of "clap-trap" and "twaddle." Religion has thus been made a play, an entertainment, too often a fashionable one, and the church turned into a petty show-house, a theatér, on whose stage the "mysteries and moralities" have been re-enacted. The result has been a very natural one; worldly men prefer good acting to bad, Shakespeare's tragedies and comedies to the poor parson's, and a first-class to a tenth-rate theater,— and so of all other entertainments,—and in the end they have too frequently gone to the genuine playhouse, with its cards, billiards, or theatricals—the playhouse that is such without hypocrisy, tho its doors open into the pit. The gospel of clap-trap has lamentably failed, and men have felt and acted upon, even where they have not acknowledged, its worthlessness; and the movement, from the highest to the lowest, has been away from at least such sanctuaries. The churches in recent times that have most

*2. The Gospel of Sensation.*

notably depended upon it have ultimately gone to pieces, thereby demonstrating the superficial character of their work, as well as the falsity of their principle.

The third class has fallen in with utilitarianism, and come under its sway. They have reasoned: "It matters neither how true, nor how new, nor how beautiful, a thing may be, if it be of no practical value; its practical worth must be clearly seen and laid hold of, and presented most pungently and directly to men." But, as the practical power of God's truth is ordinarily too vast in its workings to be summed up and expressed in figures, and estimated in dollars and cents, the so-called practicality has, from its original one-sidedness, in many cases degenerated into small scolding on subjects of the least possible importance to any human being. And so we have had our gospel of vinegar and wormwood—our Xantippe gospel. Men of taste and culture can not, and will not, long endure this; the novelty-seekers do not care for it; only small gossiping people take an interest in such things—and the tide again turns away from the pews.

*3. The Gospel of Petty Practicality.*

It needs no argument to demonstrate that none of these methods has accomplished, or ever will accomplish, the great task of reaching, swaying, and saving the multitudes in our Christian lands. Each is partial and one-sided in its assumed principle, and nugatory, if not evil, in its results. We must have a working-scheme broad enough to take into account all these forces at once, and that shall at once meet the rightful demands of all three of these prominent tendencies,—while doing vastly more than that. Discourse must in some way be made to conform to the highest principles of art, and yet be neither essay nor poem; to combine novelty with truthfulness, the "things new and old," of Scripture; and to be in the broadest, deepest, truest sense, practical and useful.

Two things render the present a favorable time for the consideration of the problem thus stated, with the view to its correct solution. The first of these is, the extensive agitation of the question, "How shall the masses be brought into the sanctuary, attached to it, and saved?" The Church sees, as it has never seen before, that it is a vital question, one touching her very existence, and she is naturally anxious to reach a true answer. The other favorable feature is, the reaction that has set in against the extreme and one-sided measures that even earnest men have been disposed to try. The gospel of esthetics, the gospel of clap-trap, and the gospel of petty scolding are not the popular things they once were in certain quarters. Common sense, the right Christian feeling, have revolted against them. Sunday-schools that once ran wild over the wares of the quack vender of novelties, now shut out everything of that kind, or meet it, when it is forced upon them, with indignation and loathing. Churches that once delighted in the dispensation of toys and gewgaws, have found these to be very worthless things in the work of building up a permanent congregation and a vigorous and healthy working membership. These two things, we say, indicate that the present is a favorable time for the consideration of the great problem, with the view to its correct solution.

It is equally true that these popular methods do not promise any better results in the direction of the evangelization of the world. Methods that are heathenizing

Christendom can not be depended upon to Christianize heathendom.

It is proposed to consider the problem of effective preaching in its twofold relation: first, to the general state of things at the present time; and secondly, to Christ's present requirement for the immediate evangelization of the world.

## SECTION SECOND.

### The Preaching Required by the General State of Things at the Present Day.

The characteristics of the times being such as already noted, and such being the stage reached in the experiment of solving the great practical problem of the Church, we are prepared to advance a step further in the discussion, and with a view to framing an answer in one degree less general, ask again the question: What is the preaching suited to these determined conditions of the case? The plain answer, which is neither unchristian nor unchurchly, is:

*God's truth, in its practical bearings, must be presented with proper artistic form, and with power, with the grand end of saving and elevating men.*

This answer would, we opine, be found not wholly new, if we could take the sense of the thinking, earnest men of the past and present; and yet we trust that, when unfolded, it will be seen to have enough of the new to meet fully the exigencies of the case. God's truth, in the proper artistic form, will meet the wants of those who have come under the influence of the scientific spirit. God's truth, in its grandeur, properly understood, contains the "things new and old"—*new* no less than *old*—with which the wants of the spirit naturally thirsting for newness must be met. God's truth, in its practical bearings, is widely and intensely practical enough for the most thorough-going of all sound utilitarians. And the one aim, in the elevation and salvation of men, subordinating everything else to itself and God's glory, furnishes the true principle of unity that will bind all together, and make the work single while it is earnest and hopeful.

In passing on to the unfolding of the proposition just laid down, it follows that, if these considerations accord with truth, certain exceedingly important topics need to be presented and emphasized.

### I. A Better Theory of the Art of Oratory Must be Grasped.

There is absolute necessity on the part of the clergy for a more correct, complete, and consistent theory of rhetoric, or the art of oratory.

One may study the laws of eloquence, solely that he may know them, and in this way attain to a *science* of the subject ; or for the purpose of applying them to any particular product of art that he may estimate it, and in this way acquire a knowledge of the *principles of criticism;* or for the purpose of instruction, development, and guidance, in attaining skill in public speaking, and in this way become master of the subject as *art.* The demand made upon the preacher can not be properly complied with without a thorough command of rhetoric in all these relations. Assuredly he ought to have a thorough mastery of the means, the forces, and the principles involved in his sublime work, as well as how they are to be applied, both in criticism and in production.

It is our firm belief that, other things being equal, a man's success, in any sphere, is, under God, in exact proportion to the correctness of the theory by which he carries forward his work; and we base our judgment on faith in that justice of the divine government, by virtue of which it is always found on the side of the right, whether it be the right in method or in action. Nor would we hesitate to make strictest application of this rule to the work of the ministry. A God of order can not delight in disorder in the highest mission assigned to man. Other things being equal, a man's success in the ministry is in exact proportion to the correctness and completeness of his working-theory. What am I to do? How, and with what am I to do it? are thus vital questions for one sent with a message from God to men. God will never fail to do his part; it is man's to see to it that his be done the best possible.

(I) Prevailing Theories and No Theories.

Leaving out of view those among the clergy who have been led to entertain intelligent and right views of the art of oratory, the remainder naturally fall into two classes: first, those who have no theory at all on the subject, and, secondly, those who hold only partial theories. Of these in their order.

It requires not even a discerning eye to advise one of the fact that there are numbers among the clergy who have no theory whatever on the important subject of their mission as God's mouthpieces in the world.

<small>1. Advocates of No Theory.</small>

Any one can recall those of his own acquaintance who scoff at all such theories when out of the pulpit, and violate everything that could be rightly embodied in them when in the pulpit. And, in self-defense, they are always resurrecting the old and senseless objections to art and the knowledge of it, that they may confront the advocates of right method with their ghosts. The familiar words of even so distinguished a man as Lord Macaulay, running in a line with the opinions of these objectors, will doubtless occur to any one at all familiar with our English literature. We refer to the passage in his critique on Bacon, in which he rails at rhetoric, logic, and grammar. Macaulay's practise is the best refutation of his theory, for in all his writings we find a *studied* adherence to the very principles at which, in this article, he scoffs.

To the class with which we are dealing, art is synonymous with artificial, or artful. They profess to plead for nature. "I must be natural—must speak out and act out my own nature." "But you are rude in manner, awkward in gesture, rough in style, harsh in voice. You ought to practise elocution, and to seek to polish your style." "But it is my own natural self. God has made me so, and I must act out myself." And thus the man deliberately persists in uttering what is at once a libel upon his nature and his God,—for he is not at all as God made him, but as man has unmade him,—and what he calls his "own natural self" is most horridly and indefensibly unnatural.

Such objections are shorn of all their force to one who has caught even a glimpse of the simple truth—that all perfect art, if not nature, is yet like and consistent with her; and who has come but to suspect that all imperfect art, so far as true, aims at this likeness and consistency. To him everything that falls short of the full likeness and consistency, is, in so far, unnatural and wrong. He finds that the principles of the highest art are merely the interpretation of the plain facts of nature. It is just by the interpretation of the facts of nature that the true, thinking man, of clear views, comes by his theory of sacred eloquence, and he therefore knows it can be neither artificial nor unnatural. The essential phenomena are before him at the outset. A right theory must take into account and embody all these facts. If, in striving to do this, he adds anything to nature, the result is inconsistency; if from nature he subtracts anything, incompleteness. He is so far true as he adheres to nature. The thing is so simple that shallow talk about being "artificial" and "unnatural" can not shake his faith in the slightest.

As we come now to judge of partial theories, held by the second class, above-mentioned, there is need that we pause a moment to contemplate those facts of eloquence of which we have spoken as patent to all, and to interpret them, in order that we may have the correct and complete as a standard by which to try the incorrect and incomplete. *2. Advocates of Partial Theories.*

In sacred eloquence we have before us a soul, in the concrete fulness of its powers and functions, possessed by God's truth and Spirit, expressing itself by means of appropriate language, to move and save other souls constituted like itself. There is first, and on either side, a soul, in the fulness of its powers, *i. e.*, mind, heart, will, taste, conscience—all these. A soul expressing itself, or a soul moved, involves all of these. Then this soul is under the controlling influence of God's truth and Spirit. That lifts its activity out of the sphere of the purely human and natural, and makes the man a divine messenger. Then there is the fit instrument of expression, appropriate language, articulate and inarticulate, including speech, tone, look, gesture, in short, whatever in the orator aids expression. And, lastly, the one grand aim, to move and save souls.

These are the facts, as any one may read them for himself. Theories of pulpit eloquence that fail to take into account any of these facts must be partial, one-sided, so far wrong. The test is simple; let us try some of them.

"Preaching," says one, "is the presentation of theological truth!" If in his practise he holds firmly and consistently to his theory, in its ordinary acceptation, a sermon with him becomes a theological essay. He evidently has a truth in his scheme, but it is only a partial truth, not even a half-truth. He has omitted the essential aim of preaching, forgotten the Divine commission, and somehow substituted an intellect for a soul. Perhaps, if he ever suspected man possessed of heart, will, taste, and conscience, he has summarily reached the conclusion that these are never affected except through cold, logical presentations of truth to the understanding, and that they have no reciprocating or reacting power. And by the phrase, "presentation of truth," such theorists too often mean, simply putting it into logical and grammatical formulas, that are intelligible to the speaker himself, and to educated, thinking men, but either unintelligible or forceless to the plain man. To them *expression* exhausts the meaning of their theory.

(1) **Presentation of Theological Truth.**

We protest that expression is not the whole of oratory. The expression of truth characterizes science and philosophy, and the expression of esthetic truth, the fine arts; but oratory is set apart from both these by the fact that it not only expresses but *transfers* truth. Before the preacher has fulfilled his mission, the theological truth must be put in fit words; into these must be breathed the quickening power of right feeling, deep moral purpose, and intense spirituality; and then this living whole must be pressed home with all the art and force of outward eloquence until that truth of God, in its clearness, completeness, warmth, and life, is left lodged in the heart of the hearer. The actual transfer of God's truth to other souls is essential to a proper oratorical presentation, and every effort that falls short of this is, so far as the highest aim of oratory is concerned, a failure.

And yet, narrow as is this view that is satisfied with mere expression in language, it is amazing to how large an extent it is the working-theory in the pulpit. We once heard a sermon after this pattern, which treated of the whole subject of the future state of God's children, answering the questions: "What is heaven?" "What of heavenly recognition?" etc., etc., quoting three or four poems—the whole discourse occupying precisely twenty minutes! We are certain that the man had never dreamed of one thing that belongs distinctively to the sermon. We grant this an extreme case, but many a discourse is constructed after a like model; and, as is always the case, the mightier the logic of the man who works after such incomplete pattern, the more rigidly does he adhere to it.

The partial truth that gives this view its power over certain minds is that man has an intellect to which the preacher must impart the knowledge of God's Word. An important truth it is admitted to be; the great, we had almost said, fatal error, is in supposing it the whole truth.

Reacting against this view, another class holds that preaching is moving the religious feelings of men by any means whatsoever. If one of this opinion hold firmly by it in his practise, a sermon with him may possibly rise to the dignity of an exhortation. There is evidently some truth in his notion, but only a modicum. Instruction is of the least possible importance in his scheme. God's Word is of no worth where a good story or a telling gesture will compass his end better. In place of a soul, in all the fulness of its powers, he puts the emotional part of man's nature, and that often not the heart in its entireness embracing those states of feeling that may be as lasting as the soul itself; but the fitful, fleeting passions of a moment, neither deep enough nor permanent enough to affect the life.

*(2) Awakening the Religious Emotions.*

The writer once listened, for a month or two, to the nightly ministrations of the once notorious Rev. John Newland Maffit, a most admirable illustration of this method. Any one who ever heard him can recall the "start and stare theatric," the moving sentimental story, the thousand little nothings in style and voice and gesture, fitted and intended to rouse the feelings of his audience; and any one who ever watched the progress of his plot to its dénouement, will readily recognize in him a complete specimen of the man who thinks it to be his mission to move the religious feelings by any means whatever.

The truth that gives this theory all its power is that

man has a heart that is to be moved and affected; the great and almost fatal error is in supposing that this is all.

Passing over the multitudinous variations of opinion, each of which has its truth, great or little, as the case may be, we find one thing more deserving special notice— the theory that no definite rules or principles are needed by the pulpit orator. *3. Freedom Requires Avoidance of Rules.*

It may appear inconsistent to call such a view a theory, when, on its very face, it professes to discard all theories. Nevertheless, it does, in fact, seek to make a theory of its no-theory. We have seen elaborate articles in the "Quarterlies" advocating it. "Let us have freedom for genius," is its cry. "Away with your formal divisions; they hamper us!" "Down with your formal rules; man is a law to himself!" "Out with your stereotyped forms; they are the dead letter that killeth!" "Give us the largest liberty!"

Unfortunately, it is seldom genius that utters the cry; ordinarily it is mediocrity—sometimes honest, industrious mediocrity, but mediocrity still. If it be a man of mark, it is ordinarily raised in reference to something of which he knows but little. A generation ago the literary world had, in another department, an illustration of the truth of these affirmations, in the Dean of Canterbury's absolution of himself from the shackles of grammatical rules, while undertaking to be an authoritive teacher of the "Queen's English." "The Dean's English," and various other brochures, demonstrated that no one had more need than Dean Alford himself to be taught these rules, and to be guided in the practise of them. This is but one case of the million.

And yet there is a value in this view, if it be considered as a reaction against a cold, rigid, dead formality, with which too many are familiar.  It has its admitted truth, that freedom is necessary to power; but it forgets that it is only a freedom under and in accordance with God's laws.  The Divine government, in every sphere, gives room for the largest freedom that is consistent with the good of the creature.  Man is a free being, tho gravitation binds him down to the earth; and one may well doubt if he would be any freer, or any better off, if there were in some way given him the power to run up the sky against gravitation.

If there is one thing evident to a thinking man, it is that freedom of discourse can never be reached by casting away the experience of ages, defying all the principles found in human nature, and running counter to all the laws of God's world.  In truth, such freedom and variety can only be secured when working under a system of rules as broad and complete as the facts of nature which center in eloquence.  These principles will always admit and prepare the way for perfect freedom and infinite variety, with the same ease with which a few ultimate chemical elements prepare for the variety of that vast realm of nature in which the great Maker never repeats himself.  It is not the sermon, but the man, that becomes stereotyped; and no taking of divisions out of the sermon will remedy that. What is needed is not freedom from rules, but freedom under rules; and this only comes by those ways, so hard to human nature—by agony of soul and sweat of brow; or, to express it in less formidable, because more familiar and less weighed phrase, which yet at bottom contains the same terrible meaning—by knowledge and practise.  Freedom without rule, at the first license, becomes, in its progress, the dullest of formality, and ends in the unhelpful liberty of the sweeping dust—utter dissolution.

(II) CORRECT THEORY EMPHASIZED AND UNFOLDED.

Such a survey of the field we have been traversing, with the application of the proper test to these partial theories, has prepared for the reaffirmation, with increased emphasis, of the necessity for a thorough knowledge, on the part of the pulpit orator, both of what is to be done by him and how it is to be done; or, in other words, of the absolute need of a more correct, complete, and consistent theory of sacred eloquence.

Taking into account all the elements properly entering into the discussion—the shortcomings of the theories and the practical evil resulting from them; the necessity of right views in order to the most successful work; the state of science and art to which the century has brought us; the imperative demand made, by the thinking and cultivated portion of society, for artistic excellence in the presentation of God's truth—the need that has been affirmed must, we think, be admitted. The principles at the foundation of this conclusion are simple. If a mechanic, working blindly, can not do worthy work, then an artist, in the sublimest of arts, can not blindly do noble work. Give him the light of true principle for his guidance. If a theory, right in its principles, is inevitably wrong in its operations, then let no man, in the highest sphere of effort, where every word is trembling with destinies immortal, attempt to deliver God's message with such a theory. Let him right the wrong. If the progress of science has made an art of oratory possible, then let not him who is sent to be an orator for Christ think to work acceptably to the Master, or successfully, without systematic knowledge of it. Give him all that may be known, to use in his great mission. If there is a right and sure method of reaching, holding, and swaying the thinking, educated men of the country by the truth of God, let no messenger of God scoff at or neglect that method. Give him the mastery of it. By rightly becoming "all things to all men," some will assuredly be saved. It is preeminently the duty of the preacher, in these times, to fail not to ascertain, at the outset, the correct method of doing God's work. He will honor just that, and, other things being equal, crown it, alone and above all, with the largest and most notable success.

A complete and consistent working-theory on this subject, such as the preacher needs, must embrace certain fundamental principles that he should understand clearly and formulate carefully, if they are to be of the utmost service to him in his preaching.

<small>Elements of Correct Working-Theory.</small>

These principles need to be the more carefully considered, because of the false and superficial views of rhetoric and oratory that have been so long in vogue. The shallow platitudes and empirical rules of the Blair school of rhetoric seem to have shaped, to a very large extent, the views of rhetoric in the public school and the university, and of the homiletics of the theological seminaries. Until the preacher is absolutely set free from the trammels imposed by this artificial system, he must attain to pulpit power, if at all, in spite of the instructions and so-called principles given him for his guidance. Hence, the importance of special attention to this subject.

In considering how truth, especially Gospel and saving truth, is rationally to be communicated to men, so as to affect and transform them, it is necessary to fix upon the practical ideas in man and the rhetorical and oratorical principles by which men are to be reached. These suggest the questions that are to be asked and answered in order to construct the right working-theory of preaching as an art.

What are the practical ideas in man, to which appeal must be made and through which the truth is to be brought to bear upon the soul? There are multitudes who apparently have never learned that there are any such ideas. 1. Practical Ideas in Man.

One reason why much of the presentation of truth is powerless is, no doubt, because it awakens no interest in the one who hears it. Unless there is something in the soul of man to which the truth appeals, it might be just as well not to present it at all. Unless there is something in the soul to which to attach the truth in such a way as to lead to action, it will certainly be vain to attempt to present it to that soul. If the hearer were a mere intellectual machine, without emotional or practical capacities or ideas, it would be vain to hope for his enlightenment or salvation through the Gospel. On the other hand, if he who presents the truth has no knowledge, or no clear knowledge, of what those capacities and ideas are—so that he can not intelligently bring the truth into connection with its natural and rational points of attachment in the man—if he accomplishes anything by the way of enlightenment or salvation, it will be by sheer accident. The great importance of gaining a clear knowledge of these practical ideas is thus made manifest.

So far as we are aware, there is but one clear and

adequate presentation of these ideas—that made by Dr. Francis Theremin of Berlin, and translated by the late Dr. William G. T. Shedd, with an Introductory Essay, in the little book entitled *Eloquence a Virtue; or, Outlines of a Systematic Rhetoric.* This book is the abstract presentation of those ideas. Later in life, Dr. Theremin published a companion volume, entitled *Demosthenes und Massillon,* which has not been translated, in which he presents these principles in concrete shape, or as embodied in the orations of Demosthenes and the sermons of Massillon.

The fundamental practical idea is that of *truth.* It is assumed that man has a natural interest in truth; an **Practical Idea of Truth.** interest that, in its abnormal development, leads to curiosity, and, in its normal, to scientific investigation and research. That which is presented to man as truth, so far as it is appreciated as such, interests him. The appeal of the orator or preacher, from the purely rational point of view, is an appeal to this practical idea of *truth.* But even if man were in an ideal intellectual and moral condition, appeals to truth would still be insufficient. Much more, evidently, must this be the case with man as he is, often stupefied by ignorance and blinded by sin. Other and more distinctively practical ideas must come in to supplement that of truth.

The practical idea to which appeal is perhaps most universally made is that of *happiness.* It may be **Practical Idea of Happiness.** assumed that every man desires happiness, or, at least, desires to avoid its opposite; and that men will act and act energetically to secure happiness or to avoid unhappiness. This is one of the powerful motive-principles in man; indeed the most powerful of these principles in man regarded from the animal and selfish side of his nature. That which promises to secure or to increase man's happiness is, therefore, of peculiar interest to him; moves and rouses him to action. The truth, the scheme of conduct, or the call to action, that appeals to this practical idea, may be expected to lead man to accept the view, pursue the course, or perform the action to which these considerations invite him, in order to secure the happiness which his nature craves.

But happiness is not one of the higher and nobler ideas. It has nothing in it that leads to the ideal. It has nothing in it that is morally or essentially elevating. The idea of *virtue*, or *perfection*, comes in to supplement those of truth and happiness. *(Practical Idea of Perfection.)* It assumes that man desires the perfect, according to his idea of perfection, which may be either good or bad, and which may have reference to either the animal, the intellectual, or the spiritual. In connection with this a man's ideal is high or low, according as his character is high or low, or his views high or low.

But even the pursuit of the ideal, or of perfection, may be merely selfish. The culture-theories lift men into egoism and indifference to the needs of humanity, and may lead them *(Practical Idea of Duty.)* only to supreme vanity and supercilious airs. It needs the idea of *duty* to supplement it with the grip of eternal obligation, and to take the man outside of and above himself. This, when one has been bound to Christ by the obligations of his redemption and the power of an endless life, becomes the supreme and all-controlling principle, taking in and subsidizing in the Christian life, faith, hope, and love, all directed toward him who is the way, the truth, and the life.

These are the great practical points of attachment for the truth, in its work of transforming character and life, as that truth reaches man in the preacher's message, emphasized by "the still, small voice," of the Spirit of God.

But what are the principles and rules of rhetorical and oratorical method that must govern the preacher, in his presentation of truth to men, if it is to be effective? This question of method is the second of the questions that must be answered by the preacher in arriving at a complete and consistent working-theory of preaching as an art.

**2. Principles of Rhetorical Method.**

Rhetorical method, according to the common notion, is a matter of style. Its essence consists in the "tricks of rhetoric." This is simply a matter of puerilities. If rhetoric has to do only with the manner of saying little or nothing, or little nothings, it is an abomination pure and simple.

A broad theory of rhetorical method must go back to the Aristotelian idea and analysis, and make the *what* of discourse the basis and end of the *how*. It must take in *invention*, which has to do with the furnishing of thought, in kind and form suited for discourse; and *style*, which has to do with the manner of molding that thought in suitable forms of speech; and it must make full note of the fact that the latter is strictly and wholly subordinate to the former.

The *Rhetoric* of Archbishop Whately, prepared originally as an article for the Encyclopædia Britannica, had the merit of restoring *invention*, as a part of rhetoric, to its rightful place; and of going back again to the old and complete Aristotelian analysis of the subject, after it has been overlaid by the shallownesses of Boileau and Blair and all the rest of their kind. It made rhetoric a matter of *brains* once more, after it had been so long a matter of mere *breath;* but Whately's attempt was encyclopedic, rather than scientific, and so of comparatively little value except as a reminder of a better way, and an index pointing along that way.

Of all the works that have been inspired by Whately, one of the most complete with which we are acquainted —and the one that presents the principles and rules of rhetorical method in the best logical and scientific form, for the preacher's use—is the *Art of Discourse,* by the late Dr. Henry N. Day of New Haven. It presents a complete working-scheme of the subject, which a writer or speaker, when once he has grasped it, can carry into and apply with ease to any department of discourse or of public speaking with which he may have to do.

Under "Invention," the work unfolds with wonderful precision the various processes by which truth, in its practical bearing, may be mediated to the human mind. First, comes "Explanation," by which the speaker, appealing to the intellect of the hearer, gives him a new conception of truth or beauty or goodness, or removes or modifies an old and dominant conception. Its methods embrace narration, description, division, partition, exemplification, and comparison and contrast. Secondly, comes "Confirmation," by which, appealing still to the intellect, the speaker leads his hearer to a new judgment regarding truth, beauty, or goodness, or removes or modifies one already dominant in the mind. The treatment embraces the entire doctrine of proof, in its positive and negative forms. Thirdly, comes

*Principles and Processes of Invention.*

"Excitation," by which, appealing to the emotional nature, the speaker seeks to rouse the feelings of his hearer toward some form of truth, beauty, or goodness, or to remove or modify some already prevailing feeling. The treatment presents the various forms of moving the feelings, as by pathetic explanation, by appeal to sympathy, etc. Lastly, comes "Persuasion," by which, appealing to the will, the speaker brings to bear reasons and motives, to rouse to some new choice or purpose or action, in view of the true, the beautiful, or the good, or endeavors to remove or dissuade from, some dominant choice or purpose or habitual mode of action.

Under "Style," with equal breadth of thought and vision, the work unfolds the properties of style. Beginning with the "Absolute Properties," or those that rise out of the very nature of style, as making use of language, it presents the entire range of oral, suggestive, and grammatical properties, as they are nowhere else presented. Proceeding to the "Relative Properties," or those that rise out of the nature of style, as related to the speaker or to the hearer, it presents the relative subjective properties, embracing significance, naturalness, and coherence; and the relative objective properties, embracing clearness, energy, and beauty.

*Principles and Essentials of Style.*

It would probably be difficult to find, anywhere else, in any language, so compendious and helpful a view of this old art, for the preacher's use in training himself for his work and directing himself in it; and it is believed that this is the unanimous judgment of the strong and solid thinkers and writers who have made the acquaintance of the book and mastered its principles.

It must not be forgotten, however, that the knowledge of the practical ideas, and of the scientific method of rhetoric, is not enough to give a public speaker power of the highest order with men. There must be a *man* back of all these, a soul conscious of a worthy mission and message and inspired by these, before the working-theory can be wrought by effectively. It used to be said that "the orator must be a good man." It is manifest that this, in its literal sense, is not in accordance with fact; but if "good man" is used in the sense of "possessed of large manhood," the meaning intended is true and valuable. Sincerity, at least for the time being, the successful speaker should have, so that he is able to throw his whole soul into his subject, with which he is heartily in sympathy—if he is to carry with him his audience to any permanent conclusion. This is most true in the case of the preacher. He, of all men, needs to be absolutely true and sincere, if his instruction or persuasion is to be of a permanent character. We have known various preachers, noted for power in producing an immediate popular effect, whose lives contradicted and neutralized their preaching; and we have found the religious results in these cases to be neither good nor permanent. There must be, then, as has just been said, a true and sincere Christian soul, possessed with its message of truth and grace, back of all the knowledge of principles and method, to give to the preacher real power, and to enable him to secure permanent spiritual results in the saving of men.

**3. Force of True Manhood.**

Too great stress can hardly be laid upon this requirement of a correct working-theory of preaching as an art, if the preacher is to be able intelligently to aim at and secure the best results.

## II. The Practise must be Conformed to the Correct Theory.

In accordance with the general answer already given to the question under consideration, the practise of the pulpit must be conformed to right theory, and to the wants of the times, so as to present God's truth to men, in its practical bearings and with freshness and vividness. Consider now *matter* and *manner*, in the respects herein involved, apart from each other, and then glance at the *spirit* of the preacher, that must help to consecrate both matter and manner.

### (I) In the Matter of Preaching.

The matter of the preaching for these times must be, at the foundation, God's truth in its great practical bearings on the actual relations of men in life.

God's truth first of all and fundamentally. It is admitted that the methods of one age are never precisely suited to the needs of another; but the great essential truths of God's Word, in their relations to man's necessities, are unchangeable.

*1. God's Truth First and Fundamental.*

We, therefore, confess to no sympathy with the tendency of Professor Draper and the neologizers of his school, who seem almost desirous, in their profound admiration for the physical sciences, to substitute the truth of nature for the truth of God's Word, in the training of the theological seminary and in the deliverances of the pulpit. It is true that, in order to be best fitted for any great mission, a man should have attained to that kind and degree of culture that will insure to him right and complete views of every department in nature, as well as in art, and in the higher sphere of theology; but that is farthest possible from justifying the claims advanced by the professor, in *The Future Civil Policy of America*, for either the predominance, or the exclusive use of, the physical sciences, in even the preliminary training of the clergy. We protest against such a view, and, while we humbly bow before him in his own department, fearlessly affirm the incapacity of Professor Draper or any other student of mere physical science, to decide what is the need of the clergy, and to mark out the course by which they must be prepared for their work. It is high time that when such men as Tyndall, Huxley, and Spencer give forth ex-cathedra utterances on subjects of which they are utterly and hopelessly ignorant—subjects entirely beyond the range of their own departments of thought—that such utterance should be given just the weight that properly belongs to them—*i. e.*, *none at all.*

We base our protest, first, upon natural unfitness; for, as a general rule, no mere mathematician or scientist is capable of forming a correct judgment concerning the great issues of the higher world of spirit. The constant repetition of the intellectual process involved in the reasoning with necessary truth, that $2+2+2=6$, or that the known and measured forces $a+b+c=d$, does not prepare a mind for moving with ease and certainty in that region where, in dealing with contingent truth, the spiritual forces combining the known and measured with the unknown and unmeasured, give us $a+x+y+\text{etc.}=z$.

We base our protest, secondly, on evident prejudice and want of knowledge in the premises, as incapacitating Professor Draper, for no one who could write one sentence that occurs in the book above referred to (p. 277), and which we quote, can pretend to have mastered the facts requisite for the formation of a judgment in such a matter. Speaking of the opposition of the leaders in religion to science, Professor Draper says :

"The result of this condition of things is that many of the most important, the most powerful and exact branches of human knowledge, have been forced into a position they never would have voluntarily assumed, and have been compelled to put themselves on their defense. Astronomy, in the case of the globular form of the earth and its position as a subordinate planet ; geology, as respects its vast antiquity ; zoology, on the problem of the origin of species ; chemistry, on the unchangeability of matter and the indestructibility of force."

We submit, that when both are rightly understood, there is no conflict between the doctrines of religion and the results of the investigation of true science. The same essential narrowness is manifest in this passage, as was exhibited at a later day, in the professor's confident belief that his *Conflict of Science and Religion* was destined to give the death-blow to the religion of the Bible!

The truth of science has its value, which we would by no means underrate, and we hail all knowledge of it as a gift of God; but nature has no revelation of salvation to make to sinners ; that, the one thing essential, is supernatural. If the Church of God has one living conviction, it is this : that nothing but the revealed truth of God's Word can save men. God himself affirms as much. God's truth, then, first of all, and above all.

And yet, guarding against another extreme, we are far from having anything like full sympathy with that tendency of mind that would reduce God's Word, as presented from the pulpit, to lifeless intellectual theory or dry abstraction.

2. God's Truth in Practical Relations.

The Bible is an intensely practical book. There are certain great questions that no thinking man can fail to ask himself—Whence am I? Upon whom can I depend? Whence the evil in the world? Is there any way of escape? What is that way? Guizot—in his *Meditations on Christianity*, in demonstrating that the Bible, in its doctrines of creation, providence, original sin, incarnation, and redemption, furnishes the only correct and satisfying answer to these questions—has at the same time brought out the essence of God's Word, and shown how prominent a thing is its perfect adaptation to our human wants. These questions have to do, principally, not with man's imaginations, not with his logic, good or bad, not with his taste, rude or cultivated; but with life and death. The Bible appeals to practical instincts, is adapted to practical needs, proposes to meet practical issues, puts its truth in concrete, practical shapes. Preaching that does not appeal to such practical instincts, that does not supply such pressing needs, that does not meet such living issues, that does not put itself in such direct and forceful shape, can not be according to the standard of God's Word. Its truth is no dead orthodoxy, but a living and life-giving thing. Not abstract, didactic theology, but God's truth, as the Bible presents it, must be the matter of the pulpit in these days. The preacher who is satisfied with the bald statement, and theological or Scriptural demonstration of a doctrine, closed up with, "this is an important truth," is not fulfilling his mission. His hearers would probably admit all that beforehand. But "science, falsely so-called," and reason, better called unreason, we admit have their cavils and objections, and these are real troubles to that hearer; and it is to meet these that he seeks aid from the pulpit. If it afford it not, it leaves him to grope on in the dark. Didactic theology is, so to speak, the skeleton, that must be clothed with living tissues, and have infused the vital fluids, and inbreathed the breath of God, before it can be a power in our world. The rightful demands of men, and of a correct theory of oratory, can only be satisfied by God's truth in its practical bearings.

But there is need of a more specific statement in unfolding what is meant by this. The aim of gospel preaching is usually stated to be "the saving of sinners and the edification of saints." As these are only different aspects of the one work of salvation, and as both are accomplished through the instrumentality of substantially the same truth, the statement may be properly varied, provided the essence of the matter be retained. It may be rightly said, then, that the aim of the message of the servant of God is to lead to the conversion of men, to develop Christian activity, and to direct the Christian work in the divinely constituted relations of the world in which it must be carried on— and it may be taken for granted that, in order to adapt itself to this aim, the appropriate message from God must be directed to the soul, from that side from which it is possible, humanly speaking, to move it. The preaching for this practical age must take into special account all these things; and, so far as the tendency to practicalness is concerned, the success of the pulpit will depend upon giving wise heed to them.

It becomes evident at once that, while all revealed truth is to be proclaimed to men, according to the proportion of faith, there are yet, so to speak, certain centers of crystallization about which that truth gathers, and in subordination to which it is to be set forth if it is to be effective.

The first aim of the Gospel is to lead to the conversion of men, or to lead to faith in the Lord Jesus Christ. The preaching that, under God, is to attain this end, must, therefore, first of all and chiefly, present the grand converting doctrine of God's word, "Christ crucified." Salvation is by belief in the Lord Jesus, and reliance upon him, not as a teacher, not as a sufferer, not as a martyr, but as the divinely appointed and divine-human substitute for sinners. Take this doctrine out of the Bible, and all that is distinctive, all that is fundamental, all that is saving, is gone. It is not merely some abstract conception of the perfection of the Savior's character, or of the beauty of his life, or of the sublimity of his teachings, or of the glory of the throne to which he is exalted as Mediator—not any or all of these, that it pleases the Holy Ghost to use chiefly in the conversion of sinners. Christ dying for our sins is the converting doctrine of the Gospel, and while all the rest must be preached, it must be with constant reference to this, and with constant aim to impress this. All this must be preached in this, and this in all. The being and nature of God and the lost condition of man are to be unfolded; the law is to be preached in all its length and breadth, and with all its terrors, and every possible motive to be plied—but this with the view of bringing the sinner to a sense of his need of Christ, and to acceptance of him.  Christ crucified for the sinner, and presented with a view to his salvation, is thus the first center of crystallization.

But the Christian is to become a worker for God, or, as Scripture has it, a co-worker with him.  To lead him to this is the second aim of the preacher.  In all true and complete religious development, Christianity must appear not only as a saving doctrine, but also as an active life.  In an age preeminently demanding action, with dead churches all around them, it should need no argument to convince the leading men that special attention must be directed to this phase of religious culture.  The question, How shall men be converted to God? is not more intensely practical than the question, How shall the energies of the Christian Church be brought out and gathered up, and directed most powerfully and efficiently to the great end of the world's salvation?

Now, the logic of Christian living, aside from the power of the Holy Ghost, is eminently simple: "Christ has lived and died for me, therefore I will live and die for him"; or, as Paul puts it, "The love of Christ constraineth us." The doctrine of the cross, as unfolding the heart of God to men, must be preached in such a way as to deepen and call forth this sense of obligation, and lead to that work for want of more of which the generations are perishing.  The ruin of the world; the mission of the Church to save it; the agencies by which this is to be accomplished; right methods of work for the heathen at home and abroad, with the progress and prospects; individual responsibility in the matter must be constantly set forth, and the appeals in view of them made urgent and irresistible by the application of the power of Christ's constraining love, until we have a Church which, by adding works to its faith, shall demonstrate that faith to be living, and not dead. All must be preached in connection with this living faith, and this living faith must be aimed at and sought in all. The doctrine of the cross, in its relations to Christian activity, is thus a second center of crystallization.

But Christian believing and working are to be done in the world as it is in connection with its divinely ordained institutions. There are three great divine institutions—the family, the Church, and the State ; the family and the State as truly of divine ordaining as the Church ; the State appointed to embrace all men; the Church to embrace all Christian men; and the family the kernel of the State and the type of the Church. The Christian is not an abstraction, but a being living in all these relations, and therefore needing direction in them all. God's law—not some human law—reaches and claims supremacy over him in every position he may occupy either in or in relation to these three institutions. *[sidenote: 3. God's Truth in the Great Human Relations. Three Divine Institutions.]*

There is a profound, and, we hold, Scriptural truth bearing on this point, and one to which this generation needs to give special heed, brought out most powerfully by Julius Müller in his *Christian Doctrine of Sin*, in the brief passage in which he insists that man is not a *legislator*, that is a justice-maker or a law-maker in the strict sense; but simply under God, who has himself made the justice and ordained the law, a *law-discerner* and *law-proclaimer*. That truth sweeps away the popular ideas: "man a law to himself"; "the Church a mere voluntary association"; "the people sovereign." God in Christ is the head of all, and God's Word the law of all.

Now, God's Word as the law of conduct is not the rule of some abstract man, but of the man in the family, the Church, and the State. The minister of God is the divinely authorized expounder of the great principles of this law that apply to all these relations and to men in them. It is not simply his privilege conceded by sufferance, but his solemn duty to bring that law to bear in all these aspects, and thus to make God's own Word the molder of sentiment in all the relations of life. We believe that the future progress of salvation in the Church will depend very much upon her recognition and appreciation of this her position and her duty.

The whole tendency of our national history has been toward putting God's messengers and his Word out of their rightful place. Reaction in the early history against much-abused authority has in the end run into impatience of all authority, even that which only aims to check the evil. The assumption of political demagogs, and of pulpit demagogs, just as truly in the interests of evil; the vulgar outcry against preaching the moral and Christian principles that should control politics and statesmanship, and the gross ultraisms of many who assume to be models in this sort of preaching, seemed to finish the work of divorcing the Christian man and preaching from all practical connection with the world, and thus to leave great vital issues to work themselves out with no proper guidance, and to spread ruin, individual, social, ecclesiastical, and national, everywhere.

It is matter of rejoicing that the terrible experience of the past has done much to open the eyes of the clergy, and to rouse them to a sense of their responsibility as God's watchmen and to reinstate them in their true position. The present and the coming years demand the presentation, plain, forcible, constant, such as the past has not known, of the principles of God's Word, applicable to all the relations of life, for after sowing the wind we are reaping the whirlwind : in the family, in new theories of marriage and divorce, of the obedience and service of children, and all that; in the Church, in independency and lawlessness, in the clogging of right work by the multiplication of voluntary associations outside of the Church, and controlled too often by irresponsible and unfit men ; and in the State—God save the State! The principles out of God's Word that furnish practical direction in all these positions in which he is a believer and worker, the Christian must especially have in this age in which the old landmarks are being removed. The law of God in the principles that apply to the social, civil, and ecclesiastical spheres of duty is thus another of the centers of crystallization.

Once more all this truth of God, whether it have in view the conversion of men, the development of Christian activity, or direction in social duty, must be addressed to what are called by Dr. Theremin *the practical ideas*. The truth must somehow be brought into living connection with the soul to which it is directed. Now, as has been seen, by virtue of his constitution, "every man ideally (tho, by reason of his sin, not actually) wills the perfect." "Every man wills the perfect in so far as it is specially determined and conditioned by his peculiar relations; this is the idea of *duty*. Every man wills to be inclined and able to realize the perfect

4. God's Truth to the Practical Ideas.

at all times and everywhere; this is the idea of *virtue*. Every man wills that each and every one of his actions result in a series of internal and external consequences that will render the realization of the perfect ideal easier for him in the future ; this is the idea of *happiness.*" (See *Eloquence a Virtue*, p. 74.)

Here is the side from which, oratorically, man may and must be approached. Show him that a thing is due to his manliness, and you have a friend within. Connect a thing inseparably with his happiness, and you have another answering voice. These times call for powerful addresses to these practical ideas. It is one of the pressing necessities. By departure from it preaching has lost much of its authority as well as much of its power. God's Word, especially as coming from the lips of Christ himself, lays tremendous stress on all of these ideas, even to that one of wo, from which the tremulous delicacy and subtle pride of this age so shrink away. Success will be won in these days only by following the example of Jesus of Nazareth in his plain dealing with the truth on these subjects.

It is an absolute necessity that the preaching of the day should take on more of this practical shape as to **The Present Duty.** its matter. What meets no living need will never reach man; for he is, after all, a practical being, and will never travel very far out of his way for that which can clearly be of no use to him. Speculate and abstract till you take all the soul and life out of God's Word, and he no longer wants it. The mightiest preachers, in moving power, have always taken advantage of the wonderful common sense of the race, and made the most of it; but somehow we of the pulpit, in this day, are slow to believe fallen men endowed with common sense and practicalness.

We have heard the broad statement made from the pulpit, and that by those credited with being thinking men, that the work of the preacher is unlike any other in the world, in that the operation of the principles of cause and effect, and of adaptation of means to end, has no place in it. Against this we plead, not for a rationalizing, much less a rationalistic view, but for a rational one; and we hold that nothing in God's universe is so perfectly adapted to the end designed as that Gospel of Christ which is confessedly the highest revelation of his wisdom.

While God is admitted sovereign, we deem it demonstrable that, in the ordinary administration of that sovereignty, the results of right work, when done in the pulpit, are not as uncertain as men seem to think. The Scriptures read: "He that goeth forth and weepeth, bearing precious seed, shall *doubtless* come again with rejoicing, bringing his sheaves with him."* "Whatsoever a man soweth, that shall he also reap." † With all possible clearness God has presented just what will save the sinner, provided he will comply with the divine conditions. He has done nothing more in any sphere. It would be madness to say that he who has provided redemption at such a cost takes less interest in the saving of souls than in the ordinary work of men. Dependence for the results is here upon the direct and supernatural power of God, secured in his promise to faith; and the man who does not wish to cast away faith will hardly claim that God's promise and direct power are less a dependence than the so-called laws of nature.

The difficulty is that, in our worldly wisdom, we have too often mistaken man, emasculated the Gospel,

* Psalm cxxvi. 6. † Gal. vi. 7.

and distrusted God: mistaken man—foolishly thinking him a fool or a puppet, to be interested by sleight-of-hand performances, rather than a being once made in God's image, and having still intense and earnest gazings upward toward the skies, and ceaseless tho undefined longings for something that he feels to be lacking; emasculated the Gospel—vainly imagining that which appeals to the lower and perishing instincts mightier than that which reaches down after what is enduring and Godlike in him; distrusted God—weakly losing confidence in that way of bearing life to men that he has declared to be the embodiment of his highest wisdom.

One thing that we of this age must learn anew, and in its full significance, is that these practical things, that have to do with the conversion of men, with the growth of Christian activity, and the direction in duty in the world, and that appeal to man's highest instincts, have not yet lost their power. They must be used more constantly and mightily in our preaching, if we are to expect great results in the Master's service. The Gospel is just what man needs; holding this, we need to preach it as if we believed it. Man, by nature, does not appreciate it; admitting this, we yet need to preach it as if he did, for God has promised to make it a light to the blind. We can not save men by preaching the Word; acknowledging this with all humility, we must yet, in some sort, preach it as if, under God, we could; for God can save and has promised to make it a word of life. The preaching whose matter shall be such as has been thus set forth can not but be a power in the world, gaining the ear of the perishing multitudes, and, by God's grace, saving their souls.

## (II) In the Manner of Preaching.

Passing from matter to manner, it is obvious that, in respect of form, the preaching for these times must be with freshness and vividness, or with power.

Professor Day has given, in his *Art of Discourse*, previously referred to, a most admirable compendium of the essential qualities of a good style, under the head of "Objective Properties of Style." First comes *clearness*, as truth must be intelligible in order to be felt. Second in order is *energy*, as truth must possess force and vividness in order to reach and stir men. Last in place is *elegance*, as what offends good taste will not readily gain access to men, even tho it be clear and powerful. Professor Day's discussion of the principles of style is commended to any one who may be desirous of an intelligent guide on the subject. The course of the present discussion does not lie in the same line with his treatise, as the aim here is, not to deal with the general qualities of style, but merely to call attention to certain special principles that have to do with adapting the style of the pulpit to the needs of the present day, and with making it more a power with the men of this age.

<small>1. Principles Giving Power.</small>

In attaining that freshness and vividness for which simplicity prepares, there are, aside from the general laws of energy, certain principles, that enter more or less into the style of the powerful preachers of all times, as an element in winning success, and that, while exceedingly important always, are especially a necessity to the pulpit of the present. They may be denominated Biblical qualities. To enumerate, in brief, some of them:

The Word of God needs to be presented more in concrete form. The idea, apparently of so many, that

**(1) Concrete Presentation of Truth.** the preacher's chief mission is to turn his text into abstract truth, or "glittering generality," with which to ply a sleepy congregation, is all wrong. However necessary the process of abstraction may be for the purpose of systematic theology, it is not the Bible method of reaching men. There was never a truer utterance than that of Coleridge, in one of the introductory aphorisms, in his *Aids to Reflection:* "To restore a commonplace truth to its first uncommon luster, you need only translate it into action." What we can *see* has power. The Lord's Supper takes advantage of this principle, and embodying the central truth of the Gospel, addresses it to reason and faith, with the added power of the senses. It is thus the most powerful of all presentations of the doctrine of the cross.

And accordingly, we find Scripture everywhere presenting its truth largely in living shape and relation, in history and individual experience and incident, and thereby attaining to a perpetual freshness and interest. The pulpit of a day in which the world presents everything in the concrete needs to model after the Bible in this regard. Volumes on faith in the abstract can never so unfold its nature to the masses of men as will the exposition of that master example in Abraham's offering of Isaac. Volumes on parental responsibility in the abstract can never so fix the idea in the hearts of men, in all its fulness, as will that terribly solemn example of a pious father's grief over a favorite son gone down to perdition through his agency, that is brought before us in David's lament over his son Absalom. For our instruction and guidance, God's Word has put its utterances in these forceful shapes, and we may find in it instances without number, applicable to every possible phase of life, whether in its faith and work or in its relations to family, State, and Church. Here is one of the powers that God has put into the hands of the ministry, to be used in their mission, and it is preeminently the demand of this age, as well as of human nature, that it be used freely and largely.

God's truth must be presented, as is the Bible manner, with apt and ample illustrations. John Ruskin (in pt. 3, vol. ii., of *Modern Painters*) has drawn out that noble theory that affirms of all inherent beauty, that it is typical of the Divine attributes. It is a magnificent thing in the metaphysical profundity of its conception, no less than in the marvelous felicity of its delineation. We take it to be the only true basis of a correct Christian art-theory. *(2) Illustrative Presentation of Truth.*

Apply the same principle to the world of fact and truth, as well as beauty, and it gives a new element of power in the pulpit. The world in which we live, in its men, in its relations, in its material aspects, becomes typical of the higher, spiritual world. As the tabernacle was fashioned after the heavenly temple, so the lower world after the higher. Not simply and arbitrarily illustrative is the world, therefore; but, to the deep and right-seeing eye, typical, and, therefore, illustrative. It is, so to speak, God's first great book for men, containing the foundations for all other revelations, and without which they could not have been—the "Dark Mirror" (*Modern Painters*, pt. 9, ch. i., in vol. v.), in which man must catch his first faint glimpses of God and heaven. "Tongues in trees, books in the running brooks, sermons in stones," is no longer the merest fancy of the poet, but the statement of veritable fact. Here is a power akin to concrete presentation of the truth, and here is furnished the clew to the mystery and force of figurative language. God has written all higher truth in some lower form, which brings it within our reach. A figure, used in illustrating, has power because it presents the very truth illustrated, as God has given it somewhere in simple and concrete shape or by way of helpful analogy.

This principle is of value, not because of Ruskin, but because of God, of whose method Ruskin has **The Bible Point of View.** simply been the interpreter; for we hold this to be the Biblical way of viewing things. The Bible makes everything typical. The soul in all its faculties and life; the family in all its relations and experiences; the nation in all its constitution and history; the Church in all its ordinances and triumphs; the earth and the material universe in all their breadth of fact and form, of change and growth—the Bible brings before us, to teach us of God and heaven, and the higher things; giving us in this wise our first glimpses of the spiritual realities and glories. One can scarcely conceive of anything that is not so used in the Bible. It is one of the secrets of the wonderful energy and perpetual freshness of style in which it surpasses all other and merely human books, and it stands out clearly as an element to be made available in the pulpit.

This Bible method is at heaven-wide remove from very much of our most pretentious human work. We deal too freely in far-fetched and much-elaborated figures that we make for ourselves, and with which manufactured stock we vainly think to illustrate in an arbitrary way what God has given us to utter. Such work is like all work purely of man, and after his pattern—forceless and lifeless, and without any real sense or significance. What this age preeminently wants is the seeing eye, the quick-discerning mind; and then, turning this down into the soul, or to the household life, or out upon the world, God will make revelations of himself to us, with which we may enforce his higher truths; and he will make them everywhere, in the flying leaf, the vanishing vapor, and the sweeping dust; in the falling sparrow, the short-lived moth, and the blooming and fading flower; in the yearning of a father over his wandering son, the watching of a mother over her helpless babe, and the heavenliness of home. So seeing, we shall no longer bear man's illustrations, but God's; and men will unconsciously recognize in them something of God's power.

Taking art and science by the hand, as aids and guides in this their sphere, religion must make the world, with all in it, tributary to the pulpit, and make full use of it, until the message of wrath and love is written, as the Bible would write it, on everything that meets man's eye, appeals to his reason, dwells in his memory, fastens to his hopes, moves his heart, and links itself with his life. Such preaching will have power with man. In the end, the distilling dew shall, from morn to morn, speak to him of the silence, the energy, the quickening, invigorating contact, and the wide-reaching influence of God's proclaimed message; the flaming course of the morning sun, as it hastens to its meridian splendor, shall show him daily the "path of the just" drawn across the skies, in its beginnings out of darkness, in its light dispelling the darkness and calling forth the life of the world, in its constant progress, and in its reaching out toward perfection; and the fading leaf, sweeping across the sky, while it speaks to him of his own withering life, shall tell him also of the accumulated work and imperishable monument, in the tall monarch of the forest standing out against the sky, left behind to bless the coming generations with its shade and protection.

Another element of power and effectiveness is to be found in the presentation of the specific truths of God's Word. We deal too much in these days in generalities. It is all wrong. Such truths, from their very nature, can possess comparatively little interest. And they are few in number; the man who deals in them must soon either exhaust or repeat himself. Moreover, it is not the Bible way; for in it everything is specific. The one who holds fast by the precise truth of each text of Scripture will always present what is fresh and new, because, unlike general truths, specific truths are infinite in number and variety.

*(3) Presentation of Specific Truth.*

Over each text a vital question is, What is the exact thing that God would teach in this message? The man who always asks it, and always presents what he ascertains as its answer, will not present the same subject in connection with all kindred texts, and will preach neither abstract theology nor philosophy, but God's Word, which is better than either or both.

*What is the Exact Point?*

Here, by way of illustration, are two texts:

Col. i. 17. "By him all things consist."

Jer. x. 23. "O Lord, I know that the way of man is not in himself; it is not in the man that walketh to direct his steps."

We have heard men preach on the same general doctrine of providence from both of them. It was not preaching God's Word. The first of the texts has nothing to say of providence in general; it only speaks of one element in the doctrine of providence —*preservation*, and is still more specific in affirming this not of God absolute, but of *Jesus Christ.* "By *Christ* all things are continued in being." The other text is still more specific, but in another direction. The emphatic words—at least in significance—are, "in man," "in himself"; and the theme from it, in its relations to providence, would be the prophet's thorough conviction of the necessity of a special providence as demonstrated to him *by the nature of man.*

Again, here are three texts :

Ps. lxii. 11. "God hath spoken once ; twice have I heard this; that power belongeth unto God."
Ps. cxi. 6. "He hath showed his people the power of his works, that he may give them the heritage of the heathen."
Jer. v. 22. "Fear ye not me ? saith the Lord ; will ye not tremble at my presence, which have placed the sand for the bound of the sea by a perpetual decree, that it can not pass it ; and tho the waves thereof toss themselves, yet can they not prevail ; tho they roar, yet can they not pass over it ? "

One might preach on the power of God from each of them, but that would by no means bring out their truth. Taking them only in their applications to the present, the *first* points rather to the abundant and clear evidence that power is God's prerogative; the *second* may turn our attention to the wonderful manner in which, by the progress of science and art God is unfolding the powers of nature to the Christian nations, and making way for the possession and conversion of the world; while the *third* speaks not specifically of the power of God, nor of the power of God to control, nor of the power of God to control the mightiest things, nor of the power of God to control the mightiest things by the most insignificant means, but of the power of God to control the mightiest forces by the most insignificant means, *as a reason why the sinner should fear him*—or, in more rhetorical form, the omnipotence of the most insignificant things in God's hands as a reason for the sinner's fearing him. The three run in wholly different lines of thought; *one* takes us out through the universe, and bids us listen for the voices of God's power everywhere, from man's soul to the sweep of the remotest star; *another* takes us along the experience of Christendom, and shows us how the forces of nature, in wind, steam, magnetism, electricity, in all their applications to the arts, to trade and intercourse, are being revealed to the Christian nations, and being used to bring the heathen to their very door for a possession for the Church and Christ; and the *third* takes us to the storm-lashed shore of the never-resting sea, and to where the minute and mysterious forces of God's vast world are working out in silence the behests of his omnipotence—and bids us sinners tremble as we see how God can hold for ages those furious and seemingly resistless waves by that shifting sand, while the adamantine rocks wear away and disappear—how he can grind up the mountains by the turn of atoms, bind the proudest with the web of a spider, take his life with a particle of dust or air, or crush him by the turning of a falling leaf.

While it is not the purpose to recommend some

superficial forms of expository preaching, as suited to this age of cheap commentaries, yet specific truth we must have, as an element of power in the pulpit, even tho it carry us all the way back to simple exposition, for that is better than generalities, however glittering, and as much better as God's Word is better than man's abstractions. We must learn to come to a text, not to see whether it may be warped to suit our purposes, but to ascertain what God says in it, and then to present and enforce that from the pulpit. *Fresh Expository Preaching.*

Such, in hasty sketch, are these simple Biblical principles that have so much to do with the effectiveness of preaching, and that the preacher must make use of to meet the demands of the times. The pulpit must hold up the practical truth of God in concrete shape, illustrated in God's way, and specific as in God's Word. The theoretical, the abstract, the indefinite, the general, have no living energy. The practical, the concrete, the illustrative, the specific, alone are always new and fresh and forceful, and so fitted to take living hold on human souls.

As a passing glance is turned to those who from the pulpit hold and control men, are found to be clearly possessed, in large measure, of at least some of these elements, and to wield influence according to the completeness of their furnishing in this respect. *2. Principles Illustrated.*

Two men stand out prominently as the popular men of the past generation in the pulpit, with reputation world-wide—Charles Haddon Spurgeon and Henry Ward Beecher. It was long the custom to call in question the power of these men, but the day passed when one could exclaim, "clap- *Beecher and Spurgeon.*

trap," with a sneer, and pass them by. The fact of their substantial and permanent success met men face to face. "Clap-trap" may attract the crowd for a twelve-month, but it has no power to hold it through the years. It is wiser to acknowledge the facts, and, while guarding against error, seek to make the most of that power, whatever it may be, by which they won their success.

Spurgeon and Beecher stand before the world as the most successful popular pulpit orators of the past generation. Wherein lay their power? Holding fast the distinction of matter and form, we should say that, in the particulars we have enumerated, Spurgeon's success was due more to the matter, Beecher's more to the form; tho each possessed, in some degree, all the elements both in matter and form. Taking Coleridge's antithesis between "science" and "poetry," Mr. Beecher's cast of mind was rather poetic than scientific. This accounted for some of his peculiarities. If he had any system of theology, it was one peculiar to himself; so that, taking him in connection with his family, the division of theologians into "the orthodox, the heterodox, and the Beecher family," is more than a witticism. As a result of this laxness and want of system, he was often to be found sneering at "orthodoxy" and "sound theology," and disparaging some of the truths most precious to the Church of God—a feature in his preaching that was deeply deplored by some of his best friends.

Spurgeon dwelt more than Beecher upon the doctrine of the cross, in its relations to the conversion of men and to the development of Christian activity. The number of conversions under his ministry was therefore greater, and the distinctively Christian activity of his church more noteworthy.

Beecher dwelt more than Spurgeon upon the duties of the Christian believer and worker in the spheres of social and civil duty—applying the truth more to the every-day home-wants of men; seeking to guide them in the world as it is, and so aiming to make them better fathers, relatives, and friends, better business men and citizens, by laying down rules for their guidance. Perhaps no man of his day attempted to apply God's Word to these practical connections of the Christian with the world, especially in the national sphere, as did Beecher; often radically and wrongly, to be sure, in consequence of attempting to go beyond the sphere of vital gospel principles to which, as has been seen, Christ and his Apostles confined themselves; but yet, men were constrained to concede, with an aim to faithfulness, and, on the whole, presenting vital truth that took hold of human hearts and made him a molder of public sentiment and a leader among men, and aroused many among the clergy to a renewed sense of neglected or forgotten duty in this direction.

Both addressed their messages to the practical ideas in man; but Spurgeon the more powerfully, speaking chiefly to duty and happiness, and appealing to the latter from its darker side with a tremendous and awful intensity of earnestness that has hardly been surpassed since Jesus of Nazareth uttered his proclamations of wo in Galilee and Judea; while Beecher addressed more the idea of virtue or manliness, as if seeking to press home dishonesty, cowardice, and meanness, as the cardinal sins.

In respect to form, both made use of all the elements of power enumerated. Both delighted to present truth in the concrete. Both held practically to the theory that the world is typical, and so both abounded in apt illustration. Beecher, born poet, yet affectionately acknowledged, in his *Star Papers*, his indebtedness to John Ruskin for the " blessings of sight " :

" We are more indebted to him for the blessings of sight than to all other men. We were, in respect to nature, of the number of those who, having eyes saw not, and ears, heard not. He taught us what to see and how to see."

Spurgeon, in one of his early sermons, gave substantial expression of his adherence to the same theory, tho coming by it in a different way. The world in all its breadth was thus tributary to both, and was made to speak most eloquently for God through them. Beecher saw it the more poetically; Spurgeon the more practically.

Both presented specific truth, and were, therefore, always fresh and novel. Of the two, Beecher was rather the man of genius and artistic excellence, and the favorite on the platform ; Spurgeon the representative of the earnest and evangelical type of piety, the model preacher of the Gospel, and the man of larger Christian influence with the masses and with evangelical Christendom. Beecher drew large audiences by the exhibitions of his genius and the fascination of his eloquence, who found much to admire in the man and in his utterances. Spurgeon gathered a vast and permanent congregation, in the literary and commercial metropolis of the English world, by the simple eloquence of the message of salvation and his personal magnetism, who consecrated themselves to organized service for Christ for the saving of the world. It should be remarked, also, that Spurgeon added to his qualities as a preacher perhaps the most extraordinary administrative power possessed by any preacher of the century; by virtue of which he was enabled to embody his gospel ideas in various forms of churchly activity and various educational and missionary institutions, that have already sent out many hundreds of ministers and Christian workers, and exerted a vast influence upon all Protestant Christendom, and that promise to continue permanently their ever-widening influence for the cause of Christ and his Gospel.

The preaching of the two, in contrasts and consequences, strongly emphasizes the larger and more permanent Christian results of that preaching, with no "uncertain sound," of Christianity as the saving power, with its two-fold message of law and Gospel, that has been already dwelt upon as the better way.

As lessons are often better learned by example than by precept, these two men are presented, as perhaps illustrating better than any other men of recent times, the elements in matter and manner that are fitted to reach the men of the present day. While insisting that no man is to be servilely copied, yet it must be regarded as a duty to lay hold of and turn to service every element of power in every man. It is granted and even affirmed, that there are objectionable elements and eccentricities in their style—especially in Mr. Beecher's and in Mr. Spurgeon's earlier efforts—that are to be avoided, at least by other men, and through mad imitation of which this country and Great Britain were at one time visited with an infliction of clergymen of the "Rev. Shallow Splurge" type. But tho these peculiarities lessened their influence, they abated not one whit from the value of the princely gifts

*How far Models.*

bestowed upon them by the Master. We have sometimes been constrained to think that, if Mr. Beecher had preached the central doctrine of the cross with the fulness and the "blood earnestness" of Spurgeon, he would have been every way the mightiest man of the modern popular pulpit.

But whatever may be the comparative estimate of Beecher and Spurgeon, there can be no question but that all who are called to stand in the pulpit should seek to make of service these powers of the two men, so far as available. Preaching, so conformed to what is right in high example, as well as to the demands of correct theory, meeting the actual needs of men in all the relations of life, will be a master-power in the world. It will have the grandest of beauty, and yet not be a gospel of esthetics; it will possess perpetual novelty, and yet not be a gospel of "clap-trap and sensation"; it will always be sublimely practical, but never a gospel of petty scolding, nor of minor morals. Such preaching will meet all the just demands of the three tendencies noted, at the beginning of this discussion, as characterizing the times in which we live.

(III) IN THE SPIRIT OF PREACHING.

Passing from matter and manner to spirit, it is clear that, in accordance with the general answer to the question proposed at the outset, the spirit of the pulpit must be conformed to the correct working-theory, so as to meet the needs of the times. It is the spirit of the preacher that transforms and glorifies both matter and manner. He must preach the Gospel with a living sense of his grand mission to save souls.

It is only necessary here barely to indicate what needs to be brought out in this connection. Dr. Francis Wayland, in his work on the *Christian Ministry*, has clearly shown that ministry to be, not a *profession*, and not on a level with the professions, but most widely separated from them in being a *calling*. A *call* to this great and solemn work, direct from the living God, is, as already insisted, the first thing requisite—a call which shall make a man cry out with Paul, under a sense of his responsibility, "Wo is unto me, if I preach not the Gospel." *

*Calling and Consecration.*

Then the vocation of the minister demands intense sympathy with Christ in the work of saving the world. It calls for an overmastering enthusiasm in the work of soul-winning. It demands an absolute consecration to that work, and an entire devotion to it. This can come only through the knowledge of God's Word, in which Christ's will is expressed, and through the rich indwelling of the Spirit of Christ. Moreover, there must be that complete knowledge of men, and sympathy with them, that can come only from intimate and constant contact with them, both as a man and a pastor.

Add to all, large expectation of results. "Preach the Word, and leave the results to God"; so we are wont to say. We hold this form of statement, as it is sometimes meant, to be neither Scriptural nor true. Preach the Word, and expect results from God, is truth and Scripture. It recognizes faith as a substantial element of power. Men must feel that their work is one of life and death, and, at the same time, a work in which God and Christ are more interested than they can be; and then, with correct theory, working in the right way and in the

*Expectation of Results.*

\* 1 Cor. ix. 16.

proper spirit, they may expect that perishing men will assuredly be reached, and, by God's grace, saved.

Would that the whole truth concerning the mission of the ministry might be written on the heart of every messenger of God with a pen of fire, and in perpetually burning words; for without it thus fixed in the soul, there can be no such thing as success in the highest and truest sense. The little work of Bonar, entitled *Words to the Winners of Souls*, already referred to, presents the idea with great force. True it is that a certain class of men cry out against what they are pleased to denominate its "legal spirit," and declaim against it as setting up an unscriptural standard by which to try the work of the ministry; but we believe that earnest and sincere men can not but plead guilty to every charge it brings against us of this day. All such men feel intensely that we need a new life in the ministry. And such men feel, too, that without such a new life, without such men, there is no salvation for us!

If the consecrated spirit shall thus crown the Scriptural and divine matter and the intelligent and wise manner, the divine blessing and resultant large success may be confidently expected.

## SECTION THIRD.

### The Preaching for Immediately Evangelizing the World.

The preaching of the Gospel has been considered in its general relations to the times in which we live. It is vastly more important that it be considered in its special relations to the present meaning of the Great Commission, in the light of God's Word and of God's providences. That calls for a preaching that shall keep in view the obligation of the ministry, and of the Church, to give the Gospel to all mankind without delay.

The preaching that is to have this in view must manifestly be preaching for awakening and revival—not for emotional or hysterical revival, nor even for sporadic and local revival of the genuine sort; but for a great awakening, such as the Church has never hitherto known, that shall reach and rouse and set to work the Church of Christendom for the accomplishment of this one object.

From this point of view, the supreme thing to be emphasized in the preaching of the day, if it is to meet the present needs, fulfil the preacher's commission, and be effective, is that it must be essentially and directly evangelistic, and with constant reference to the present status of that commission. The Gospel must be preached as a regenerating and saving power, of present efficacy for the individual sinner and for all mankind. Now, if ever, preaching should intelligently and constantly aim at the immediate conversion of sinners and of the world. It should be heartily and intensely Gospel-preaching, in this awakening and saving sense.

Such preaching will doubtless rouse opposition, as it always has in the past; but that opposition will be God's testimony and Satan's testimony to the necessity for it. It will not excuse the preacher from faithfully delivering the message Christ has committed to him. The "carnal mind" has never ceased to be at "enmity against God," * and never will cease to be so. It will never listen to the complete presentation of God's truth concerning man's sinful and lost condi-

* Rom. viii. 7.

tion, without reluctance or resentment, varying in intensity and virulence according to circumstances. A method of questioning young evangelists, on their return from a preaching tour, in order to test their success—which we have heard attributed to John Wesley—is highly suggestive of man's condition and need, as well as of keen discernment of human nature. It was by three questions and their answers: "Has your preaching resulted in the conversion of any sinner?" "No." "Has it resulted in the conviction of any sinner?" "No." "Has it made any one mad?" "No." "Then you will not do for a preacher of the Gospel."

Such opposition will doubtless be strongest where the pews are filled with the rich and so-called culti-
*The Wickedest Sinners.* vated classes; and it will be thereby proved of greater need just there, if these souls are not to be lost. The preacher needs to remember that the great sinners are not necessarily the ragged denizens of the slums, and to be judged by their rags and squalor—as so many in these days seem to think. Righteousness does not consist in external decency and good clothes; nor sin simply in poverty, filth, and wretchedness. Paul, by inspiration, declared himself to be the greatest of all sinners (1 Tim. i. 15, 16), and affirmed that God had, for this very reason, saved him and set him up as an example for all sinners in all ages, of the power of divine grace. The "wickedest man," as the gospel standards measure wickedness, is rather the man of great brain and great enlightenment and great gospel opportunities and privileges, who, notwithstanding all these, remains an unbeliever and rebel against God, and a hater and rejecter of Christ's claims and commands and en-

treaties; and he is more likely to be found in the "best pew" in the fashionable church than in the slums or the prison, unless, as is sometimes the case, he has passed from the first to the last.

That his plain message from God might have stirred up opposition will furnish no adequate excuse at the judgment bar for the preacher who has for this reason failed to deliver it. Perishing souls need the message, and the compassionate Savior, knowing this, commissioned the preacher to deliver it, that lost souls might be saved. Ezekiel's judgment upon the watchman is the divine judgment upon the unfaithful watchmen on the walls of Zion to-day: *The Watchman's Responsibility.*

"But if the watchman see the sword coming and blow not the trumpet and the people be not warned; if the sword come and take any person from among them, he is taken away in his iniquity; but his blood will I require at the watchman's hand."*

I. STATED PREACHING FOR IMMEDIATE SALVATION, GOD'S METHOD.

Preaching the Gospel as a saving and regenerating power, by the stated ministry, for the immediate saving of men, is, we take it, the true and normal method, and the only healthful method, of progress in the work of the Church for the lost world. Such preaching is the only provision for laying, in the minds of the mass of men, the deep, rational, and permanent foundation for the proper results of the Gospel in conscience and character. *The Normal Method.*

* Ezekiel xxxiii. 6.

## (I) Limitations of Special Revivalism.

The lack of such preaching has doubtless made the necessity for the work of the special revivalist. Such revival work is necessarily brief, and its limitations of time are such that it can not be other than superficial. Little of permanent value can be expected of it, unless there has been a previous thorough preparation in the preaching of the stated minister; and it is to be noted that ministers who depend upon such special work of revivalists are not commonly of the kind who lay such solid foundations in their own preaching.

When this rational foundation for religion is lacking, the temptation and tendency to introduce powerful stimulants and excitements, to produce the action that should be secured in a reasonable way, are almost overwhelming. Of course the masses of so-called converts, in such circumstances, can only be expected to illustrate the character and faith of the "stony-ground hearers," of the parable of the sower.

In very many cases, all rational basis for religion is left out; and the mere machinery is all that is left to accomplish the work of so-called conversion. Instead of strong presentation of truth, there is the funny story and the clap-trap method, the boy-preacher and the lay-evangelist, the praying-band and the gospel singer, to take the place of the exposition and enforcement of the Word of God by the preacher of the Gospel. We have known hundreds of so-called conversions, the result of such methods, to disappear again in the mass of worldliness, without adding anything to the membership of the Church. When Dr. Asahel Nettleton began his preaching, in eastern Connecticut, he found there, in the dreadful spiritual barrenness that made his work hopeless, the results of the ill-advised methods of the evangelist Davenport, of the previous century. One who had occasion to follow the track of even the sainted John Summerfield in such hasty evangelistic work, found that the region over which he had passed had come to be designated the "burnt region"!

Now, it is true that there are revivals and revivals; that there are revivalists and revivalists. To the right kind of both the Church owes a vast debt, and the testimony to their value has come from the best of her preachers. Dr. Lyman Beecher, in one of his last public addresses, said: "I feel that, if I had a thousand lives to live, they should all be devoted to the ministry and to revivals." Dr. Porter of Farmington, Conn., once said: "Those who remain of Dr. Nettleton's revival converts are the chief strength of our church." His son, President Porter of Yale College, said: "I deem it all-important that ministers should be revival men." Bishop McIlvaine once said: "Whatever I possess of religion came in a revival." President Heman Humphrey of Amherst College said: "After all that our eyes have seen and our ears have heard, I marvel that any should look with suspicion on revivals. Rather let us hail them in this midnight of tribulation as the harbinger of the 'light of seven days'" ¡*

The Church owes an immense debt to revivalists of the better kind. But even tho they be of that class, their work is, so far as it is necessary, a proof of the failure of the regular ministry to reach, in a normal way, the results contemplated by the Head of the

*See *Revivals: How and When.* By Rev. W. W. Newell, D. D., pp. 21-23.

Church. That in these days they should be almost universally resorted to, when men are to be gathered into the Church, is proof of a wide-reaching defect in the present methods. It must be noted, however, that the testimonies just cited are-not mainly to professional revivalism and revivalists, but to religious awakenings in connection with the regular ministrations of the pastor. It is the latter kind of revivalist that has universal commendation.

(II) NEEDED RETURN TO THE NORMAL METHOD.

In a return to such revival preaching of the stated ministry is to be found the only safety for the Church. It can hardly be questioned that the influence which this work gives to him who engages in it is needed to maintain the minister's authority and influence at their best with his people. It is certainly needed, if there is to be the proper, rational, and intelligent basis for a Christian life in the hearer, when he becomes a Christian.

Moreover, the minister and the Church both need it in order to be prepared to take proper care of new converts when made. The one process—that of bringing the sinner to Christ—is the necessary preparation for the other—that of training him in the service of Christ; and the one is the necessary presupposition of the other, as the mother-love is for the proper nurture of the child.

It can not be reasonably doubted that observation of the results of this normal and Christian method has shown it to be the true method. At the same time, it seems to be almost demonstrable that the present state of things is, in large measure, the natural result of ministerial failure in this direction. The converting and saving doctrines of Christianity are the great conscience-rousing and character-making agencies. The withdrawal of these doctrines from prominence, in preachers' deliverances, has naturally been followed by a lack of intelligence in the hearer on the subjects of conscience and character. It has led to his practical release from the internal and moral pressure that holds to right principle and right conduct—of originating and manifesting which pressure the pulpit has always been the main agency. It has led, in greater or less degree, to the elimination of the religious, spiritual, and distinctively Christian element from the services of the sanctuary, so that the Christian side of the environment of the church-goers has largely dropped out. If, as has been estimated, the worldly side of that environment presses upon the business man "with a force some twenty-five times greater than it did before the age of steam," the pressure must necessarily have come to be pretty much all one way—and that away from God and Christ and evangelical religion. Men who want religious and Christian teaching naturally complain that they get very little of it from many of the pulpits.

Is it any wonder that, in this condition of affairs, there is much complaint because so few of the leaders among men, in business and in the professions, are in the churches? The substitution of mere exhortation and Sunday-school talk for the vigorous doctrinal and practical presentation of Bible truth fails to satisfy, nay, disgusts, men of intellectual grasp and moral earnestness.

Often the preacher who falls into this vicious method is not himself aware of it. A well-known preacher and pastor, who had been somewhat dazed by a temporary outside popularity, once said to the writer:

"I was out of my study all last week, and did not get home from lecturing abroad until late Saturday night. So I went into the pulpit on Sabbath morning, took as my text a familiar passage of Scripture, and extemporized for an hour. I have never before had such freedom and satisfaction in my pulpit-work in all my life."

That was the view from the pulpit. A few days later, a member of that preacher's congregation, a distinguished lawyer, said of that morning service :

"Our minister is running hither and thither all the week, and when the Sabbath comes he has no preparation for his preaching. He went into the pulpit last Sabbath morning, after such a week, and sputtered extemporaneous exhortations at us over the corners of the pulpit, for more than an hour. I am tired of it."

That was the view from the pew!

The substitution of esthetics, minor morals, and sensationalism generally, for the great themes that

*Sensationalism a Failure.* should be supreme in the pulpit, fail to satisfy intelligent, strong men. They do not find anything in such froth and foam that meets their needs or cravings. There is nothing in such preaching to induce a really intelligent man to go to church. If such a hearer is inclined to sensationalism and excitement, he can get it in more approved form at the theater. If he has literary or esthetic inclinations, he has the best of these things at his command outside the pulpit, and of such superior character that the preacher can not be expected to compete successfully with the literati and the artists. And of what interest to him are the ten thousand pettinesses, if he is at all conscious that he has a soul and is on his way to the presence of him who is to judge "the quick and the dead"? We once heard a man of national reputation, whose pastor was such a preacher, say :

"I go to church because my family want me to. I never hear anything the minister says. He never says anything. I let it all go in at one ear and out at the other."

Naturally, the old feeling that the Church has a message of overwhelming importance is gradually passing from the minds of men, and multitudes are turning their attention toward other sources of Sabbath instruction and amusement. Naturally, too, the moral bottom is dropping out of the society, the business, the politics, and all the rest of the things in which these men have control. And so, largely in this way, we have come to what a distinguished Boston clergyman has characterized as "our present state of desperate need," extrication from which calls for the use of every possible agency of the Gospel.

Hence, the growing and deepening conviction of many of those who best understand the character of the times that there is needed a great and powerful religious awakening and quickening, such as the Church has not known for a generation, or even for a century and more—an awakening that shall begin with and work out from the pastors and the churches. *A Great Awakening Needed.*

## II. Preaching for the Immediate Salvation of the World.

The supreme question of the hour for the preacher is, then : How can I, the ordained preacher and leader of the Church, so preach the Gospel as to do my part in bringing about these results, in the saving of sinful men just around me, and of the world of sinners besides ?

(I) REQUIREMENTS MADE OF THE INDIVIDUAL PREACHER.

The first necessity is that each individual minister shall answer this question for himself, and, having found the answer, shall proceed to do his individual duty in his appointed place.

There are certain general requirements (elsewhere emphasized), to begin with. He must take in fully the situation. He must understand the commission and message that have been entrusted to him. He must become possessed with the unhesitating conviction that divine regeneration, by the power of the Gospel, is the only thing that can bring about the needed change. He must become deeply and solemnly conscious of his position as the appointed mouthpiece of God in proclaiming the Gospel. He must firmly and irrevocably determine that he will do his duty and his whole duty, as required by the Master who has sent him. Then he must consecrate himself to the carrying out of his determination, in absolute and unwavering reliance on divine grace to give the word and work success. All this is just as necessary for the minister as is the business man's outlook when he enters upon any enterprise. God is a God of order, and Christian work and preaching are rational procedures.

*General Requirements.*

Having secured such command of the situation, and such divine girding for the work, the preacher is ready to do the one thing he is just now called upon to do as a preacher. *That one thing* is to direct his Gospel message, immediately and persistently, to the members of his congregation, saints and sinners, in precisely the doctrinal aspect and form required to meet their sins and the sins of the age, and to arouse and quicken conscience.

This assumes that all revivals begin with the awakening of the church members and extend from them to the sinners beyond. This is a commonplace with those familiar with revival work. It assumes that the preaching should be intelligently aimed at the desired results, and that the preacher is warranted to expect that such preaching will, by the grace of God, be followed by such results. None but a hyper-Calvinist has any ground for doubting this. It assumes that there are certain great doctrines, or forms or aspects of doctrine, that the Holy Spirit is accustomed to use and bless, in stemming and turning back the tide of sin, and in saving sinners. This may not be so readily admitted; but this is the point to which the special attention of the preacher needs to be directed.

## *1. A Preparatory Study of Principles.*

In making ready for this kind of work, now so imperatively demanded, the preacher needs, therefore, to study the principles of genuine revivals of religion in the light of historical and inductive observation, in order to their methodical and practical application in his own work.

It is as true in revivals as elsewhere that "history is philosophy teaching by example." Their history constitutes an object-lesson of peculiar instructiveness. There have been three great eras of general revival in the history of the American Church, each of which has been characterized by certain peculiar features. *(Three Eras of General Revival.)*

*First.* There has been, in each case, a providential preparation, in the revival of faith in the dogmatic authority of the Sacred Scriptures as the Word of God— a genuine and general religious revival being apparently impossible with shaken or shattered faith in divine revelation. This revival of faith in the Word has brought the Church and the world to the test of the "Law and the Testimony," and awakened and roused them by the exposure of current errors, the uncovering of churchly formality and hypocrisy, and the judgment and condemnation of all sin.

*Secondly.* There have been, in each case, special phases of error and sin, having their clearly marked differences, and calling for peculiar and appropriate treatment.

*Thirdly.* There have been, in each case, specific differences in the doctrines presented by preachers and blessed by the Holy Spirit, in remedying the evils by rousing the Church and saving sinners—these doctrines being exactly suited to counteract the peculiar errors and sins of the period.

The first era of American revivals was that under Edwards and Whitefield and their successors, contemporaneous with the movement in England under Whitefield and the Wesleys, and dating back to 1740.

The philosophical English deism, which, in the course of a long controversy, had largely undermined the faith of the English-speaking peoples, and resulted in general religious stupor, received its logical death-blow in the publication of Butler's *Analogy of Religion*, in 1738. In New England, which, in the eighteenth century, in consequence of the immigration of much of the better Puritan element from England, became the great center of theological

*The State of Things.*

thought, the skepticism showed itself in the prevalence of mere formalism in religion, in place of the system of gospel grace that lays stress on regeneration and vital piety; and in the consequent prevalence of open immorality in the conduct or of trust in mere morality, in place of a life of Christian virtue. The world had been largely received into the Church, in consequence of ignoring the doctrine of the new birth, of the baptism of the children of those who were not members of the Church and their admission to the Lord's Supper, of regarding the sacraments as saving ordinances, and of other like irregularities. There had thus grown up a system of works that, in the American Church of Edwards' day, had produced the same fruits that were produced by it in the early church at Rome, and to the remedying of which Paul had directed the Epistle to the Romans—that is, they had "made the grace of God without effect." *

In the Great Awakening, as it has been called, Edwards, Bellamy, and their contemporaries planted themselves solidly on the assumption and distinct reaffirmation of the authority of the Word of God. They met the ultra Arminianism and churchly legalism by appealing to Paul's doctrine to the Romans in analogous circumstances—the doctrine of justification by faith in the Divine Redeemer. This was the one common burden of the preaching of the day. As essentially connected with justification, tremendous stress was laid, in this era, upon the condemning power of the law, and the lost condition of the sinner, in order to leave the sinner hopeless, unless he could obtain justification through the righteousness of the crucified Savior, and find refuge in him; while the necessity for the new birth was emphasized, in order to bring the formal and godless professor to despair of deliverance and salvation except by the power of the Holy Ghost. These were the distinctive dogmatic features of the first era of revivals, and these were the specific doctrines blessed by the Holy Spirit, in connection with the Great Awakening.

The second era of American revivals—that in which President Dwight, Dr. Edward Dorr Griffin, and others were among the leaders in its earlier phase; and Drs. Nettleton and Finney the leading revivalists in its later phase—may be reckoned from 1797, and it extended well into the nineteenth century.

<small>Second Era of Revivals.</small>

A period of backsliding and moral defection followed the Great Awakening. The errors and sins of this period were again of a peculiar character. A blatant and scoffing form of skepticism had taken the place of the old, reasoned deism, and had sought to undermine Christianity and the authority of the Bible in another way. The French skeptics and their followers had laughed the Word of God out of court, had gone squarely to the polls and voted, "There is no God," and then had formally repudiated the sovereign rule of God. In connection with the American and French revolutions, and in consequence of the sympathy resulting from the generous aid we had received from the French during our Revolutionary War, this infidelity had spread widely in this country, either in its more popular and scoffing form, as represented by Voltaire and his compeers, or in its coarser and more brutal form, as represented by Tom Paine. It had gained a hold, especially among many of those who laid claim to high intelligence and culture, and who were proud to be considered "free-thinkers"; and it had greatly affected a large number of the public men and of the young men in the colleges and seminaries of learning. There was a wide-spread revolt against authority in every form, but especially in religion, against the authority of God and his Word. The practical creed of these men may be summed up in the sentence : " We will not have God to reign over us."

But error in faith and practise had come in from another side. The preaching in the Great Awakening naturally erred by defect. In keeping their minds intently fixed upon the central truth of justification by faith, as furnishing the antidote to the corrupting influence of formality and legality, the preachers had not, perhaps, laid sufficient stress upon the necessity for an active life of Christian duty, as the necessary result of the true life of faith. At all events the Church, after the day of Edwards, fell into this error. " Dead orthodoxy " had been the result, accompanied too often by open immoralities, or at least by their advocacy in the sacred name of liberty.

Moreover, the success and prosperity that had attended the American Republic had led to boastful pride and arrogance. The nation that had " whipped England could whip the world," and did not feel like acknowledging any sovereign but the "sovereign people." Reaction was inevitable. The dreadful excesses of the French Revolution, acknowledged and boasted of as the legitimate fruit of the skeptical theories, the equally dreadful licentiousness of the leading skeptics themselves, and the threatened dissolution of society and of Christian civilization, drove men back to the Bible and Christianity by the contrast, and forced upon the masses, almost unconsciously to themselves, a firm conviction of the absolute necessity for the authority of God as a foundation for life and religion. The influence of that great Christian philanthropist, Wilberforce, in introducing the knowledge of a higher Christian life among the nobility and the educated classes abroad, together with the disgust with which the folly and corruption that had characterized the leaders and literature and society of the time of the Restoration and of the Georges, had caused many of the more intelligent to turn to the Bible and Christianity for refuge and help.

The leaders in the reaction—such men as Dwight, Griffin, and the elder Mills—fell back once more upon the Bible, assuming, affirming, or proving, by unanswerable arguments, its divine authority, and they directed their preaching intelligently against the prevailing errors and sin. The peculiar dogmatic feature of this era, appearing to a large extent in all the preaching, was necessarily the sovereignty of God. The people had largely revolted against God, and needed to be made to feel, to the utmost, that there is an infinite God above all and controlling all, and the arbiter of future destiny. The Spirit of God made use of this doctrine of the sovereignty of God in the preaching of that age of revival; and, in the teaching of the strong men of the day, it became a trumpet-call to repentance and judgment. The message was: "Submit to God, your rightful sovereign." "Throw down the weapons of your rebellion."

The churchly and personal errors and sins of the times were met by emphasizing the doctrines of repentance and of a holy life, and the personal duty to love and serve God with all the soul, might, mind, and strength. The message became: "Repent, and turn yourselves from all your transgressions." "Son, give me thine heart." "Devote yourself and your life to the service of God."

The Holy Spirit led the preachers to use just the doctrines needed to meet the case. It is obvious that the natural tendency of the call to submission and duty was to make *practical Christians.* Great reform movements sprang up against intemperance, profanity, Sabbath desecration, licentiousness, slavery, war, etc. The great benevolent and missionary agencies came into existence—the Bible Society, Tract Society, mission societies, etc. A powerful and permanent impulse was given to home missions and to foreign missions. The opening half of the century witnessed a marked elevation in Christian ideals, character, and activity.

The third era of American revivals began with the great awakening of 1858. It was a revival among the people. It made revivalists, rather than was made by them, and has been estimated to have added a million members to the churches. {Third Era of Revivals.}

A reaction had followed the second era of revivals. The authority of the Sacred Scriptures was attacked from a new point of view. Certain advocates of immature science, or of "science falsely so called," insisted that the latest discoveries of astronomy, geology, and other sciences contradicted the Bible, and that, therefore, the Bible must be every way false, untrustworthy, and worthless. The wide publication of their views, and their loud advocacy in the newspapers, at the post-offices and corner groceries and gathering-places, and even in the rationalistic pulpits, led to a rapid extension of their influence and the consequent weakening of the faith of many.

It was during this period that German rationalistic criticism began to exert a large influence against the acceptance of the Scriptures as the Word of God. A special agent in introducing it was Theodore Parker, then of Boston, whose work in this direction culminated in the translation of De Wette's *Introduction to the Old Testament.* That English scholar, Frederick W. Newman, also did much toward undermining faith in the Scriptures by presenting, in *Phases of Faith,* the universal religion common to all creeds—a view that at once appealed to and embodied the philosophical *zeitgeist.* More than all else, perhaps, the philosophy of August Comte acted as a disintegrating and undermining power. Positivism was silent about the existence of a Deity, and thus practically atheistic. It made nature's laws the only providence, and obedience to them the only piety. It thus brought in the sway of naturalism and anti-supernaturalism.

Moreover, out of the preaching of the previous era there had resulted, by emphasis of responsibility and human duty, a tendency to undue exaltation of human ability, and a characteristic self-sufficiency on the part of the impenitent, in the assurance that they could repent when they pleased, and so did not need any special help from God. The emphasis laid upon duty had resulted in the depreciation of faith; and this again had reacted upon the sense of duty, to such an extent as to threaten its annihilation and the reduction of Christian activity to the mere management of the machinery of organization.

Besides, new secularizing forces had come in and changed the whole face of society. The great goldfields of California had been discovered and their riches developed. Science in various forms had begun to be widely applied to the arts and industries—in the chemical laboratory, in the mines, and in the magnetic telegraph, and in innumerable other inventions. The application of steam to locomotion and machine-production had covered the rivers and oceans with steamers, gridironed the continent with railways, and opened the way to possibilities of almost fabulous production of the means of enjoyment and luxury. Intense worldliness threatened to engulf the Church.

The attacks upon the Scriptures by the scientists and the rationalists were met, their objections answered, and their arguments refuted, by such men as Thomas Chalmers, John Pye Smith, Hugh Miller, Pritchard, Edward Hitchcock, Arnold Guyot, and James D. Dana, and by such men as Charles Hodge, Henry B. Smith, Ezra Abbot, Mark Hopkins, Tayler Lewis, and many others; so that the intelligent and educated were quite generally satisfied that both science and reason had failed to impugn the authority of God's Word.

But the religious awakening came in a most unusual way, and took on an entirely new aspect. The previous movements, already considered, were intimately connected with some special presentation of dogmatic truth, or with the appearance of great leaders; but the revival of 1858 came as one result of the pressure of a peculiar providence. A great financial crisis had some time before prostrated the industries of the country; the depression continued and increased until vast numbers, left without work, were on the verge of abject want. In tneir despair they were driven to turn to God in prayer. God, who has many ways of accomplishing his purposes, had this time roused men by smiting their idol, Mammon!

New York City, the center of commercial depression, was the place in which the movement originated. The Fulton Street Noon Prayer-meeting, established October 8, 1857, with a layman, Mr. J. C. Lanphier, in charge, was the point of origin. That meeting was itself an inspiration. In three months after it was opened the great revival had already begun. In six months noon prayer-meetings had spread across the continent, in all the cities and centers, and the revival went with them. Dr. A. P. Marvin, in the *Bibliotheca Sacra*, for 1859, says :

"Perhaps there was no period of four months' duration, in the time of Edwards, when the results were so great and astonishing as during the four months which followed the opening of February in the year 1858. And as the present work is still going forward with power, may we not hope that its final results will mark it as the grandest since the planting of Christianity in the midst of pagan darkness and pollution !"

The work spread from the prayer-meetings to the churches, and the preachers added their messages to the sympathetic influence of the union gatherings. In Philadelphia alone ten thousand new members were gathered into the churches at that time. Dr. T. W. Chambers, in his memorial volume on *The Noon Prayer-meeting*, in Fulton Street, during its first year, gives an account of a memorable sermon by the lamented Rev. Dudley A. Tyng,

"where the congregation numbered more than five thousand persons, and where 'the slain of the Lord' were more perhaps as the result of a single sermon than almost any sermon in modern times."

Dr. W. W. Newell—in *Revivals : How and When*—estimates that "more than a million of souls were saved."

It was not a revival for preaching the doctrines of dogmatic theology, but for the Spirit to write certain needed practical doctrines in the heart of the Church. It demonstrated for Christendom the power of prayer. It was a great sympathetic, social movement, that brought Christians of all denominations together heart to heart, and demonstrated and realized the essential unity of Christendom and the power that lies in this unity. It brought to the knowledge of the Church sources of untold power hitherto unrecognized. It fixed in the hearts of all Christians the doctrine that every member of the Church of Christ is a coworker with Christ in the work of saving the world, and that a "manifestation of the Spirit is given to each one for the profit" of the Church. It thus awakened and led to the development and organization of the *lay element*, which in church and mission work, and in the organized effort of the Young Men's Christian Association and the various young people's societies, and in the Salvation Army movement, has made it such an incalculable power in Gospel work.

<small>Brought out the Lay Element.</small>

Apparently the Spirit, with wise purpose, kept the mind of Christians generally centered on the great practical principles that were being wrought into the life of the Church; directing the preachers, in their regular or revival ministrations, in supplementing the work and giving it to some extent a solid basis in the law of God and in the great doctrines of grace.

On the whole, it is easy to see, at this later day, that the revival of 1858 transformed the life and work of Protestant Christendom, and gathered its forces together to hold them in readiness for some mighty future enterprise that should need the combined effort of all Christians in the entire Holy Catholic Church. It has been seen, in the discussion of "the Preacher's

Commission," that the Church of to-day is confronted by such an enterprise, in which ministers are God's appointed heralds and leaders of the people.

## 2. *Application of the Ascertained Principles.*

**Need of a Fourth Era of Revivals.** Having investigated the principles that have prevailed in recent great and confessedly genuine revivals of religion, the preacher is prepared for the methodical and practical application of these principles to the great enterprise that immediately confronts him; and to aid thereby in bringing about the *fourth and greater era of revivals* now called for.

So much space has been devoted to the survey just made, in order to assist in grasping the situation, and understanding, in the light of the history of past awakenings, just what is needed, in the preaching of to-day, to make most powerfully for an awakening that may bring the Church to the summit of its achievement, in that immediate, final, and complete carrying out of the Great Commission that seems to be clearly called for by the "signs of the times."

It can not be too strongly emphasized that, in view of the imperative demand made upon the preacher **Gravity of the Situation.** and the Church, in the present status of the commission under which they are acting, the situation is one of peculiar gravity. The work to be done manifestly surpasses everything that has heretofore been attempted. The obstacles in the way are immense. No half-hearted consecration, no half-intelligent purpose, no half-way effort, will either win or deserve success. Nothing short of a mighty awakening, that shall rouse all Christendom, can possibly lead to the accomplishment of the divinely appointed task of the Church.

There is need that every preacher should bravely face the situation and fearlessly direct his preaching so as to meet the peculiar exigencies. The needs in various regions will differ, *The Exigencies to be Met.* but the doctrinal preaching for hastening the coming fourth era of revivals, must meet the peculiar exigencies. These exigencies, that must be fairly met, can be taken in at a glance.

Powerful influences are operating directly upon the outside world to unsettle faith in the Scriptures as the Word of God, and at the same time largely molding the unintelligent and unthinking churchly and Christian opinion in the same direction. Atomism, materialistic evolution, secularism, are in the air; so also are the so-called principles of the rationalistic higher criticism. The two tendencies conspire in seeking to eliminate the supernatural from what Christians regard as the world of God and the Word of God. The men under their influence are always asking : "What is written in the Book of Herbert Spencer, or of John Stuart Mill?" "What is written in the Book of Kuenen, or of Robertson Smith?" instead of the Christian question: "What is written in the Book of God?"

The immense development of mere material wealth; the infatuated devotion of men and means to its increase; the creation of gigantic combinations, at once soulless and conscienceless, for its rapid and vast accumulation; and the idleness, luxury, vice, and ruin that follow upon its possession and misuse, seem to have doomed the age to the service of Mammon—a servitude the most cruel and degrading of all the modern idolatries.

The demoralization resulting from the greatest of modern wars still rests like an awful shadow and blight upon the nation; and helps on the general tide of vice and crime.

Almost equally powerful influences are operating on the Church from within. The shaking of faith in God and the Scriptures, and the tide of worldliness, have affected most seriously the popular conceptions of the Christian life. The views of fifty years ago regarding social usages and amusements, regarding theater-going, dancing, card-playing, and all that, have been very radically changed. What was then regarded as essentially Christian is now in many quarters sneeringly pronounced "Puritanical." The materialist and sensationalist views of right and wrong have revolutionized the views of sin and crime, and the treatment of them in Church and State.

The sympathetic character of the revival of 1858, so far as not counteracted by the preaching of the pastors, has had its marked molding effects on the character of the church members. Men were not driven to God, in that revival, by a sense of sin, but by a sense of need and helplessness. Some have designated it "The Revival of Love." There was little or no preaching of law, or of justification by faith, or of the necessity of the new birth; the first three chapters of Paul's Epistle to the Romans were skipped; hence, there was comparatively little sense of sin or of spiritual need. The rousing and soul-stirring messages of the Edwardian era were conspicuously absent during all this time; nor were those of the later period, under Dwight and Nettleton and Finney, much heard. Often the only cry was: "Come to Jesus, poor, needy, helpless soul! He

*Depreciation of Doctrine.*

wants you to come; he needs you!" The tendency to decry doctrine and the authority of the Scriptures was very marked and has sensibly increased.

And in all the years since, the ingatherings in the churches, in the schools and colleges, at the mission stations, in the young people's meetings, have been largely by this same sympathetic method. The social spirit and the rage for organization have obviously too often largely overlaid and partially smothered and hindered the spiritual life and activities, or preoccupied the attention and exhausted the energies with the mere machinery of an activity mainly churchly or worldly. The perfected machinery remains as a permanent result, which may be of great service in the future.

The great prominence given to lay effort, on the part of old and young, while fixing in the mind of the Church the call of every Christian to work for Christ, has naturally had the effect upon "novices" against which Paul warned Timothy to guard in his selection of leaders for the churches.*

These peculiar exigencies and needs the preacher should aim to meet in his message. He should seek to remedy all these defects and to lead men, in the Church and out of it, to right views of sin, as a thing to be abhorred and repented of, and he should endeavor to bring to bear all the sympathy, and Christian activity, and machinery of organization, and power of prayer, in carrying out immediately Christ's command.

The needs in various regions will differ, but the doctrinal preaching for hastening the coming fourth era of revivals, will be required to emphasize, in special manner, the following points: **Doctrines for the Fourth Era.**

*First*, the divine authority of the Bible as the Word of God, by which all light, whether in the Church or in the world, is to be judged; and the supreme and sovereign authority of God himself, the Creator, Lawgiver, and Judge of the world. This is required in order to restore the faith shaken by the senseless materialism and criticism of the passing time, and to give God his rightful place back of law and conscience and life. Moreover, it is needed to lift Christian doctrine—which is merely Bible teaching, and as necessary to man's spiritual life as air or bread to his physical life—from the discredited position that has resulted from the defects of the teachings of the last great revival; and restore it to its true place, as the very basis and ground of all powerful Christian life and activity. There are already clear indications of a reaction in this direction, in the wide-spread repudiation of rationalistic criticism and socialistic secularism, and in the increasing interest in systematic study of the Word of God. So marked are the signs of change in this regard that some of the prophets are already predicting the speedy coming of what is needed to save the Church life from degenerating into mere sentimentalism—*a great dogmatic revival.*

*Secondly*, the requirements and obligations of the Law of God. This is requisite, if sinners are ever to understand and appreciate their lost condition, and their need of Bible salvation as something infinitely different from a mere sentimental salvation; and are ever to "flee from the wrath to come," to find refuge in Christ as their Savior. The dreadful lawlessness and consciencelessness of the age emphasize the call for "law-work" as profound and thorough as in the age of Edwards or of Nettleton and Finney, or as in the age when Paul had to deal with Roman sinners in his epistle—and for law-work with a trumpet-call to repentance added.

*Thirdly*, the Bible teaching concerning justification by faith and regeneration by the Holy Spirit, as the only way in any age to vital piety and a genuine Christian life. The defect of the revival of 1858 in this regard needs to be remedied by the revival of the closing decade of the nineteenth century. In this way alone can the superficial and mechanical character be eliminated from the various phases of churchly life and work.

*Fourthly*, the necessity for a new baptism of the Holy Ghost, to counteract the swelling tide of worldliness, and to lead the Christian Church to understand that its supreme business is the saving of the world by the Gospel, and that to this end its wealth, its energies, and its members are to be consecrated. Nothing else can stop the mad worship at the shrine of Mammon and turn men back to God. Nothing else can lead the Church to furnish what is needed for the carrying out of Christ's command. Nothing else can transform the present spirit of self-seeking and self-indulgence into the spirit of self-denial and self-sacrifice, of which Christ himself set the example and without which his work can not be done as it should be done; and lead to the spiritual service of Christ in the saving of humanity, in which the work of the Gospel consists. Most of all is it to be emphasized that such baptism of the Holy Ghost is the very thing now needed to make available for spiritual results the power of prayer, the sympathetic and social forces, all the rising tides of Christian unity, and all the perfected machinery of religious effort and activity—

giving force and fervor and divine direction to them all in the conquest of the world for Christ. This is the only way of becoming endued with power from on high !

*Fifthly*, the present and immediate obligation of the Church to give the Gospel to all the world. This is absolutely fundamental; since it would be irrational to expect Christians to do what had not been brought home to them as their duty to Christ.

*Sixthly*, the necessity that the ministry and the officers of the Church should take their places as the called, appointed, and authorized leaders and directors in the gospel work that must be done. Their failure in this respect was, as already seen, a main defect in the awakening of 1858, and in the subsequent years. There was doubtless a providential necessity for this, in order that the lay element in the Church might be brought to understand their duties and responsibilities in the work of the Gospel, into which they had hitherto entered to a very limited extent only; and in order that a sympathetic and social element, which is so powerful a factor in all social and religious movements, might be developed and given the large place that belongs to it in our Christianity. The incompleteness of the results was also doubtless intended to teach the Church in general—especially the more active lay element and the ministers themselves—the absolute necessity for the leadership of the ministry, as doctrinal instructors and as pastors and guides, in all substantial and complete Christian work. The experience of the past generation has furnished an example, on a grand scale, of what Paul illustrated when, in writing to the Church at Corinth, he represented the Church as a "body," in which rational and effective activity requires all the members, from head to feet, to cooperate, each in its own sphere and to the utmost extent of its capabilities.* The day has now come for bringing out and emphasizing this essential ecclesiastical organism, and giving to each part its proper sphere and play, in a combined effort of Protestant Christendom for evangelizing the world.

### (II) Requirements Made of the Entire Ministry.

A second necessity, no less pressing than the one already presented as resting upon the individual preacher, is the organization of a great preaching campaign—into which every preacher and leader in the Church shall enter—having in view the immediate conquest of the world for Christ, in fulfilment of the Great Commission. A few hints must suffice on this topic.

The work can not be accomplished without the most comprehensive union of effort. It is too late in the history of the world for even the greatest of men to expect, unaided, to accomplish any great public task. Union and organization are in the air, and the great man's greatness and wisdom at once are shown by his subsidizing the largest possible number of coadjutors and the largest possible amount of assistance, in carrying out his purposes.

The work must be wisely planned. It is too late to expect great things to be accomplished by desultory efforts. The choicest business wisdom must be exercised in carrying out, as a business enterprise and by business methods, this greatest of all undertakings that has been delegated to the preacher.

* 1 Cor. xii. 12-31.

The plan must be designed with the aim of reaching and setting in motion every Christian and every Christian organization and agency, and subsidizing every possible legitimate force and influence, secular and social, for the accomplishment of the results sought, in the conversion of the world.

Recourse must be had, by the ministry unitedly, to the Spirit of God, from whom must come the enduement with power and the dispensation of the requisite spiritual gifts. The results sought are incalculably great, but, under the direction and impulse of the Spirit of God, their ultimate attainment may be very simple and direct.

Let any preacher get into his mind and heart the real aim of Gospel-preaching in this age, and let him *Course of an Individual Minister.* proceed at once to bend his preaching to its attainment. This is the starting-point. True, it may render it necessary for him to change his whole method and spirit. Several years ago the Rev. Dr. Robert Russell Booth, then pastor of the University Place Presbyterian Church, New York City, was deeply impressed with the value of the revival at that time going forward in the city, under the direction of Mr. Moody. He said to a convention of ministers:

"Such a thing as an inquiry-meeting had never taken place under my sober ministry in my staid Church ; but I resolved that I would appoint one. On Sabbath morning I preached frm the text, 'Come, for all things are now ready.' I said to them, 'This sermon presupposes and involves an invitation, now and here, . . . that now and here you are to have an opportunity for accepting Christ.' The inquiry-meeting was appointed, and ten persons came in and accepted Christ. . . Brethren, have we not to revolutionize the whole system of preaching, and change somewhat our mode of operations ? The trouble is, our sermons do not mount to the climax. If they are mere orations, and theories of Christianity, an invitation to such a meeting is incongruous and absurd."*

A hearty affirmative reply, on the part of the preacher, to Dr. Booth's interrogatory, would doubtless be the needed initial impulse to the work to be done. The practical carrying out of this affirmation would be the initial movement in that work.

If it is asked, What is to be done beyond this? let any Christian minister, who appreciates the situation and the responsibility, stir up the man next to him, in his own church and in the ministry. In this way the circle of influence will grow and widen. The greatest and most genuine revivals that we have ever known have originated and extended in this simple way, without thought of the presence or help of the special revivalist.

Let every preacher who is fully roused carry his own ideas on this subject and his own spirit into the ecclesiastical convention and organization with which he is connected, and thus reach and rouse the whole brotherhood, until all are ready to unite in the work.

Let Christian officers and laymen stir up their associates and neighbors, and consider this great question of present duty with them, until the whole Church is roused and girded for the work. Let the united wisdom of all be employed in planning and pushing the campaign.

The Spirit of God can be relied upon for the proper guidance of the grand work, and for the enduement with the "power from on high" with which to carry it forward. And, in the accomplishment of the great individual tasks that enter into the whole work of

* *Revivals : How and When*, pp. 17, 18.

Christ for the world, we can see no good reason why that commanding genius of reputed Christian men, such as those who have used their genius in iniquitously organizing great Sugar Trusts and Standard Oil Trusts, should not be wrested by the Spirit of God from the service of Mammon and Satan, and employed in such greater, reputable, and holy enterprises as the rapid evangelization of China or of the Dark Continent.

All these are but hints and suggestions thrown out to those who have the promise that they will be made wise to understand the will of God, if they are ready to do that will.* The accomplishment of the glorious work will undoubtedly require the spiritual awakening and quickening of every individual preacher of the Gospel; his intelligent apprehension and appreciation of Christ's present call to carry out his commission now; and the wisest application of his consecrated powers to the accomplishment of the task set before him. It will require the consecrated and combined effort of all the ministry, and of all the Church, embracing the hosts of able laymen of large business capacity and experience, and the great lay organizations of old and young, in the carrying out of the purpose of Christ by the present generation; and the persistent and unwearied pushing of the work along all lines until it is accomplished.

### *Retrospect and Prospect.*

To present the possibility and the feasibility of the immediate accomplishment of this great work of the Gospel for the world of mankind, and to make clear the responsibility of the Church for its being done *now*, these chapters have been written. The command

---
* John vii. 17.

of Christ, that it be done now, is unmistakable. The evidence of the providential readiness of all that is necessary for the work is overwhelming. The signs of the times indicate the presence of the conditions of the glorious coming of the Master to victory, and emphasize the imminence of his coming.

In the light of all these considerations, the glance that a living Church casts down from the eminence to which the ages have brought her, can not but be an anxious one. Looking out upon the world, and noting the signs of the times, it is impossible to resist the conviction that she is at the dawning of an eventful period in her history. The growth of the modern missionary movement has been confessedly one of the marvels of the world. That God, for the coming of whose Kingdom all things are working together, has prepared the way for it by the progress of science, art, and civilization is already noted. There has always been this same perishing world, but it has heretofore been a far-off world. The later centuries have been bringing it nearer and into living contact with the Church, until, at last, by that mysterious electric power that with equal ease spans the continents and oceans God is gathering the nations into one mighty audience chamber of the Gospel, to the remotest aisles of which every voice in the Church may reach, and the touch of every hand vibrate. The rapidity of the flight of the angel of the Apocalypse, bearing the everlasting Gospel, seems about to be realized.

And in the movements of God's Kingdom this nation has, by its geographical position, its political character, its commercial connection, and the orderings of Providence, been made a center. Upon us the Old World has poured out its superabundant population. Besides the myriads brought near by the wonderfully increased means of intercommunication, here are the millions from darkened Africa, thrown into direct contact with the Church; furnishing, so to speak, the links in the chain of sympathy that is to bind her to the destinies of the world. Here, in control of the Church, is the learning requisite to translate the Bible into every tongue, within the lifetime of a single generation. Here is the printing-press, with which to print a copy of it for every son and daughter of Adam within the same period. Saying nothing of the rest of Christendom, here are the men from whom messengers might in the same time be sent to every hamlet on the face of the globe; and here is the beginning of the very work itself in the present spontaneous uprising and consecration to the work of Christ of great multitudes of young men and women, who are either preparing to go or are already waiting to be sent. And here is the gold with which to accomplish all this work in so brief space. The great thoroughfares by which the missionaries and Bibles might be sent are open. These considerations and facts open to us the glorious possibilities—what shall the actual be? A complete Christianity, working with full power in the Church of this land, and out from it, would, we doubt not, in the course of the next quarter century, compass the globe with its saving and elevating influences, and usher in the millennial glory. Shall all this be?

The answer will depend, in chief measure, under God, upon what the *ministry* shall be for these coming years, and upon what the character of the *preaching* shall be. Providence has prepared the universal mines for shattering with equal ease and completeness the newest and most formidable strongholds of iniquity in the centers of Christendom, and the intrenched citadels of paganism hoary with age. The trains have been laid and are waiting for the impulse, the leadership, the moral inspiration of the ministry, with the "tongues of fire" and the lips touched with the live coals from off the altar of God, to rouse the Church, fire the train, and complete the great consummation. What will the preacher and the Church have wherewith to answer the Master, if the work be not done without delay?

# CHAPTER V.

## THE PREACHER AS A PASTOR IN THESE TIMES.

PREACHING is admittedly a most important, as well as a most solemn work; but the gathering of its fruits into the Church of Christ, and their conservation there, depend upon the preacher's office of pastor, or shepherd of the flock of God. Christ's threefold charge to Peter, on the shores of the Lake of Tiberias, was: "Feed my sheep." "Feed my lambs." "Shepherd my sheep." That charge is on the preacher and pastor still. The preacher's commission, message, and furnishing prepare for his preaching; but the preaching and all the rest for his work in the care of souls, including their ingathering into the Church and their nurture and direction in the work of the Church. If the question be asked, What is the work of the preacher as pastor in these times? the answer may be given:

*The ingathering and shepherding of those who are saved by the preaching of the Gospel, and their wise organization and direction in the great campaign for the immediate salvation of the world.*

The problem of the pastorate for these times—how to accomplish this work—is certainly one whose im-
**The Problem of the Pastorate.** portance is only equaled by its difficulty. The minister, in his twofold character of preacher and pastor, and as the divinely appointed

leader in the work of the Church, must have an intense and abiding interest in its discussion and solution.

It is proposed to consider the question of the efficiency of the pastorate in its relations to the circumstances and the wants, the great difficulties and the imperative demands, of the present age, in order to ascertain, if possible, what needs to be done to bring it up to the requisite efficiency for completing the successful carrying out of the preacher's commission, and obtaining the desired results from the preacher's message.

In dealing with this subject, we shall consider the work of the pastorate as embracing all the duties of the minister resulting from his office, except those that have to do directly with the pulpit and preparation for it; and shall take it for granted that, under God, the efficiency of the work of the Church depends very much upon it; the two offices mutually presupposing and involving each other. It may also be said, at the outset, that this discussion has nothing to do with finding some new method of doing God's work that shall be better than the ordinary method; for, in the workings of grace, no less than of creation, the rule laid down by God for guidance is always broad enough to meet the wants of all ages; so that the Gospel and the essential law of the pastorate can as little need to be changed, improved, or supplemented as can the law of gravitation. In short, the highest that the Church can hope to do is to hold fast by God's method, and to adjust that method to the needs of the times in which we live.

## SECTION FIRST.

### Changed Pastoral Conditions and Popular Ways of Meeting Them.

Before considering either the Divine Law of the pastorate or the required adjustment to present needs, it is necessary to take account of some of the altered circumstances that have materially modified the conditions of pastoral work, and to glance at some popular ways of regarding the law of the pastorate and adapting it to meet existing wants.

### I. Revolution in Pastoral Conditions.

In taking a survey of the state of things in our own land, as bearing upon this subject, it becomes clear that a great revolution has been going forward, in the business, the character, the social usages, and the methods of Christian work, and that, while this revolution has materially changed the elements that are to be taken into account in solving the problem of bringing the Gospel to bear more effectively upon the masses through the pastorate, it has also greatly enhanced the difficulty of that solution.

We note, first, the revolution in business. The modern advance in the arts, that has brought and bound all nations together, has extended the arena on which the daily strife of business is carried on, from the narrow limits of the single town to the confines of the world. Out of this transaction of business for the world, rather than for the village, has come an activity proportionally increased, and therefore by so much the more intense and engrossing.

*Revolution in Business.*

And besides this immense expansion, there has taken place an entire change in the controlling principle in the pursuit of wealth. William Cunningham, in *Politics and Economics* (lectures delivered in Cambridge University, England), has pointed out clearly that three periods are to be distinguished in English economic history:

1. When the methods of pursuing wealth were determined in accordance with Christian morality.

2. When they were directed in accordance with national policy.

3. When free play was allowed to individuals to pursue the courses they preferred.

An understanding of these is necessary to any proper appreciation of the present business situation and problems. The first was the medieval method, when the Christian doctrine of right was applied to prices of labor and commodities and to rates of interest, by both canon and civil law, and when labor was honored and the great industrial gilds flourished, and English industrial interests were at the front. The second method came into vogue in the sixteenth century, when the new continents had been discovered and opened up, the European nationalities developed, and national rivalry brought in, and the application of the Christian doctrines of economics, as embodied in canon and civil law, discredited in the casting off of the shackles of Romanism. The result was the exaltation of English national economic interests and of great chartered monopolies—the whole system being directed against conflicting interests of foreign nations. The third, or *laissez-faire*, method, came in with the changed ideas and conditions of the eighteenth century, and was the result of the effort of constitutionally free England to break down the old monopolies and give the citizen a chance once more in the competitions of trade and industry. During the present century it has been mainly a struggle to restrict the evils of free competition, in its unmoral or immoral aspects, by law, and to comprehend and adjust individual and public interests not yet thoroughly comprehended and adjusted.

In this country, where we are just in the midst of this struggle, the development of the *laissez-faire* principle, as immoral, cut-throat competition, has reached the extreme; so that, in the opinion of many able economists and business men, legitimate business, on Christian principles, has become well-nigh impossible. Speculation has become the order of the day in everything. The road to wealth is no longer by the old slow way of waiting for the legitimate increase of demand, or of adding to value by actual change of place or form; but rather, by forcing a fictitious demand, by taking advantage of the pressing necessities of men. In Wall Street and "on change," and in all other trade, a grand game is being played, involving as the stake every staple article of food and clothing, every necessary and every luxury of life, and the privileges of land, water, and air. From the sudden and extraordinary changes brought about by these speculative operations, there results a risk in the transactions of the smaller tradesmen that was formerly unknown. There is no escape from such risk, for, in bringing about the ends of the speculation, combinations are daily formed that command their millions and control the price of everything, and that are equally ready to take the proceeds of the broker's gambling and to snatch the hard-earned bread from the mouth of the starving poor. Corners, pools, combines, trusts—these are threatening the life of the individual and the life of the nation.

In this anxious whirl, men of business have little time for religious intercourse or thought, and are almost inaccessible to a pastor.

A revolution in character and social usages has followed upon this change in trade. Sentiment is fast outgrowing principle. The merchant or tradesman, worried by the business of the world and absorbed in it, has neither time nor disposition to lay a solid basis of principle in himself or in the members of his household, or in those connected with his business establishment. It is neither easy nor comfortable to think closely of principles when the life is so abnormal. *(Revolution in Character and Usages.)*

This has been superficially designated a day of "introspection"; but it is this only as to feelings, not as to principles. Principles do not trouble the mass of men much. They have been in many cases deeply overlaid by the increase of imposing religious forms and ceremonies, or forgotten in the hurry of work carried even into the Church. Rogers, in the *Greyson Letters*, suggests to his novel-reading niece that to save herself from imbecility from overmuch novel-reading, she keep a debtor and creditor account of sentimental indulgence and practical benevolence, with occasional memoranda running thus :

"For the sweet tears I shed over the romantic sorrows of Charlotte Devereaux ; sent three basins of gruel and a flannel petticoat to poor old Molly Brown."

The suggestion might be happily applied to much of our life, to bring it back to reality and truth again.

Busy men aver that they have not time to think on the great religious and theological topics. They protest against their minister's setting them to thinking, on the Sabbath-day. They are too weary for that. This is true on both sides of the ocean. A generation ago, a visitor asked a noted judge in Edinburgh: "Who is the greatest preacher in your city?" "Dr. Candlish," was the answer. "Do you attend his church?" "Oh, no!" was the reply; "I am tired when the Sabbath comes, and do not want to be made to think. I go to hear Dr. Guthrie. He does not require me to think." The old foundations of strong doctrine having thus been lost out, a pastor now too seldom finds, in the basis of character, the earnestness of the stern old Puritan by which to lay hold of men and mold them.

At the same time the rapid changes in social position have introduced new barriers between pastor and people. The changes resulting from the false modes of business have given rise to a mass of conventionalities—chiefly as a fashion in the uncultivated rising families, and partly as a defense in those already occupying the high places of society—that clog the whole interior and better life, and have induced a contempt and a disrelish for honest work, that tends to the destruction of strength and manliness.

The old-fashioned home of half a century ago, with all the family gathered around one hearthstone, is less and less seen in the mansions of the opulent; while the closet is at the same time crowded out by the fashion and the constant round of excitement. In the winter, the family must break up and the main part of it go South, while the father goes to the hotel or the club-house; in the summer, they must flit to the mountains or to the sea-side resort; between the coming and the going there are perhaps a few days or weeks of rest, in what passes under the name of *home*, but has lost its sacredness and its attractions. Or perhaps most of the household go to Europe for a few years, leaving the husband and father, and possibly the oldest son, to remain homeless during that long period, and to carry on the business necessary to support the extravagant outlay. In the mean time, there have grown up, in this so-called democratic country, the pretentious display and glittering vice of the great demoralizing club-houses, and the supreme sillinesses of the social four hundreds, and all that. In many of the families involved, all worthy aim in life is taken from the young; idleness begets imbecility, worthlessness, and positive vice; and, with the increased temptations of the day, the tendency of much of the wealthy society is veering rapidly away from religion and downward.

These and many other things conspire, in some cases, to make the home and the every-day life almost inaccessible to the pastor; and perhaps, in most instances, to an absolute divorce of the home and family from the Church and church life, that places them practically beyond the reach of religion. In the mean time there has been an immense influx into our country of peoples of foreign nationality, in which there are, to say the least, some very undesirable elements, whose presence has increased the hindrances in the way of the pastor's work. These elements have imported with them their foreign notions of morality and formal religion, and of the Sabbath as a day of recreation and amusement, and their foreign drinking usages and habits; and they have added a vast mass of dense ignorance and extreme corruption to the social body. They have entered into business and social alliances with the native-born citizens, and have become a powerful factor in shaping public sentiment in favor of liberalism, socialism, and anarchism. Whole communities have thus been foreignized, and brought into open opposition to all that is best in our Christian civilization. As some of these people are very thrifty in a business way, they have been able to set up new social barriers in the way of the approach of any evangelical minister, and have thus made themselves practically inaccessible to such. Almost every community has, in these various ways, come to have a dead weight of irreligion and immorality (perhaps glossed over), and of more or less open infidelity, resting upon it, and the difficulty of the work of the pastor has been greatly increased thereby.

There has taken place a corresponding change in the methods of Christian work. We have a vivid recollection of the impression made upon us, several years since, relative to this very subject of the work of the Church, by that admirable little book of Dr. Fish, *Primitive Piety Revived.* The want of "individualism" was set forth as one of the great wants of the piety of the age. But if that could have been written then, how much more now, when our labor-saving machinery in the Church has become as perfect as that in the factory or on the farm! The conversion of the world is rightly our great work. But how often, alas! is the little work of the individual lost in this complicated machinery. Organizations have an indispensable place. It is not, however, to supersede, but to evoke and systemize, the Christian work of individual men;

*Changed Christian Methods.*

not as a substitute for personal effort, but as the instruments for insuring it and rendering it effective. It is too much the case that everything can be done by machinery and by proxy now. There is some way by which every one can give his money and withhold his personal presence and effort, while securing a substitute to carry on the work of every department of moral reform, Christian philanthropy, and religious instruction. The children of the family are to be taught. They can be turned over to the Sunday-school. The masses outside of the Church are to be looked after and saved. That can be given over to the mission-school and hired missionary. The Church of God is to be built up. That work is safe in the hands of the pastor. The tide of vice in the community is to be stayed. Instead of having the trouble of going to the victims, and by personal Christian kindliness lifting them up and saving them, and then by personal influence and example elevating the tone of society till it shall be an efficient aid in this work, the power of legislation rather is relied upon, and the whole matter turned over to the civil government, to legislate the moral evil out of existence, and the individual Christian conscience into quiet sleep. All this change in the method of the work has put the individual further from the reach of pastoral effort.

While these changes have been taking place, there has arisen an increased demand upon the pulpit. Perhaps this may not be owing to greater intelligence and culture in some of the hearers; but rather to the general diffusion of the Bible and religious literature, and of information on all subjects. When the Pilgrim Fathers came to this country, the first English translation of

*Increased Demand on the Pulpit.*

the Bible (Coverdale's) had been read only eighty-five years, and King James's version had been published but nine years, and had not been much used as yet. Every child had not a Bible then, as he has now. What was acceptable and edifying to the men of that age, as dispensed from the pulpit, may be commonplace and unimportant now, even to the child. This increased demand upon the preacher has rendered it more difficult to meet the requirements made of the pastor, by so much abridging the time at his command.

II. POPULAR METHODS OF MEETING THE CHANGES.

With this glance at some of the altered circumstances of the age, that most seriously affect the pastoral work, we turn to inquire briefly, What has been done toward the adjustment of the energies of the pastorate to these changed conditions?

It is hard to divest oneself of the conviction that much remains to be done in this direction, both in the task of formulating the law of the pastorate, and in making the proper adjustment of it to present conditions. Touching the twofold work of the minister, as preacher and pastor, we have had our "homiletics" and "pastoral theology"; but in the old treatment of the subjects involved in them, while the sphere of the pulpit is plainly and adequately defined, the scope of the pastorate is not so clearly determined. There are certain duties somehow connected with the twofold work—and all-important duties they are in this day—which the authors have not seemed to know exactly how to deal with, or to which part to assign them, even when conscious of their existence.

Almost thirty years ago, Dr. Horace Bushnell, in an address before the Porter Rhetorical Society of Andover Theological Seminary, on "Pulpit Talent," brought forward and emphasized one of these duties—that of *administration*—in making "administrative or organizing capacity" one of his "preaching talents." He evidently did it with hesitancy, altho he said not. In the ordinary schemes there was no place assigned for any such talent; perhaps the ordinary definitions excluded it. That address appeared to be the first revelation of it to many. Dr. Shedd, while showing in his work on *Homiletical and Pastoral Theology*—from his point of view so admirable—that he was conscious of the existence of such a side to pastoral work, was content to say, in his definition, that the office of a pastor "is to give private and personal advice from house to house and to make his influence felt in the social and domestic life of his congregation"; and then, in his further development of the subject, to recognize the negative and subjective side of this work of administration by making "decision" one of the necessary qualities of the pastor's character in his relation to the Church. This point, like many others, seems to have been only gradually working its way into the teaching-consciousness of the Church. Now we do not, either in Christian doctrine or in the law of the pastorate, believe in any change by way of improvement upon God's Word; but we do believe in change, by way of development and growth in knowledge, and by way of adaptation to the varying wants and characters of men. Were we to venture a criticism upon the old view of this subject, it would be that it failed to take into account the necessity and fact of change by way of adaptation to

*[margin: Administrative Talent.]*

the changing circumstances of living men, so that it sent the pastor to the oversight of an *abstract man* (perhaps it should be said a *student*), just as it often sent the preacher to preach to an *abstract sinner*.

It is sufficiently obvious that, in some quarters, the changed condition of things, to which attention has just been called, has not been noted at all. When it is reported, for example, that the additions in membership to one large branch of the Church, for a certain year, were all in one-half the churches in that denomination, the information is sadly significant. In other quarters, the revolution spoken of has been marked and taken into account, and has led to various experiments by way of remedy, sometimes in apparent ignorance or neglect of the great Divine principles that should govern all Christian work. It falls in with the present purpose briefly to notice some of these experiments.

Men of one class have sought to increase the efficiency of the pastorate by grasping after larger personal influence, through letting themselves down to the level of the world and its demands. Reference is not to men of the stripe of "Rev. Joseph Bellamy Stoker" of Holmes, or "Parson Stiggins" of Dickens; for we believe that such rarely exist, save in the imagination of men who know but little of the character of an evangelical ministry, or who have learned to despise all that was noble in their own ancestry. But there has been among the younger clergy, in some instances, a reckless grasping after popularity, at the expense of Christian character and influence, truly alarming. In the pulpit, or out among the people, they are ready to bring to market just the wares for which there is the most ready sale—extravagant story and theatrical ges-

*1. By Descending to the Level of the World.*

ture for the Sabbath and the sacred desk; vulgar familiarity and shameless jest for the week-day and the home. We have known the same man to startle an audience on the Sabbath by shouting from the pulpit: "The motto of the world is, every man for himself, and the devil take the hindermost!" and then, on the week-day, to confirm his right to the character thus won, by securing the setting up of a billiard-table in the rooms of a Christian organization.

Now, putting the best construction possible upon such conduct, the course taken must be pronounced a ruinous blunder; for, in attaining the notoriety that such a method brings, the man casts away all religious power among the people by forfeiting all claim to their respect. In the cases of this kind that have come under our observation,—and they have been somewhat numerous,—the next step has been an open breach with evangelical Christianity and a quick passage to the ranks of infidelity.

Men of another class have attempted to bring the whirl of the world, with the secular spirit, into the Church, and to restore the power of the Church over the world by making concessions to the world and conforming to it. 2. By Bringing the World into the Church. The amusement question, that has been so much under discussion in some quarters, had its origin, in its connection with the Church, in the time-serving, world-serving spirit of this class of men. The leaven is to be put into the lump; card-playing and billiard-playing are to be sanctified; Paul's rule of refraining from eating meat, when it makes a brother to stumble, is to give way to Christian "liberty," so called. We have heard men in high places favor the establishment of religious club rooms, with all the approved appliances of a club room, for reclaiming the young men of our cities and furnishing them society! Articles advocating these things, having not even the poor merit of ability to atone for their error, have filled the secular journals, and have even been admitted to places in leading religious papers. Be it recorded to the honor of the Christian young men of the country that, when, more than twenty-five years ago, the matter came to be pressed upon their attention at the national convention held at Montreal, they emphatically pronounced against all complicity with such time-serving schemes.

This is but one of the ways in which men of the spirit here deprecated have set about their work of secularizing the Church. More recently it has been seriously proposed, by a prominent city clergyman, to found saloons, under church control, for the saving of young men! It is self-evident that all such schemes must be futile, as they can only result in worldliness, or in worldly power, if in any power at all.

Men of still another class have sought to devise new methods of Christian work to meet the obvious wants of the day. These have been put in the place of the simple and divinely ordained method of the Church. In some regions the aim has been to introduce some popular service in the place of the second preaching service. Organization upon organization has been added to the regular church machinery, to make it equal to its mission. We knew of one pastor who organized the young members of his congregation into what a good mother in Israel called a "singing-gang," and sent them out to spend the Sabbath afternoons in singing to the sick people of the parish. It was somewhat barren of spiritual fruits, but resulted in as many weddings as

*By Devising New Methods.*

there were couples in the "singing-gang." It seems indeed to have been almost forgotten in many quarters, that all the methods given by God to the Church are none the less perfect and adequate because of their simplicity, so that nothing needs to be added to them.

But the innumerable conventions and conferences, and the much discussion, have shown that the Church at large is conscious of not having reached the right method of adjustment, while at the same time it has come to realize in some degree the increased difficulty in reaching men, and the real lack of efficiency and adequacy in the work of the pastorate, as it is now understood and wrought. It sees that things are going wrong, but it has not yet hit upon a remedy; hence the protracted discussion grows in interest and earnestness. And it must be noted, by the way, that such discussion, while it is the harbinger of coming progress, is at the same time an indispensable condition to such progress. Every generation—we might with truth say, every man—must discuss and solve each practical, moral, and social problem for itself, before the truth involved in it can find a place of power in the consciousness and hearts of men. The ministry should, therefore, always hail the agitation of such a subject as an ally in the work of God.

Meanwhile, for the pastor to go on his course in the way the fathers went, ignoring or giving no heed to all such recurring agitation growing out of changing circumstances, were as unwise as for the military man to cling to his old-fashioned guns and his wooden ships, regardless of the revolution wrought by earthworks and steel armored cruisers. And hence, by just so much as any one interested in the results of such movement delays to enter into it, and make the requisite investigation of principles and adjustment of forces, he suffers serious loss. What needs to be done should be done at the earliest possible moment. The ministry, the Church, should certainly meet the situation fairly, and if we find ourselves, our principles, or our methods, at fault, in directing the forces ordained of God for the work of the Church, neither pride of consistency nor love of conservatism should be allowed to prevent us from righting whatever is found wrong.

## SECTION SECOND.

**The Requisites to the Increased Efficiency Demanded.**

This preliminary discussion has prepared for the treatment of the practical question, *What is to be done to bring the pastorate, in efficiency, up to the requirements of the times?*

Its shortcomings in efficiency or adequacy may result either from the departure of the Church from the Divine law laid down for the guidance of the work; or from failure, on the part of the one who holds the office of pastor, to come up to the demands of his position. The subject at this point, therefore, naturally falls into two parts: first, the Divine law of the pastorate, and then, the pastor for the place and age.

### I. The Divine Law of the Pastorate, and how Observed.

The Divine law of the pastorate must first be clearly defined and affirmed. The place must be considered, first, to prepare for ascertaining the qualities that fit the man for the place. In order to reach any satisfactory view on this subject, it is obviously a first necessity that there should be a return to the Biblical idea of the Church as "the body of Christ," and to learn from this its organization and work, for on this wise only can the place of the pastorate, in its relation to the whole, be ascertained. The only right mode of procedure is to ascertain, first, what the office is, and then make the definition to suit; not, as is so often done, to construct first the definition; and then warp or dwarf the thing to suit it.

There are three commonly received propositions in this connection that are held to be fundamental:

1. In the Church of Christ, in the entire membership, are to be found the human energies that are to be directed to the accomplishment of Christ's work of salvation in the world. *Three Fundamental Propositions.*

2. The prerogative and duty of directing these energies inheres in that Church in its organized capacity.

3. The pastorate holds, under Christ, the chief place in that work of direction.

These three propositions, while they mark off the sphere and authority of the pastorate, furnish, it is believed, at the same time, the logical and Scriptural basis on which the Church is to build.

(I) THE ENERGIES IN THE MEMBERSHIP.

In the Church of Christ, in its entire membership, are to be found the human energies which are to be directed to the accomplishment of Christ's work in the world.

In opening this discussion, the place of the Spirit

of God is, of course, to be carefully guarded. The preaching of the word of Christ and work for Christ, both attended by the Holy Ghost, are the two great instrumentalities in the extension of Christ's kingdom, and without the Holy Ghost the work is as worthless as the preaching is ineffectual. But, under the Spirit, the working element is to be found in the Church of Christ, and takes in the entirety of its membership.

And by this it is meant to include the two aspects of the truth: that each member of the Church is a worker sent of Christ on a special mission, and that all the members in their united capacity are coworkers with Christ. Individual effort and combined effort are the two sides of the law that governs all the work of the universe. The illimitable forests that cover the hills like the shadow of God have been built by the combined work of the single leaves; the mighty tides that gird the globe are but the sum of the flow of the single drops; the tempests that sweep over the earth with resistless force only combine the momentum of single particles of the viewless air; the force of gravitation that hurls the innumerable starry train along with such fearful velocity only sums up the power of the single atoms, each of which pulls for itself. In precisely the same way, the vast work of the Church in bringing the world back to God, is only the sum of single efforts, the combined work of single Christians. The whole frame-work of Christianity presupposes this twofold principle. The mission and structure of the Church embody it. The history of the early Christian converts conspicuously exhibited its practical working.

Paul, in his Epistles, takes special pains to present and enforce both its aspects. A "manifestation of the Spirit is given to every man for the profit" of the Church and the world.* This is one aspect. It contemplates man as an individual. As each man is to repent for himself, believe for himself, live for himself, and die and give an account for himself; so the Holy Ghost gives each man a gift peculiar to himself, and assigns to him a place and work suited to himself, in carrying on the great work of the Church for the salvation of a lost world.

Paul exhibits, by the relation of the parts of the body to the whole, the relation of the work of each man to the whole work of the Church.† This is the other aspect. God has so arranged the parts of the human body as to constitute one living organic whole, in which harmonious cooperation is added to the action of the individual parts. If any one part refuses to perform its office,—if the eye refuses to see, or the ear to hear, or the hand to work at the bidding of the soul,—the power and completeness of the body are destroyed and its mission made a failure. Just so God has fixed the position and gifts of every member of Christ's body, the Church,—the endowments being as various as the places,—and the harmonious cooperation of all in their places is as essential in the Church as the united working of the eye, the ear, and the hand, in their places in the human frame.

The Church is thus to be regarded as a great working institution, in which each member is to be a workman for God, with the ability given him in his own appointed place; and in which all together are to be regarded as cooperating in carrying out the one plan of God. This is the divine law of the work of the Church, and here are to be found, in the individual

* 1 Cor. xii. 8.  † 1 Cor. xii. 12-27.

members and their gifts from the Holy Spirit, the energies that are to be directed to the accomplishment of Christ's designs in the world.

(II) THE AUTHORITY IN THE ORGANIZED CHURCH.

Believing that this needs little more than to be stated fully and clearly, to gain admission, we pass to the second proposition: that the prerogative and duty of directing its own energies in its work inhere in the Church in its organized capacity. All forms of Church government imply this, at least to the extent to which it is here desirable to affirm it. All churches assume it as fundamental. Christ has organized and endowed the Church for this mission. It has this right in virtue of Christ indwelling.

There are three conceivable ways of proceeding in all our Christian work : *first*, that by independent individual effort ; *secondly*, that by voluntary organized effort ; *thirdly*, that by organized Church effort.

The *first method*—that by independent individual effort—has the advantage of simplicity. Its doctrine is : " Let every man work with his might in his own sphere. God deals with men, not in the mass, but as single souls. They are regenerated, sanctified, and saved, as individuals. Every man whom God saves, he saves and sends forth to work for him in the world. All power must, in the last analysis, be resolved into individual power—the power of gravitation into the pull of the single atoms ; the power of the Church into the energies of its separate members. Let every man labor for Christ, to the extent of his ability, in his place, and the work will go forward. It requires no officers, no cumbrous machinery."

Now this method has a most important truth at its foundation, one of the truths embraced in our first proposition, but not both. It is certainly a great advantage to have a simple way of doing our work; but just as certainly there are things that men, as individuals and working alone, can not accomplish. Sometimes the power of many individuals needs to be gathered up and directed to one end, in order to do what must be done. We must have all the individual effort; but, in addition to that, we must have organized effort too.

The *second method*—that of voluntary organization—has been proposed to meet this necessity. The doctrine is : " Let those, who choose to do it, combine together voluntarily for that purpose, devise their plans, and prepare their machinery for carrying out those plans. Union is strength. Together men can accomplish what, working singly, is beyond far their power to compass."

This method has the advantage over the other of organizing effort, of combining the single and separate; and it takes into account both sides of the truth of our first proposition. But theoretically it involves a fatal error, in departing from the truth of our second proposition. It assumes that it is not the duty and prerogative of the Church, as organized by Christ, to direct its own energies in its appointed work. It assumes that the Church, to which Christ has given the mission of saving the world, is not fitted for its work, or is not equal to it, and that man can devise some better way of doing God's work. Practically, it is against economy, against unity, dangerous in its tendencies, and must prove a failure ; against *economy*, for it introduces a new set of machinery, and every new set requires so much the more power in managing it; against *unity*, for it divides the energies of the Church, and weakens it by so much disorganizing in organizing ; *dangerous* in its tendencies, for it is irresponsible in its direction and control, and must fail at last, for nothing can succeed that is not done in Christ's appointed way.

The *third method*—that of organized Church effort—is believed to be the Scriptural method, and the one applicable in all ordinary work. It was to the Church as organized by Christ that the Great Commission, to preach the Gospel to every creature, was given, and, with that commission, there was conferred upon it the authority to devise all the plans, and to invent all the mechanism and direct all the power required in its execution.

It can not be denied that this way has the advantage of simplicity. It does not divide the energies of the Church; but, recognizing the fact that its work is one, it unites and concentrates all its power. Moreover, it keeps everything out of irresponsible hands, by giving the control to those whom Christ, in and through the Church, calls to the positions of authority, and who are directly subject to the Church and responsible to it. More than all, it is willing to accept Christ's way as the best way, tho it be an old and plain way. It has thus all the advantages of unity and concentration, simplicity and directness, organization and responsibility, scripturalness and the consequent divine approval.

We hold it, therefore, to be fundamental, vital truth, that it is at once the prerogative and the duty of the Church, as constituted of Christ, to direct its own energies in its appointed work.

## (III) The Pastor in the Leadership.

Our third proposition is that the pastorate holds, under Christ, the chief place in the direction of the energies of the Church in its mission.

The pastor is properly at the head of the directing element, whatever it may be. It can hardly be doubted that this is in accordance with the teaching of the Scriptures. Christ's words to Peter, when he restored him after his fall, were: "Feed my sheep"; "Feed my lambs"; "Shepherd my sheep."* These words unfold the work for the old and the young, and add to instruction the office of guarding, directing, in short, whatever is included in "shepherding" the sheep. In his charge to the elders at Ephesus, Paul exhorts them to "take heed to all the flock, over which the Holy Ghost hath made you overseers."† Christ is the shepherd and bishop of our souls. Under him, the minister is the under-shepherd and bishop; as Christ's representative, the head of the particular Church over which God places him. This has been substantially the working-theory of all the branches of the evangelical Church in this country. Methodism assumed this as the basis, and doubtless owes much of its efficiency in the past to its rigid adherence to it. The Protestant Episcopal body, altho adhering to what Dr. Samuel Hanson Cox once characterized as "the doctrine of the threefold disorder of the clergy," and even when manifesting a hierarchical bent, has always given to the ministry the chief place in the direction of the energies of the Church in the work of Christ. Congregationalism in this country, tho starting from another

\* John xxi. 15–18.   † Acts xx. 28.

theory in the abstract, has been compelled, in its actual working, to come to the basis so well expressed in the Saybrook Platform, which reads thus, on this point : "We agree that the ministerial office is instituted by Jesus Christ for the gathering, guiding, edifying, and governing of his Church ; and continue to the end of the world." The Presbyterian Church gives no uncertain sound, as it makes the pastor the head of the session, which is over the church and everything in it, from the choir to the Sabbath-school.

Our third proposition, may, therefore, be taken to accord at once with the Scriptures and with the general views of the evangelical churches.

### (IV) Failure to Conform to the Divine Law.

If these three fundamental propositions are true, it must be evident that departure from any one of them must destroy or impair the efficiency of the pastorate, while it must also cripple the work of the Church. If, in the estimation of Christians, the mission of the Church, and every member in it, is not one of earnest work for Christ ; then there is a lack of the full energies for the Church to direct. If it be not considered the prerogative and duty of the Church, as organized by its great head, to direct those energies in the work; then they are, to say the least, out of the reach of the pastorate. If the chief place in directing be not accorded to the pastorate, aided by other office-bearers; then the pastor at once sinks to the level of any private member, and there is no one in the Church who embodies the idea of unity that is so essential to success.

But to turn from what should be to what has been,

from theory to practise—too often the Church has not conformed to this Scriptural theory, and failure or inefficiency has, therefore, been the too common result.

Practically, the majority of the churches do not hold by our first proposition. The Church is looked upon too exclusively as a great ark, in which men are to be borne safely to heaven; and too little as a body of workmen, sent to use all its energies for the spread and prevalence of the Gospel. We see no reason why a church of many hundred members, filled with the Holy Ghost and conscious of their commission, should not to-day, with the grander facilities for work and influence, make themselves felt in the world even more powerfully than did those hundreds who went forth on that first mission for Christ; yet who does not know many a a church with such a membership that scarcely holds its own from year to year? The elders, deacons, and private members practically all unite in saying: "We have nothing to do, and will do nothing"; and there are therefore no living energies to be directed. *First Principle Neglected.*

Practically there has also been a wide departure from the truth of our second proposition. The Church, as organized of Christ and fitted for the work of directing its own energies in his work, and gifted with the prerogative and duty of directing them, has been very largely denied its place in practise, or has failed to come up to its duty. The great number of voluntary organizations existing for the purpose of doing the work that God has made the special duty of the Church—which often aim to control the Church rather than to be controlled by it, and which are wholly beyond the reach of the divinely given government of the Church—is proof in point. *Second Principle Disregarded.*

It is freely admitted that such organizations have had their origin in the failure of the Church to do its work, or sometimes even in its refusal; and that they have been devised by earnest men in the Church, under the apparent pressure of necessity; and we insist that the Church, in allowing its work to call for any such new methods, is guilty before God. But it is true, nevertheless, that there is a better way of remedying the evil; for, while it is admitted that organization is invaluable, since two working together can accomplish more than twice what each one could if working alone, yet it can hardly be disputed that the same energy, in the Church and working in Christ's appointed way, will do more than working in any way that man can possibly devise. Where collision and conflict have not resulted from the voluntary and divisive course, the life has either been drained from the Church, or its energies divided, and the elements of power God has given it for his glory practically placed beyond its reach.

But even where the first two principles have been acknowledged, that involved in the third proposition has too often been ignored or denied.

*Third Principle Ignored.*

The pastor is widely looked upon too much as a hireling of the people. With many disposed to give him a higher place, he is still merely a member of an honorable profession. Many who honor him still more, confine the sphere of the pastorate to the narrow limit of ministering to the sick and afflicted, and influencing the people in their social and domestic relations. Few are inclined to concede to him, beyond this, the larger and more important sphere of presiding and governing in the work of bending the energies of the Church to the task of the world's salvation.

This is doubtless in great measure the fault of the ministry themselves; they have often given up their headship voluntarily, because of the amount of labor involved in it, and have been only too glad to let the Church take its own course or no course at all, as best suited it; but in many instances the pastor has been denied his true place, in all the work of the Church, and even put out of it. The Reformation justly cast out the idea of *priesthood* from its conception of the ministry. In its failure to discriminate clearly, Protestantism has since almost cast out the ideas of *direction* and *control*. With both *priesthood* and *headship* retained, the papacy wields a marvelous power; with neither, the Protestant Church is largely shorn of its vigor and efficiency.

Now it is evident that the first adjustment demanded by these times is a threefold adjustment of the practise of the Church to this divine law. *The Adjustment Required.*

The Reformation, under Luther, fixed in the heart of the Church the vital truth that man can only be saved by personal faith in the Lord Jesus Christ. There seems almost to be needed a second reformation, to fix in the soul of every member of the Church the vital truth that he has been saved in order that he may become a personal worker for the Lord Jesus Christ, and that every Christian, if he is not to forfeit his title to the name, must go to work for Christ. This will give the energies to be directed. Christians must be brought to understand, and feel too, that the Church is a Divine institution, ordained of Christ for the mission of the world's conversion; gifted with the requisite powers; containing in its simple organization all the machinery necessary, and at once competent to the direction of those powers and the wielding of that machinery; and irrevocably under obligation to carry forward the work at once in obedience to Christ's command. And then the Church, with this consciousness of its mission, instead of planting itself immovably across the track of progress, must carry forward the work with all its powers in God's way.

And the Church obviously needs to rise to that larger conception of the sphere of the pastorate that shall clearly take in all its functions and recognize the sacredness of the office; and then to seek, in its schools of training, to mold and fashion those sent of God to fill that office in accordance with such larger conception, so that the right man may be prepared for the place. And the pastor needs to take his place of direction; and when he does so—with a working membership, organized in the church and under one chief director—we may expect glorious progress for the Kingdom of God on earth.

## II. The Pastor for this Age.

We are thus brought to the second part of our subject; the pastor for the age and place. What sort of man must he be in his Christian character? What in his place of direction? What must be his training?

In general, it will be admitted that we must have a Christian soul inspired, energized, and molded by God's Word and Spirit, and fitted at once to reach out through a Christian life and activity, and impress the Church with his own Christlikeness, and to direct that Church in doing like work. Success will depend, other things being equal, upon the dignity and intensity of the life; upon its directing power and the energy given it of the Holy Ghost; and upon the bent and development resulting from its training and its contact with men.

### (I) A Better Christian Man and Worker.

In giving a more specific answer to the first of the questions proposed above, it may be said that the first and pressing demand of the times is for a better Christian man and worker in the pastoral office. This has already been emphasized from the side of the preacher; it needs to be emphasized from that of the pastor.

The "world," which the early disciples were to overcome by faith, had a mighty meaning. It was the iron world of Rome, embracing everything included in that, from the emperor to the slave, from the gods to the passions over which they presided, and from the laws to the legions. *1. Stronger Man and Unmistakable Calling.* But the subtle, unprincipled, unimpressible world of to-day, sweeping to perdition under pressure of steam and electricity with awful momentum, is quite as hard a world to deal with. To impress this world at all, there is demanded a higher style of man, a man after Christ's own pattern, more pervaded by Christ's spirit as a spirit of wisdom and power, a spirit of boundless love and self-sacrifice, and put in his place in Christ's own way.

To sum up in a single period—there is needed in the pastorate a man called of God, cultured and guided and energized of God, for his work; upheld and directed by the promised personal presence of God; and possessed with an abiding and overwhelming sense of his mission from heaven. In a word, there is emphatic call for a minister of that new order that we have already seen to be demanded by these times. Nothing less can meet the needs of the age and forward the solution of its problems. These requirements are therefore to be insisted upon strenuously and emphasized distinctly.

It would not be easy to lay too great stress upon an unmistakable call from Christ to the work of the pastorate. In the past generation of ministers, there was much timely and earnest discussion of the nature of the office of the ministry, by Dr. Wayland and others. We heard much about an "overstocked ministry." In one respect not without reason. Speaking to his class on this theme, Dr. Joseph Addison Alexander once said: "The pastor is sent to feed the flock of Christ; but some men only drive the sheep about and fleece them." It is to be hoped that this is true of comparatively few of the accredited evangelical ministry of this age; but doubtless it is still true that there is a large class, proved uncalled by their lifelong idleness or uselessness, who give some color to the complaint of an "overstocked ministry." In view of these facts, there is no possibility of emphasizing too strongly the worthlessness of an uncalled ministry. The pastoral work tests such men. They have no interest in the pastoral vocation; and it is in this sphere that they are peculiarly a source of evil to the Church. "Wo be to the pastors that destroy and scatter the sheep of my pasture! saith the Lord."\* The way in which the minister carries himself in the pastorate is perhaps the severest test of his divine call.

It is manifest that no man can speak or act with the authority with which men must speak and act in this

\* Jer. xxiii. 1.

day, to be heard above the thunder of the world's traffic and heeded, without a call as real, if not as articulate, as had the prophets in the olden times.

Secondly, there is equal need to emphasize the importance, in the pastorate of the present day, of a man led of God to that higher Christian life in which a constant Divine presence is realized in speech and action, in all the life and work. **2. A Higher Christian Life.** There is perhaps valid reason to fear that much of the so-called Christian work of the day draws too little of its inspiration from the communion of the closet and the approbation of the God who sees in secret. The "right hands" too often spend quite as much time in telling the "left hands"* what they have been doing as they occupy in the work itself; and, as might be anticipated, the workmen frequently acquire a greater facility in telling than in doing. It shows a state of things all wrong.

The perfectionism, advocated by various parties, and put into systematic shape by Upham, in the *Interior Life* and *Life of Faith*, and the books that have recently followed in the same line, we are inclined to think partly the result of a dawning sense of the need of a higher and better life in the Church. In the growing consciousness of this need we find the explanation of the hearty response with which Boardman's *Higher Christian Life* was met by so many Christians. Now it is the advance in Christian attainment which the latter book urges—however greatly one may differ from it in its terms and modes of explanation—that is needed in the sacred office; the style of Christian life that comes from complete understanding and acceptance of Christ. Too many are living with only half a Christ, and that the half

* Matt. vi. 3.

which has least to do with girding the Christian for the work of life. The tendency is to stop with the doctrine of justification by the blood of Jesus. The heathen Festus, in rehearsing to Agrippa the grounds of dispute between Paul and his Jewish accusers, said that it had to do with "one *dead* Jesus, whom Paul affirmed to be *alive* again."\* It takes the two, the dying and dead Jesus, and the risen and living Jesus, to lay a complete foundation for a Christian life—the dying Jesus, by whose righteousness the law and justice of God are satisfied, and forgiveness and restoration to the Divine favor secured—and the risen, living, interceding, reigning Jesus, by whose promised personal presence, along with and in the Christian, he is girded for all the struggle of life—it takes the two to make the strong man in the service of God. Too many of us have only a "*dead* Jesus."

We are persuaded that this is a vital matter—that just here is the secret of the inefficiency of many pastors. The completeness with which a man receives, is is made alive by, and lives by Christ, will, other things being equal, measure his power in influencing and molding men. Christ sends his followers to be 'living epistles, known and read of all men.' The pastor of this age has got to take more note of the imperial power of a right Christian life. There are things too great, too deep, and too sacred for him to speak them to men in all their fulness with mere words—he can only live them. It is not, of course, to be denied that truth is beautiful and forceful in its own unfading light; but it is when embodied in a life, and so made itself a living thing, that it shines with its richest splendor. While the life of Paul is a grander epic than Homer or Milton could produce, it is also as

\* Acts xxv. 19.

cogent an argument for the power of his religion as any he ever penned, and added tenfold to that argument as penned by him. While the career of the incarnate Son of God is a sublimer tragedy than Æschylus or Shakespeare could imagine, it is also a clearer and grander expression of the love of God than the most significant of human words could voice. As Holland's poem, *Kathrina*, so beautifully showed, there is no logic of infidelity that can refute or resist a downright earnest, loving Christian life, embodying the principles of the Gospel.

Let us not be mistaken here. We believe in creeds—and in creeds that utter no uncertain sound—but the source of the pastor's power is not so much in the right creed printed in his *Confession of Faith*, as in that right creed embodied and enforced in his life. The work of Christ demands that every one called to the pastor's office, in this day, should rise to a life that shall have its source in implicit trust in the merit of a dying Christ, and find its strength in sublime confidence in a living, reigning, indwelling Christ, inspiring and aiding him in all his work. The infatuated world will give heed to no other life than one right from God.

And it would be impossible to lay too great stress upon the necessity, in the pastor of this day, of a constant and overwhelming sense of his mission for Christ to men. This has been emphasized for the preacher; it needs equally to be emphasized for the pastor.

**3. A Profound Sense of his Mission.**

The man called of God, and filled of God with Christ, must have his gaze turned constantly in the direction of his work. An ambassador for Christ, beseeching men in Christ's stead to be reconciled to God, his mission is the grandest one ever given to man. He needs to have such a sense of it that everything shall be made to have reference to this work of saving souls; that every moment, every talent, every energy, every breath shall be consecrated to this; that the whole career shall be decided and shaped by this.

And let this be urged the more earnestly, because nothing but a sense of a Divine mission can take away the hankering of men after their own self-devised missions; nothing but this feeling that the moments are Christ's, and given for the saving of souls, can preserve the clergy from the indolence and loss of studious habits that ruin so many and threaten the ruin of so many more; nothing but this living conviction, that every energy is Christ's for the highest work, can save the clergy from the petty social and literary ambitions that prove fatal in so many cases; nothing but this perpetual sense of responsibility for souls can save the clergy from that silence of indifference on things spiritual, in their intercourse with the people, that is leaving the multitudes to hurry in their own unhindered way to perdition; and nothing but this can transform the whole pastoral work into what it should be—*a seeking for souls.*

Given the unmistakable call from God, the appropriation of a complete Christ, and his embodiment in the Christian life, and this perpetual sense of his sublime mission from God, and you have the better man and better worker imperatively demanded in the pastorate at the present time. Such a man will have power even in an age like this. Men will not scoff at him and put him out of his place. He will make himself felt through all the barriers of business and fashion and of religious indifference.

(II) A MAN OF LARGER ADMINISTRATIVE ABILITY.

The second question, touching the man for the pastorate of the day, concerned his adaptation to the place of direction. The second pressing want in the pastorate is the development and application of a larger administrative ability.

It is evident that, whatever his character, the pastor alone can not overtake this steam-driven, giddy world. He can do it only by summoning all the Church to his aid and directing them in the work. In Dr. Bushnell's address,* to which reference has already been made, occurs the following passage:

1. Necessary to Gather the Forces.

"Our preacher, therefore, is not a mere public speaker,—far from that as possible,—but he is to have a capacity of being and doing; an administrative, organizing capacity; a power to contrive and lead, and put the saints in work, and keep the work aglow, and so to roll up a cause by ingatherings and careful incrementations. The success and power of the preacher, considering his fixed settlement in a place, will not seldom depend even more on a great administrative capacity than it will on his preaching. And with good reason; for it really takes more high manhood, more wisdom, firmness, character, and right-seeing ability to administer well in the cause than it does to preach well. No matter what seeming talent there may be in the preaching, if there is no administrative talent, then the man is a boy, and the boy will have a boy's weight—nothing more. On the other hand, being a true man, able to be felt by his manly direction, his mediocrity in the sermon will be made up by respect for his always right-seeing activity. In this office, then, of preaching, one of the very highest talents demanded is an administrative talent. Every preacher wants it, even more than he would in the governing of a State."

With the qualification that we look upon it from the side of the pastorate rather than of the pulpit, and

* On "Pulpit Talent."

with some exceptions elsewhere noted, we are ready to indorse the thought of this passage most heartily. Admitting the importance of the duties ordinarily assigned to the pastor, still we do not hesitate to affirm that the work of the pastorate in this age must be made chiefly one of direction. The pastor is to accomplish more by wielding the energies of the Church than by his own personal effort. He can not in any other way do what is waiting to be done. It is evident to one who discerns the signs of the times that we have come upon the day when the administrative talent of the clergy needs to be developed, along with the individual activity of the membership. The attempts made to remedy the existing defects show this. Hence has arisen the long-continued and all-important discussion of the responsibility and agency of the laity in the service of Christ—a discussion upon the decision of which, as one can readily see, the future of the Church must to a very large degree depend.

As in connection with all great religious movements there are great errors to be guarded against, so in this there are such, patent to all discerning men, that it will require all the wisdom of God's people to avoid. The Church all workers; the Church with the prerogative and duty of directing its own energies to Christ's work; the pastor at the head of the directing element,— we have seen to be the Divine law that should govern Christian effort. Any departure from this, even on what may seem the best of human grounds, must, in the last result, be fraught with evil. Least of all can the regulative, administrative capacity, lodged in the organized Church and in the divinely appointed leader, be dispensed with. There is reason for fearing that this is not enough taken into account in some of the current Church movements.

An increased development and application of administrative capacity in the pastorate must then be insisted upon, as essential to the highest success in pushing the immediate evangelization of the world in obedience to Christ's last command. *Administrative* is the word rather than *organizing*. That minister is a rare man who has come to even a slight appreciation of the command of Christ, " Feed my sheep"; but the man called for by the exigencies of the present day is the much rarer man, who has come to some slight understanding of that more comprehensive command, " *Shepherd* my sheep," with which Christ followed up the former command. That is where the administrative talent comes in. That is just where ministerial development needs to be brought into sympathy with the spirit of the age, as manifested in business and all other practical activities—in the wielding and directing of organized masses and forces. There is need of power, not to make new machinery, but to use efficiently that which has already been given to the Church by Christ.

<small>2. Necessary to Push the Work.</small>

<small>"Shepherd my Sheep."</small>

This demand for increased administrative ability is enforced by the fact that there has been no period in modern times that afforded such facilities as the present for the exercise and direction of individual Christian activity. Of the change that had then taken place in individual Christian activity, Dr. Enoch Pond said, thirty years ago, in his *Lectures on Pastoral Theology:*

<small>" I count it one of the peculiar privileges of the present age that it presents so many opportunities for labor in the cause of Christ— labor not only for the officers of the Church, but for all the members.</small>

Every one who has a hand and heart to labor in the Lord's vineyard can now find something appropriate for him to do. In this respect the times are very different from what they were two generations ago."

The thirty years that have since elapsed have wrought a still more marvelous change, not only in the breadth and scope and variety of Christian activity, but also in its organization and definiteness of aim. This movement has included the extensive work of the various tract, Sunday-school, and mission agencies, by which it has been sought to extend the influence of the Gospel to all regions and all classes. We recognize the latest phase of it in "Silent Evangelism," which is practically the old tract work brought into touch with the present time, and bringing well-directed personal effort within the reach of those who have not the gift of tongue. The movement has also included the thorough organizing of the youthful working forces in the Church, in the great agencies that now belt the globe,—the Y. M. C. A., the Y. P. S. C. E., etc.,—the spiritual value of which must always depend upon their yielding an increase of genuine Christian work, and the ability and wisdom of the directory that is back of them.

It is thus a special problem of the day how best to develop and direct the activity of the membership, and how best to use all these new agencies in accomplishing this object.

*In Directing the Membership.*

The spheres are various. In the home-church and congregation there is always a wide field for Christian effort. The multitudes within the scope of the home-pastorate are to be reached and influenced and shaped by personal and constant intercourse with the pastor and officers; are to be led by Christian communion and interchange of views, sentiments, and experiences, to a higher piety and a larger and more intelligent benevolence; are to be brought together, and all the varied and even discordant elements to be molded into unity and harmony and efficiency, and then pervaded with that indescribable but irresistible *esprit de corps* to which nothing by way of organized and energetic effort is impossible.

In this scheme every man finds his place, and there need no longer be occasion for the impression of the honest Scotchman, that the only use of a deacon or an elder is to be at the bottom of all the Church quarrels, and the only use of the members to furnish the material for quarrels.

Within this general work there is the special function that has to do with the preparation for the Church of the next generation, in training the young; which is perhaps the most important that comes within the reach of the preacher as pastor. *In Training the Young.* The younger element in the membership requires of the pastor practical instruction, that shall restrain the ruinous tendency to withdraw from spiritual activity and to fall into laxity of views, and the not less ruinous tendency to conceit,—by laying in them a solid basis in doctrine, by giving them intelligent conceptions of their mission, and by leading them to the early formation of right habits of Christian usefulness. There is, besides, a duty to the children of the Church, to be performed through the Sabbath-school and family. To use the Sunday-school aright, as a place for training the church members to work for Christ, while leading the children to a knowledge of Bible-truth; to give interest and efficiency to its work without a library of tenth-rate novels, a concert of theatricals, and a teaching made up of petty gossip and clever story—must demand of the pastor the exercise of an administrative capacity that can lay hold of and employ all the piety and talent and energy of the Church.

There is perhaps no command of Christ that is of greater importance to the minister to-day than the command, "Feed my lambs"; and there is perhaps no command just now in more danger of being forgotten. Bishop John H. Vincent of the Methodist Episcopal Church, whose life-long work for the young has made him a recognized authority in that department of Christian effort, has recently uttered some wise words of warning, to which the ministry will do well to give full heed. He says : *

*"Feed My Lambs."*

"There is, I fear, in our day a tendency on the part of certain ministers to remand the Sunday-schools to the care of the superintendent and the teachers, and to 'patronize' the school occasionally by an official visit. There are pastors who hold no teachers' meeting, who rarely visit the teachers' meeting, if there be one, who have organized no normal class, and who have no voice whatever in the selection of the men and women, who, as representatives of the pastor, are to teach and shepherd that important part of the flock.

"It is a painful fact that in many of our churches no children's meetings are held for special religious services except those which come under the care of laymen, and often very young laymen, in Christian Endeavor, Epworth League, and other young people's associations. The Sunday-school and the Christian Endeavor have taken charge of the young folks, and, in many cases, immature and irresponsible people are the only teachers of religious things whom the youth of the Church recognize. In many families, even in Christian families, I am told, family prayer is a reminiscence. In many

---

* See Article on "The Pastor in the Sunday-school—his Place, Work and Influence," in the *Homiletic Review* for February, 1896, pp. 104–05.

churches there are no longer classes of catechumens. In many Methodist Episcopal churches, altho the *Book of Discipline* of that Church is very explicit on the subject, there are no classes of children and youth in which the pastor conforms to the well-known Paragraph 46, which reads as follows : ' The pastor shall organize the baptized children of the Church, when they are at the age of ten years or younger, into classes, and appoint suitable leaders (male or female), whose duty it shall be to meet them in class once a week, and instruct them in the nature, design, and obligations of baptism, and in the truths of religion necessary to make them ' wise unto salvation '; urge them to give regular attendance upon the means of grace ; advise, exhort, and encourage them to an immediate consecration of their hearts and lives to God, and inquire into the state of their religious experience.' This same pregnant paragraph provides, 'that children unbaptized are not to be excluded from these classes.' The fear which I express is that the pastor does not organize young people and bring them under his personal direction and teaching, as the statutes of most churches require, and as the very fact of his pastoral relation renders imperative. To the Sunday-school and the young people's organization is turned over all this important work, and instead of the pastor we have untaught, inexperienced, and, too often, worldly men and women, and these not always wise with the experience of age, to fulfil functions of the most delicate and sacred character.

" The pastor should therefore *find* his place in the Sunday-school as pastor, and proceed to organize such classes, to provide such courses of instruction and himself to supervise them, that he may remove from the thought of the Church, and especially from the thought of childhood, that somehow the Sunday-school is a substitute for the pastorate, and that Sunday-school teachers are sufficient to do the work which the commission of the Master imposes upon the ministry—the feeding of the lambs, the teaching of Holy Scriptures which make ' wise unto salvation,' and which teach, reprove, correct, and instruct in righteousness those who are to be, if they are not already, formally enrolled as disciples of Christ."

Moreover, to bring back home instruction to be what it should be, an efficient aid in training for the Church; to show parents, and make them feel, that the work committed to them—for which God has prepared them by the deepest and tenderest love, and the most constant and winning example, and the strongest and most absolute authority—can not possibly be turned over with safety to any one else; and to give the new impulse, so much needed, to home religion—will require of the pastor a weight of influence that shall shape the sentiment of the whole community.

In bringing up the Church to this various work, private communion and consultation and systematic visitation will be needed—in short, every means of exerting influence, and of leading others to active cooperation, will be called into requisition.

Moreover, in the outlying and destitute regions, beyond the bounds of the immediate congregation, is an almost unlimited field of effort. In the cities this vast work is as yet almost untouched. There are greater numbers yet to be reached by the Gospel than are now found in all our congregations. To reach and bring them in will require the most wise and tactful application of every legitimate method. But, in the opinion of many the "territorial method"—introduced by Chalmers, advocated and presented by Guthrie, in *Out of Harness*, and *Sketches of the Cowgate*—is to be the chief and most efficient mode of reaching these multitudes. The Church seems to be settling upon it with a firmer conviction. It takes into account all the principles that, in the discussion of the law of the pastorate, have been seen to be essential. In the work of the teachers, and of the helpers of the missionary pastors, is furnished a channel into which an amount of energy may be turned that shall bring greater results than have been seen to flow from our efforts, by way of mission schools, and street, and dock, and theater preaching, in all the past. And in reaching the masses in our great cities "the institutional church," just now becoming so important a factor, will doubtless in the near future have a large development and application.

Then there is a great world beyond, to which we can send a substitute if we can not go ourselves, and to the immediate evangelization of which Christ calls his Church.

Is it not patent to every one that there has never been an age that admitted and called for such development in the right direction? The work is waiting on every hand. The channels are already prepared; but this rushing world will never be overtaken without all the energies the Church can furnish, united and directed in the right way.

The call is for men, in the pastor's place, fitted by enlarged administrative capacity to be leaders of Christ's hosts. Wherever such men are found in the place, progress is made. The grandest successes of the day are won by them. We have had examples in the heart of London—in Newman Hall, with his twenty mission places, and in Spurgeon, wielding, in ceaseless activity and in every direction at once, the largest membership in any one Church organization in Christendom. It was clearly in just this qualification, that Mr. Spurgeon greatly surpassed that other splendid preacher, Henry Ward Beecher, and in virtue of this he was able to lay the foundations of a work involving many institutions and vast and complicated machinery for instruction and training for ministers and Christian workers, and for missionary and philanthropic effort, that remains as an enduring monument of his administrative genius, while still continuing to bless the whole world. In this age, there is a mission for some second Luther, in rousing the Church to a sense of the grandeur of her present opportunities, and impressing upon her the divine law of right work under right direction. Meanwhile the absence of some one mighty soul, sent for this end, casts the responsibility upon all who are in the ranks of the ministry.

### (III) A Man of Broader and Better Pastoral Training.

The third question, touching the man for the pastor in these times, had to do with his training. This fertile subject must be passed over with a few brief hints. Three things enter into the idea intended—increased vigor of soul, enlarged sympathy with men, and more practical knowledge of the work; the first to meet the requirement for a higher style of man for the place, and the other two to secure a better adaptation to his place of influence and direction. The proper training must intelligently seek the production of these. That training should send the pastor to his work with a larger soul; that is, with an increase both of mental and spiritual power.

There is need of a more vigorous thinker, with both greater acuteness and broader comprehensiveness.

**1. A More Vigorous Thinker.** Let it not be said that this is a requirement for the pulpit only; it is as much a necessity for the pastorate, for problems more difficult are constantly presenting themselves there for solution—problems involving at once a keener logic and a more subtle metaphysics. As Dr. Bushnell has well indicated, the pastorate is the place calling for the stronger man. We must have stronger men and more of them.

It is related by Rev. Thomas Williams, the eccentric clergyman who preached the funeral sermon of Dr. Emmons, that one of Dr. Emmons' members, who contemplated entering the ministry, broached the matter to his pastor in this wise: "I have been trying my gifts, and find that I have reason to conclude, I think without conceit, that I would make a tolerably good minister. What do you think about it?" The answer of Dr. Emmons was characteristic: "I haven't a doubt of it, sir; but the difficulty is that we have too many '*tolerably* good ministers' already!" There is need of something better than *tolerably* good ministers in the pastorate of this age.

Strong habits of practical analytic and synthetic thought alone can fit for the present work of the pastorate. In fact, the insight and comprehension called for in the place of administration are only analysis and synthesis under other names.

But we should err, if we failed to insist on a better spiritual nurture for those who are looking to the ministry. It has been already seen that the style of the Christian man most seriously affects the result of his efforts. Theological students should be directed and aided, intelligently and constantly, in growing in that preparation of heart that is, after all, more important than the preparation of intellect.

2. A Better Spiritual Nurture.

There is likewise a special call upon the schools for the production of an enlarged sympathy with man, and an increased acquaintance with the actual work of the pastorate, by way of adapting the man to the place. Mere acquaintance

3. An Enlarged Sympathy.

with correct theory is not enough. The pastor must have his right theory clearly defined, and besides this there must be the existing bond of sympathy between him and the people, and then practical acquaintance with the ways of molding them. The lack of these things, in a large number of those who enter the ministry, has been deeply felt on all hands. It was originally difficult to retain all the features of the theological seminary as an educational institution, and to add these essential features of ministerial training. It has become all the more difficult, because of the increased number of studies embraced in the curriculum. The solution of the problem will doubtless be found in the systematic devotion of the long vacations of the student to Christian work, organization, and exhortation, in Sunday-school and mission work, under the wise direction of pastors.

As this defect in practical training arose from the substitution of the theological school for the old method of preparing for the ministry under the direction of some pastor, it has required time to bring about the proper adjustment to the new conditions. That such adjustment is exceedingly important goes with the saying; that it will be brought about in due time may be confidently expected.

With the Divine blessing attending, a ministry trained with a clear and intelligent conception of the place and of the man for that place, can not fail to make of the pastorate a power for good such as it has not been since Apostolic days. Under a large minded, thoroughly cultured, and wholly consecrated leader, there may be expected, with God's blessing, a return to the working Church of primitive Christianity.

In the family, the state, and the Church, this is a

day of questions involving grave issues, but among them all there is none more momentous and far-reaching in its consequences than the one here under discussion. The success of the work of the Church of the present day must be won by return to the Divine idea of the pastorate, and by the raising up and training of men adapted to meet the demands of the position, as defined by God's Word.

By glancing along the line of progress by which the Church has come to the present vantage ground, and noting God's methods of forwarding his purpose concerning Zion, by successive stages of trial and preparation, we shall be the better prepared to understand her position at the present, and shall get a clearer view of the momentous importance of what we have been pleading for. In the progress of trial, we first see Christianity brought face to face with the law and the legions, the culture and the gods, of the old world; then, itself enthroned above all these and in possession of the place of ease and power, molding the empire in its own way; again, in fierce struggle with barbarian force and overcoming it in subduing for Christ the Gothic and Slavic nations that overran the empire; once more, in the hour of its faintness, at the time of the Renaissance, meeting the forces of reawakened reason and rising to a mightier life in the Reformation; still further on, coming out of the battle with the later Rationalism, girded for the modern missionary movement. To-day, when we see it grappling with the dizzy, headlong, terrible energy of the world—what, we ask, will be the result?

Turning to her progress of preparation for the world's conversion, we find the Church first defining and formulating her doctrine, while the world that is to receive the doctrine is yet unknown and inaccessible; then advancing to the Reformation, while, through the mariner's compass, the world in its preparation for the doctrine of Christ keeps pace in becoming a known world; then rousing herself for the mission movement, while, by the discovery of steam and its application to printing and locomotion, the world is being made accessible to the Gospel of Christ. Now, when we see the energies of the world being developed as never before, and heightened by the manifold adaptations of science and the direction of the mightiest and most subtle forces of nature, to the work of life; and when, along with this, innumerable channels are open for Christian effort, and waiting for this energy to be guided through them to the accomplishment of Christ's great purpose—what, we are constrained to ask, will be the result?

This vast store of human energy indicates, in its development and accumulation, the preparation for a final stage of progress. Sanctified and owned of God, it is just what is needed to hasten the work of the world's immediate evangelization. Even now much of it is waiting to be directed into the ways of Christian effort and enterprise. Christ is waiting to give it all to the Church when she sincerely and believingly asks for it, and shows herself ready to wield it for his glory. Upon the pastorate of these coming years, even more than upon the pulpit, will depend the progress of the Church and the hopes of the world. With the right man in the right place everywhere in the Church Catholic, and with the Divine blessing, the signs of the times would indicate the near approach of the great consummation; and the pastors now just entering upon their work may confidently hope to witness that consummation in the effective preaching of the Gospel to every creature.

### Concluding Outlook.

The present outlook upon humanity reveals an awful crisis in human affairs. Two mighty hosts are confronting each other in hostile array.

On the one side, the armies of the spiritual Babylon are gathering, and the forces and spirits of evil, human and Satanic, are mass- *The Hosts of Darkness.* ing as if for the great final struggle of Armageddon:

" The three unclean spirits like frogs come out of the mouth of the dragon, and out of the mouth of the beast, and out of the mouth of the false prophet . . . the spirits of devils, working miracles, which go forth unto the kings of the earth and of the whole world, to gather them to the battle of that great day of God Almighty." *

Anarchism is hastening to its fruition in anarchy, and the massing of the forces of evil portend "the end of an age."

From a merely human point of view the times are portentous. Figure apart, for the moment—the writer in the *Quarterly Review*, already referred to, calls earnest attention to the fact that the conditions that preceded, prepared for, and precipitated the French Revolution with its agony and blood, are now reproduced on the scale of the civilized world. He says : †

" It would be interesting to trace the resemblance between our time and the latter years of Louis XV., or those which went before

---

\* Rev. xvi. 13, 14.

† *Quarterly Review*, Article " Anarchist Literature," January, 1894, p. 4.

the great Revolution. In both cases, we should find ourselves dwelling on the 'fair humanities,' the 'mild manners,' the toleration of conflicting ideals, the dreams of everlasting peace, and, above all, the dilettante, bric-a-brac, and pseudo-artistic mania, from which the whole of society was suffering. Everywhere we should hear the prophet's cry, 'Watchman, what of the night?' while those whose ears were keenest might catch his oracular response, 'The morning cometh—and also the night'—such a night as a hundred years ago hung over the Place de la Révolution for months together."

On the other side, the host of the King of kings, the Church, is gathering in opposing array, with every needed equipment of power and grace at her command; bearing the sharp and omnipotent sword of the Spirit, the Word of God, with its double edge of judgment and grace, in the law and the Gospel; and with her great leader summoning her, by his Word and his providence, to present victory over all the forces of evil, and to the immediate conquest of the world.

*The Hosts of Light.*

As the battle is about to be joined, men ask with bated breath: What is to be the result? Shall it be the reenactment, on the scale of the world, of the scenes of the French Revolution? The titanic, volcanic forces are all there, and only a touch of evil is needed to bring the tremendous results, in the defeat of the good and in social, civil, and moral destruction. How light a touch may serve the purpose, and how hopeless the defeat and ruin may become, the experience in the Pittsburg riots and the later uprisings of labor and anarchism in Chicago may suggest. Or shall it be the final victory of him who has "on his thigh a name written, King of kings, and Lord of lords"?* That will all depend upon the response of the Church to her Leader's call. She is commissioned to wield "the two-

*The Leader's Call.*

\* Rev. xix. 16.

edged sword" for Christ. She has the promise and assurance of certain, complete, and speedy victory. Every obstacle has been removed; every excuse for delay has been swept away. Will she obey the command "Go ye," and move on without delay to the triumph and conquest?

*Whether she will do it or not will depend, most of all, upon what her appointed leaders, under Christ—*the ministry—*will do.* They bear up the standard of the cross; they hold the key to the situation, the talisman of victory, the commission for commanding and sounding the forward movement; and **upon the ministry can not therefore fail to rest the chief weight of responsibility!**

THE END.

# INDEX.

Administrative ability, large development of, 29; Bushnell on, 315, 339; larger measure needed by the pastor, 339, 348; examples of, 347
Alexander, Archibald, on popularity, 212
Alexander, Joseph Addison, on the mercenary pastor, 334
Alford, Dean, "The Queen's English," 229
Anarchism, Age of, 147; characteristics, 147-151
Anarchist literature, 149
"Anna Karenina," characterized, 211
Apologists meeting scientists and rationalists, 287
Apostles, the, their Commission, 3; the first "missionaries," 8; view of giving, 40; were preachers, 195
Apostolic, rule of giving, 41; rule in preaching, 62
Argyll, Duke of, on "Christian Socialism," 62, 209
Aristotle, "The Modern," 208
Arithmetic, some problems in, 43
Arnold, Matthew, 182
Augustine, 199
Authority, modern revolt against, 147

"Back to the Law," the need of the age, 75; not merely as the battle-cry of reform, 80
Beecher, Henry Ward, characteristics of, 261-266; debt to Ruskin, 264

Beecher, Lyman, on value of revivals, 273
Bellamy, Joseph, Bible as word of God, 281
Bible Christianity, as a saving power, the preacher's theme, 53; in doctrinal form, essential to preaching, 110
Bible, text-books of salvation, 72; as the Book of God, 188; as theology, 190; as practical truth, 192; intensely practical, 193; a practical book, 243; answers in its doctrines the great human questions, 243; makes all material things typical, 256
Biblical knowledge, preacher's need of a better, 188; from three points of view, 188-194
Blackstone, view of tithes, 41
Blair, William, rhetoric of, 208-237
Bonar, Dr. Horatius, "Words to the Winners of Souls," 128, 198, 200, 268
Booth, Robert Russell, experience in revival, 298
Bushnell, Horace, his famous epigram, 55; on duty of administration, 315, 339
Butler, Joseph, "Analogy of Religion," 280

Call to the ministry, essential, 160; from Christ and constraining, 161; the brilliant preacher without, 162
Candlish, Dr. Robert S., the judge's estimate of his preaching, 310

Carlyle, Thomas, on "bankruptcy of science" and mechanical era, 148
Chalmers, Dr. Thomas, "expulsive power of a new affection," 63; failure to solve the problem of poverty, 66; estimate of reform preaching, 64; failure in, 69
Chambers, Talbot W., The Noon Prayer Meeting, 288
Changes in Christian methods, 312
Christ, his command, and his authority, 3; his statement of his mission, 53; method of preaching, 62, 67; his principle of unity of aim, 85; emphasis on repentance, 97; his emphasis on regeneration, 104; on the enmity of the world, 133; on prayer for more laborers in the vineyard, 161; his threefold charge to Peter, 304; his requirement of pastoral care for the young, 344; his "Leader's call," 354
Christian giving, the Scriptural law of, 34-48; false theories, 35; the Church's practical theory, 35; Christian the steward of Christ in, 37; Old Testament rule, 37; New Testament rule, 39; Christ's view of, 39; Apostles' view, 40; Apostolic rule, 41; Church's unscriptural theory, 42; Scriptural law of, makes ample provision for evangelizing the world, 43
Christianity, its proposals, 59; reconstructs, 60; mode of transforming man, 62; a doctrine and a life, 98; its basis the Bible, as God's word, 112; antagonized by the New Secularism, 142; recognizes original sin, 142; has a principle of recovery, which heathenism lacks, 157; its progress in the plan of God, 351
Christian living, the logic of, 246

Church, her commission and responsibility, 34; requirement to furnish pecuniary means, 6; missionary opportunity, 8; immense wealth, 21; failure in the work, 51; a spiritual agency, 54; decline of power, 133; causes at work, 133; influence of skepticism, 136; why young men don't go to, 146; the retrospect and prospect, 300; what her future, humanly speaking, dependent upon the ministry, 302; her critical position, 354
Church of Scotland, confession of, 198
Clifford, Professor, his atheism, 136
Coleridge, S. T., on wealth, 21; aphorism, 254
Collatia, illustration of consecration from, 199
Columbian exposition, 45
Columbus, Christopher, voyage of, 16, 17
Comte, Auguste, atheistic philosophy, 286
Consecration, preacher's need of more complete, 197-204; God's call for, 200
Constantinople, the fall of, 18
Constructive training, importance of, 171; neglect of, 176; essential, 177; method of, 178, 179
Corporations and law, 81
Covetousness, God's hatred of, 50
Cui bono? the motto of the age, 214
Cunningham, W., the Anglo-Saxon problem, 87; historical economic changes, 307

Day, Henry N., "Art of Discourse," 237; principles of style, 253
Dead orthodoxy, its worthlessness, 118
Definition, value of exact, 170
Deism, English, prevalence of, 280
De Quincey, Thomas, "Biographical Essays," 21

INDEX. 359

Despotic sway of militarism and monopoly, 155, 156
De Wette, "Introduction," 286
Doctrinal preaching, its partial abandonment and the reasons, 110–119; return to, a necessity, 119–127; the three R's of salvation, 121
Doctrine, schism of, and ethics, 77; linked with life, 98; four fundamental doctrines, 105; essential to preaching, 110–119; return to, in preaching a necessity, 119–121; and ideal Christian life, Paul's view, 122; Peter's view, 123; Froude's view, 124; essential to rational religious life, 128; central in preaching, 245; present depreciation of, 295; what now required, 293–297
Dogma, unreasonable sneers at, 98
Dornerism, defects of, 78; tends to Universalism, *post-mortem* probation, etc., 79
Draper, John W., physical sciences in training the clergy, 240; "Conflict of Science and Religion," 242

Earnestness, intense, demanded of the preacher, 202; illustrated by Xavier, 202; Paul's example of, 203; essential to the leadership of the ministry, 204
Economics, moral law over, 89; historical principles of, 307
Edwards, Jonathan, character of his age, 96
Egoism and Altruism, 76
Electricity, agency in opening the world, 11
Eloquence, various study of, 222; elements of sacred, 225; need of correct theory of, 231; working-theory of, 232
Emmons, Dr. Nathaniel, on "tolerably good ministers," 349
Enthusiasm, demanded of the preacher, 200; illustrated by Michelangelo, 201
Era of Revival, need of a fourth era, 290; exigencies to be met, 291; doctrines required to promote it, 293
Eras of Revival, 279; peculiar features of, 280; first era, 280; second era, 282; third era, 285
Ethics of selfishness, crystallized by Paley, etc., 76; illustrated, 117

Faith, justification by, the test of Protestantism, 102; importance illustrated, 103; relations to reason and philosophy; not blind trust, but rational, 113
Farrar, F. W., "The Message of the Books," 189
Finney, Charles G., secret of power, 96, 292
Fish, Dr. Henry C., "Primitive Piety Revived," 127, 128, 312
Flint, Robert, "Philosophy of History," 208
French, skepticism, prevalence of, 282
Fulton Street Prayer-meeting, its origin, 288; memorial volume on, 288; its development of the laity, 289
Furnishing of the preacher, what essential, 130; in knowledge and oratorical skill, 180–197; in science and philosophy, 181; in Biblical knowledge, 188; in special power to preach, 194
Future punishment, disbelief of the age in, 151; examination of a candidate on, 152

Germanizing theological seminaries, 172
Germany, influence of, methods, 174; present tendency of theology in, 174
God's law, the rule of family, Church, and State, 248
Gonçalo de Cordova, genius of, 17

Gospel, scientific and esthetic, 217; of sensation, 218; of petty practicality, 219; its twofold aim, 244
"Great Awakening," character of the preaching, 127
Great awakening, now needed, 277
Great Britain at the front, 18
Great Commission, its terms, 2; its requirements of the Church, 4; test questions, 5, 6; standing objections, 8
Great truths at basis of great life, 125
Guizot, "Meditations on Christianity," 243
Guthrie, Thomas, a judge's estimate of, 310; "Sketches of the Cowgate," 346

Harris, Dr. John, "The Great Commission," 12
Higher criticism and new theology, 141
Hodge, Dr. Charles, "Preaching the Gospel to the Poor," 138
Hugo, Victor, illustration from, 143
Huxley, Thomas, 185, 241

Ideas, practical, in man, 233; of truth, 234; of happiness, 234; of perfection, 235; of duty, 235; presenting God's truth to, 249
Immediate evangelization of the world, required of the Church, 5; providential preparation of the world for, 8–34; Scriptural law of giving provides the means for, 34–47; the missionary call to, 47; the needed baptism of the Holy Spirit for, 49; the only real obstacle to, 51; old excuses removed, 51
Institutions, three divine, 247
Invention, in rhetoric, 237; processes of, 237
Isaiah, his preaching in a crisis like the present, 92; vision in the Temple, 131; his response to God's call, 164

James, his man with the gold ring, 139
Jerome, view of tithes, 38
Josephus, view of tithes, 38
Justification, by faith, the principle of Protestanism, 101

Kingdom of God, new doctrine of, 147
Knowledge, necessity for definite, 170; a professor's protest against 170
Knox, John, his call, 161

"Labor Church," 144
Laissez-faire principle in English history, 307; influence of, 308;
Lanphier, Mr. J. C., and Fulton Street Prayer-meeting, 288
Law, God's, the starting-point in preaching, 74; neglect of preaching, 74; basis of morality, 75; preaching to sinners, 80; relation to human societies, 81; way of life, 93; standard of judgment, 94; its preaching illustrated, 95
Laymen, agency of, in the Gospel, 67; in reform movements, 67; brought forward by third era of revivals, 289
Lea, Mr. Henry C., on Murder in Christendom, 150
Licentiousness flooding literature and intrenching itself, 149, 150
Lilly, Mr. W. S., "On Shibboleths," quoted on retributive justice, 90; on American political corruption, 91; on the coming revolution, 157
Living pictures, as culmination of depravity, 212
Logical training, importance of a better, 166
Lombroso, fatal errors of his sociology, 83; demoralizing influence of, 83
Love, defective analysis of, 78
Lowell, James Russell, on the Great Avenger, 158

Luke, record of promise of the Holy Spirit, 49
Luther and the devil, 137; need of a, 348

Macaulay, T. B., opinion of rhetoric, 224
Magellan, his voyage, 18
Magnetism, agency in opening the world, 10
Mallock, W. H., "Physics and Sociology," 84
Manhood, importance of, in preaching, 239
Mark,"The Great Commission," 2
Marvin, Dr. A. P., on revivals, 288
Matter of preaching, God's truth, 240; in practical relations, 243; in human relations, 247; to practical ideas, 249
Means needed for evangelization, in the hands of the Church, 20
Message, of the preacher, 53-129; both law and Gospel, essential, 71
Michelangelo, illustrating enthusiasm, 201
Mill, John Stuart, a logical wreck, 183
Minister, "active," illustrated, 275-276; the present duty of each, 298; to do what the Commission requires, 296; to rouse and lead the Church, 297; the "tolerably good," 349
Ministry, cause of present inadequacy of, 133-153; the remedy, 153-204; periods of decline in, 198; not a profession, 267; calling and consecration of, 267; expectation of results in preaching, 267; Bonar on the spirit of, 268; requirements made of all the, 298; an "overstocked," 334; present power and responsibility of, 355
Mohammedanism, check of, 16
Monthly concert, 12; providences following upon, 12

Moody, Dwight L., representing lay movement, 29
Moral disorder, in man, 55; its extent, 56; involves both wreck and wretchedness, 57; various proposed remedies, 58; Christianity the only remedy, 59
Moral Law, over society, 89; over economics, 89; over politics, 91; binds man to God only, 76
Moses, on giving, 37; on the benevolence of God's law, 93; patronized, 167-169
Müller, Julius, man not a legislator, 247
Murder, age of, statistics of, 150

Naturalness, false sense of, 224
Newell, W.W., "Revivals: How and When," 273, 288
Newman, F. W., influence of, 286
Normal method of conversion, 271; need of return to, 274
Novels, the era of, 210
Novelty, the rage for, 209; in the pulpit, 212; the Greek rage for, 214

Oratory, better theory of, needed, 222; prevailing theories and no theories, 223; partial theories, 225; freedom in, 229; correct theory, 231-239; elements of correct theory, 232; practical ideas in, 233

Parker, Theodore, influence of, 286
Pastor, preacher as, 304-355; his special work, 304; hindrances to the work of, 306; need of administrative talent, 315; false modes of meeting changed conditions, 316-320; how to make efficient, 320; law of his work, 320; the energies of the membership to be directed by, 322; in the leadership, 327; breaches of the divine law of, 328; lead-

ership of, denied, 331; for this age, 332; a mercenary, 334; an unmistakable call, 333; a higher Christian life, 335; a profound sense of his mission, 337; larger administrative ability, 339-348; broader and better pastoral training for, 348-353; in training the young, 343; call for enlarged sympathy in, 349

Pastorate, problem of, 304; changed conditions of, 306; divine law of, 320-332

Paul, the Apostle, view of preaching, 1; his statement of Christ's mission, 53; statement of man's moral disorder, 55; treatise on the way of salvation, 55; his exposure of legalism, 65; his three Bible text-books of salvation, 72; his presentation of law, 75; his statement of the Christian's obligations to mankind, 80; his principle of unity in Gospel work, 85; his statement of the godward side of salvation, 99; his answer to the jailer's question, 99; of the manward side, 101; his three great "therefores," 101; on the new life, 104; his view of the legal aspect of redemption, 105; the legal aspect of redemption, 107; the relations of preaching, doctrine, and faith, 122; his ideal Christian, 122; weeping over sinners, 138; his sense of his call, 161; his earnestness; 203; the greatest sinner, 270

Paxton, Dr. William M., on the aim in sermonizing, 163; on the preaching now required, 196

Pentecostal power in New Testament, 164

Peter, his ideal Christian, 123; Christ's threefold charge to, 304

Philosophy and faith, as sources of truth, 112; distinction between, 112; need of better knowledge of, 181; false, how to be met, 182-186

Pierson, Dr. Arthur T., "Play of Missions," 52; "Crisis of Missions," 128

Plutocracy, danger from, 156

Politics, relation of preaching to, 64; the moral law over, 191

Power to preach, preacher's need of more, 194

Practical, ideas in man, Theremin's view of, 233; the Bible, 243; Christians, from second era of revivals of, 285

Preacher, the, his present commission, 1-52; his anxious questions, 1; his leadership, 5; present duty, 50; his message, 53-129; salvation the key-note, 53; Bible Christianity as a saving power, his theme, 55; regeneration fundamental, 55; both law and gospel essential, 71; duty to preach doctrine, 127; pressure of secularism on, 153; the furnishing needed, 153-204; intellectual mastery of the situation, 154; more Scriptural working-theory, 159; a different and better training, 165; more of knowledge and oratorical skill, 180; a more complete consecration, 197; present requirements of, 278; his relation to revivals, 278; need to study principles of revivals, 279; as a pastor in these times, 304-355; his work in gathering and shepherding, 304

Preaching, its place in Gospel scheme, 1; that leads to legalism, 64; two opposite modes of, 65; the law to sinners, 80; distinguished from reading, 195; for the masses, 196; Dr. W. M. Paxton on, 196; for these times, 205-303; the times as a factor in, 205; required by the state of things, 221; cor-

rect theory of, 231 ; in its matter, 240 ; expectation of results in, 251-261 ; in its manner, 253 ; expository, 261 ; in its spirit, 266 ; for immediately evangelizing the world, 268-303; should keep in view the Great Commission, 268 ; Wesley's test of success in, 270; stated, God's method, 271 ; without preparation, danger of, 275, 276 ; for saving the world, 277-300 ; doctrines now called for in, 293-297
Principles, importance of knowledge of, 186 ; of rhetorical method, 236 ; of invention, 237; of style, 238 ; giving power in preaching, 253 ; present lack of interest in, 309; of the pastorate, 320
Problems of society, 82 ; of the Anglo-Saxon race, 87
Protestantism, perversions of, 154 ; dominance of, in commerce, 14; in the nations, 15 ; at the front, 19; its original aims, 154; perversions of, 154 ; and democracy, 155
Providences opening the world, nature providences in magnetism, steam, and electricity, 9 ; removing hostile barriers, 12 ; Columbian providences making Protestantism dominant, 16 ; immense increase of wealth, 20 ; setting free the messengers needed, 27 ; development of administrative and organizing ability, 27 ; preparing for the world's immediate evangelization, 301

Quarterly Review, on Max Nordau's " Degeneration," 148 ; illustration of anarchist literature from Swinburne, Oscar Wilde, Tolstoi, Ibsen, etc., 148 ; on the present situation, 353

Rally, the final, of the century, 48

Redemption, its Godward side, 99; its manward side as given by Paul, 101-106 ; its manifold aspects, legal, governmental, moral, dynamic, of service, sacrificial, 107-110
Reform, relation of preaching to, 60 ; Gospel not subsidiary to, 62 ; true relation of preacher to, 66 ; futility of popular preaching of, 65
Regeneration, fundamental in preaching, 55 ; requirements of the case, 58 ; ignoring it fatal, 60
Repentance, vital to Christianity, 96, 97 ; stress on, by Finney and Henry B. Smith, and by John Baptist, Christ, and the Apostles, 96, 97.
Retributive justice the law of the world, 90
Revivalism, special, its limitations, 272; legitimate, testimony concerning, 273
Revivalists, the debt of the Church to, 273
Revival of Learning, 19
Revival of 1858, agency of commercial depression in, 287; Dr. A. P. Marvin's estimate of, 288; outcome in Christian organizations of the laity, 289; called a " Revival of Love," 292; failure of ministry as leaders in, 296
Revivals, principles of, 279; three recent eras of, 279
Revolution, in business, 306; in character and usages, 309
Rhetorical method, principles of, 236
Righteousness, the supreme thing, 75
" Robert Elsmere," characterized, 211
Robertson, F. W., sense of responsibility, 216
Rogers, Henry, " Greyson Letters," 309
Romanism, decline of, 16

Romans, epistle to, the way of salvation, 55; text-book of salvation, especially for the Roman and Englishman, 72; as text-book of salvation, nearest universal, 72; as defining the preacher's message, 73; summary statement of the Godward side of redemption, 99; the three great "therefores," 101; legal aspect of redemption, 107
Romish preaching, by Protestants, 64
R's, the three, of salvation, 121
Ruskin, John, "Modern Painters," 208; on utility, 215; theory of beauty, 255; debt of Beecher to, 264

Sacrificial aspect of redemption, 109
Salvation the key-note of the Gospel, 53; Bible text-books of, 72; law the starting-point, 74; *from*, and not *in*, sin, 96; its Godward side, 99; its manward side, 101; relation to doctrine, 120; the three R's of, 121
Schodde, Dr. George P., "Theological Thought in Germany," 174
Science and philosophy, the preacher's need of better knowledge of, 181–188
Science, belongs to the Church, 134; its great expounders Christian, 134; falsely so called, 134; modern triumphs of, 206; no revelation of salvation, 242
Scientific, method, value of, 171; spirit, activity of, 206
Secularism, this an age of, 133; its materialistic scientism, 134; its shallow philosophy, 133; influence on the Church, 136; age of socialistic, 140; the old, dead, 141; characteristics, 140–147; the new, crystallizing in the Labor Church, 144; manifestations in the Church, 146

Selfishness, new ethics of, 117; unbridled, 149
Sensationalism a failure, 276
Service of man, demanded by the law, 80; as an aspect of redemption, 109; and self-sacrifice, 109
Sexton, a, who did not know broadcloth, 139
Shedd, W. G. T., "Homiletic and Pastoral Theology," 315
Shepard, Elliot F., example of, 31
Sinners, against preaching the law, 152; Paul the greatest of, 270
Smith, Dr. Henry B., stress on repentance, 96; on relation of faith to philosophy, 112
Smith, John Pye, 287
Society, problems of, 82; social progress of, not social evolution, 84; not an organism, 84; moral law over, 89
Sociological fallacies, 83; Mallock on, 84
Sociology, positivist, dangers of, 82
Spain, her glory and decadence, 17, 18
Specialism, tendency of mere, 175; leads to neglect of constructive training and thinking, 176
Spencer, Herbert, unwarranted estimate of, 114; all-pervasive false teaching, 115, 182, 183, 241, 291
Sphinx riddles, 130; of religion the greatest, 131
Spring, Dr. Gardner, on purpose in sermonizing, 163
Spurgeon, C. H., characteristics of, 261–266
Stated preaching for conversion the normal method, 271
Stead, Mr., "Civic Church," 61.
Steam, agency in opening the world, 11; in the hands of Protestants, 10
Strong, Dr. Josiah, "Our Country," 128

Style, principles and essentials of, 253; principles giving power in, 253; Biblical qualities, concrete, illustrative, and specific presentation, 254-261; principles illustrated in Beecher and Spurgeon, 261-266

Tappan, Lewis, "Is it Right to be Rich?" 25
Territorial Method, in reaching the world, 346
Texts, specific truths in, illustrated, 258-260
Theological training, need of better, 172; danger from Germanizing tendency, 172; from mere specialism, 175; from neglect of constructive thinking, 176
Theology, shallowness and impudence of the rationalistic, 166-168
Therefores, Paul's three great, 101
Theremin, Francis, "Eloquence a Virtue," 234; "Demosthenes and Massillon," practical ideas, 249
Thinking, indefinite, influence of, 116
This-world-ism, 133
This-worldliness, Walter Walsh on, 140, 145
Times, the, as a factor in preaching, 205; practical characteristics of these, 206-216; results in the preaching, 216-220
Tithe, expressions for, in New Testament, 41
Tithe-system, errors regarding, 37-39; abrogated, 39-41; Blackstone's view, 41
Tobit, view of tithes, 38
Tolstoi, "The Kreutzer Sonata," 149
Transcendentalism, shallow, 111; rational, legitimate, 112; rationalistic, baseless, 114
Triad, the Christian and the pagan, 145

Truth, in order to holiness, 117; essential to rational and religious life, 124

Ueberweg, "History of Philosophy," 116
Universalist pew-holder, power of a, 152
Utility the rage for, 214 ; John Ruskin's distinction, 215

Vasco da Gama; voyage of, 17
Vincent, Bishop John H., on pastor's duty of training the young, 344

Walsh, Walter, on "The New Secularism," 140-145
Warren, Bishop H. W., view of ethics, 77
Watchman's responsibility, 271
Wayland, Francis, ministry not a profession, 267, 334
Wealth of the Church, revolution and its causes, 21 ; the world's treasure-fields given to Protestantism, 23 ; results of the revolution, 24 ; consequent Christian duty, 25 ; dangers from hoarded, 45 ; perils from misused, 46 ; the present problem of, 47 ; and the age-temptation, 89
Well-being, its two senses, 78 ; the sense chosen decides the morality and the theology, 79 ; the wrong view of, wrecks morals and life, 79
Wesley, John, tests of success, 270
Westminster Review, on "The Sexual Problem," 149
Whately, Archbishop, "Rhetoric," 236
Wickedest sinners, 270
Wuttke, "Christian Ethics, 77

Xavier, Francis, earnestness of, 202

Zola, M., as anarchist novelist, 211

www.ingramcontent.com/pod-product-compliance
Lightning Source LLC
Chambersburg PA
CBHW020309240426
43673CB00039B/747